ARISTOTLE ON THE COMMON SENSE

OXFORD ARISTOTLE STUDIES

General Editors
Julia Annas and Lindsay Judson

PUBLISHED IN THE SERIES

Space, Time, Matter, and Form
Essays on Aristotle's Physics
David Bostock

Aristotle on Meaning and Essence
David Charles

Time for Aristotle
Ursula Coope

Aristotle on Teleology
Monte Ransome Johnson

On Location
Aristotle's Concept of Place
Benjamin Morison

Political Authority and Obligation in Aristotle
Andres Rosler

Order in Multiplicity
Homonymy in the Philosophy of Aristotle
Christopher Shields

Aristotle's Theory of Substance
The Categories *and* Metaphysics *Zeta*
Michael V. Wedin

Aristotle's *De Interpretatione*
Contradiction and Dialectic
C. W. A. Whitaker

Aristotle on the Common Sense

PAVEL GREGORIC

OXFORD
UNIVERSITY PRESS

OXFORD
UNIVERSITY PRESS

Great Clarendon Street, Oxford OX2 6DP

Oxford University Press is a department of the University of Oxford.
It furthers the University's objective of excellence in research, scholarship,
and education by publishing worldwide in

Oxford New York

Auckland Cape Town Dar es Salaam Hong Kong Karachi
Kuala Lumpur Madrid Melbourne Mexico City Nairobi
New Delhi Shanghai Taipei Toronto

With offices in

Argentina Austria Brazil Chile Czech Republic France Greece
Guatemala Hungary Italy Japan Poland Portugal Singapore
South Korea Switzerland Thailand Turkey Ukraine Vietnam

Oxford is a registered trade mark of Oxford University Press
in the UK and in certain other countries

Published in the United States
by Oxford University Press Inc., New York

First published 2007

British Library Cataloguing in Publication Data

Data available

Library of Congress Cataloging in Publication Data

Data available

Typeset by Laserwords Private Limited, Chennai, India
Printed in Great Britain
on acid-free paper by
Biddles Ltd., King's Lynn, Norfolk

ISBN 978–0–19–927737–7

1 3 5 7 9 10 8 6 4 2

For Marta, Mia, and Maks

Preface

It is customary to preface one's work on the so-called 'common sense' in Aristotle with the warning that it has nothing to do with our notion of 'plain common sense'. Although opportune, this warning calls for an explanation. Common sense, as we understand it, seems to be a very basic ability of rational beings to follow their experience in discerning some obvious things, making elementary connections among them, and avoiding patent contradictions. Because this ability is so basic, it is shared by all rational beings, and that is why it is called 'common'. On the other hand, it is called 'sense' because it is developed naturally and because its operations are intuitive, not because it is a perceptual ability properly speaking.

In the context of Aristotle's psychology, the expression 'common sense' refers to a distinct perceptual capacity in which the five senses are integrated. It is called 'common' because it is shared by the five senses, and it is called a 'sense' because it is indeed a perceptual ability properly speaking. And because it is a perceptual ability, rather than a rational ability, it is shared by all animals, non-rational and rational alike. Obviously, what Aristotle calls the 'common sense' is very different from what we call 'common sense'.

It is a linguistic coincidence that these two very different notions have the same name. The Aristotelian expression *κοινὴ αἴσθησις* is translated, quite literally, as *sensus communis* in Latin and as 'common sense' in English. Here the Latin *sensus* and the English 'sense' are used in their primary connotation of a perceptual ability strictly speaking. However, in the current use of the expression 'common sense', the English word 'sense' has a wider connotation which goes far beyond the sphere of perceptual abilities. This wider connotation is found in the Latin word *sensus*, and those modern European languages that took over the Latin word—such as English, French, or Italian—adopted the wider connotation with it. The Greek word *αἴσθησις*, by contrast, does not permit this wider connotation, and that is why the Greek expression *κοινὴ αἴσθησις* never refers to the same thing to which the corresponding English expression refers nowadays.

That is not to say, however, that what we call 'common sense' is a modern invention. The Latin classical writers, such as Cicero, Horace, and Seneca, used the expression *sensus communis* in a way reminiscent of our notion of common sense. Moreover, our notion of common sense has been traced back to Greek philosophers, especially the Stoics, and the germs of that notion have been found in Aristotle himself. However, the Greek origins of our notion of common sense will vainly be sought under the heading of κοινὴ αἴσθησις in ancient Greek philosophy.

Apart from attempts to trace our notion of common sense back to Aristotle, in the literature one will find the general claim that Aristotle is a philosopher of common sense. I find that claim plausible because it seems to me, to put it in a nutshell, that Aristotle sought to preserve as many beliefs warranted by experience as his subject-matter permitted. This is brought out by Aristotle's memorable methodological remark in the *Generation of Animals*: 'Such appears to be the truth about the generation of bees, judging from theory and from what are believed to be the facts about them; the facts, however, have not yet been sufficiently grasped; if ever they are, then credit must be given rather to observation than to theories, and to theories only if what they affirm agrees with the observed facts.'[1] Why, and to what extent, Aristotle is a philosopher of common sense would make an excellent topic for a book. However, that is not the topic of this book. This book is dedicated to *Aristotle's* notion of the common sense, not ours.

Such a book, I think, has long been due. The common sense is an important notion in Aristotle's psychology and one of his most enduring contributions to the history of psychology. Yet Aristotle says precious little about it, and what he does say is unsystematic and often ambiguous. It is little wonder, then, that scholars from antiquity to the present day have been in disagreement about the exact content of this notion. To get a firm grip on Aristotle's notion of the common sense, one needs to understand the wider framework in which it is embedded and to analyse painstakingly a dozen or so passages from Aristotle, many of which are unusually dense and textually problematic. Such an undertaking requires no less than a book-length study.

I hope that this book will fill the gap. It is a thoroughly revised text of my doctoral dissertation submitted to the University of Oxford in 2003. Without my supervisor, Michael Frede, the book would not have been written. He insisted that I stick with the topic of my BPhil. thesis, and he guided my work with scholarly rigour and philosophical acumen

[1] *GA* III.10 760^{b}27–33, trans. A. Platt.

for which I can find no parallel. I flatter myself that in the course of my BPhil. and DPhil. studies in Oxford Michael had taught me 'how to go about things in philosophy', to use an expression of his, and I shall always be grateful to him.

The dissertation was examined by David Charles and David Sedley. Apart from their joint report which contained many valuable observations and criticisms, I received an additional five pages of detailed comments from David Sedley that proved particularly useful in the process of revising. The dissertation was subsequently read by Myles Burnyeat and Péter Lautner. I had the benefit of their incisive oral and written comments respectively, which led to further improvements. Myles was also kind enough to read and comment on the penultimate version of Part III, Chapters 3 and 4, which may be regarded as central. Two anonymous readers for Oxford University Press gave me a number of useful suggestions in point of content and structure. I also owe a word of gratitude to the colleagues who read and commented on parts of the revised manuscript: Ursula Coope, Filip Grgić, James Harris, and Thomas Johansen. Having mentioned Filip Grgić, with whom I have closely collaborated on several projects, I wish to add that without him my professional life in Zagreb would be greatly impoverished, so I feel very much in his debt. Thanks also to Luka Boršić for sharing his knowledge of Greek and Latin with me. Of course, none of the individuals here mentioned should be held responsible for any fault that this book contains.

In the winter semester of the academic year 2005–6 I held a Junior Research Fellowship at Central European University in Budapest. The fellowship relieved me of my teaching duties in Zagreb and enabled me to dedicate myself to the final stages of revising. I am thankful to the Special Project Office and the Department of Philosophy of CEU for the fellowship and flexibility in arranging it to suit my needs. A special thanks goes to István Bodnár, who read the whole of the revised manuscript and saved me from a number of blunders, some innocuous and some substantial. I presented a paper based on Part I of the book before a well-informed audience at CEU, and I profited from the lively discussion that followed.

Finally, I would like to thank my family, in particular my parents, Tanja Kolar-Gregorić and Goran Gregorić, for their support and encouragement over the years. The people whose presence meant most to me in the course of preparing this book were those who suffered most from my absence due to long working-hours. It is to them, my wife Marta and my daughter Mia, that I dedicate this book with all my love. Maks was fortunate enough to be born after the book had been written. In fact, expectation of his birth hastened the final stages of writing; that alone would have secured him a place in the dedication.

P. G.

Zagreb
November 2006

Contents

Abbreviations

The following abbreviations are used in this book:

Cat.	*Categoriae*
APr.	*Analytica Priora*
APo.	*Analytica Posteriora*
Top.	*Topica*
Phy.	*Physica*
Cael.	*De Caelo*
GC	*De Generatione et Corruptione*
Mete.	*Meteorologica*
DA	*De Anima*
PN	*Parva Naturalia*
DS	*De Sensu et Sensibilibus*
DM	*De Memoria et Reminiscentia*
DSV	*De Somno et Vigilia*
DI	*De Insomniis*
DDS	*De Divinatione per Somnum*
DLBV	*De Longitudine et Brevitate Vitae*
DJS	*De Juventute et Senectute, de Vita et Morte*
DR	*De Respiratione*
HA	*Historia Animalium*
PA	*De Partibus Animalium*
MA	*De Motu Animalium*
IA	*De Incessu Animalium*
GA	*De Generatione Animalium*
Met.	*Metaphysica*
EN	*Ethica Nicomachea*
EE	*Ethica Eudemia*
Pol.	*Politica*
Rhet.	*Ars Rhetorica*
Prot.	*Protrepticus*

References to Aristotle's works are given in the following form: abbreviated title, book (if available), chapter, followed by page, column, and lines in Bekker's edition; e.g. *DA* I.1 402^a1–4, *DSV* 1 454^b31–$^a3$.

References to other works, ancient and modern, aim to be as short as possible, and they have the following format: author's name, followed by parentheses containing the year of publication, page, and lines (if available); e.g. Alexander (1887: 64.1–5), Kahn (1966: 60), Brunschwig (1996: 218). References to ancient works of disputed authorship are given according to their traditional attributions in standard editions, e.g. Philoponus (1887: 460.17–19), Simplicius (1882: 185.7–20). Introductions, notes, and commentaries by editors and translators of Aristotle's texts are cited by the editor's or translator's name followed by 'ed.' in parentheses, e.g. Ross ((ed.)1961: 33), Hamlyn ((ed.)1968: 102). Details of all cited works can be found in the Bibliography, which is organized so as to facilitate following up of references; notably, the list of editions and translations of Aristotle's works is ordered alphabetically by names of the editors and translators.

All translations are mine unless otherwise stated. Many of my translations derive, sometimes with minimal modifications, from those already published. Translations of the textually most problematic passages are accompanied by the Greek text in the Appendix. The Greek text is furnished with a selective apparatus for the reader's convenience. The apparatus is compiled from various modern editions and makes no claim to comprehensiveness.

Introduction

Imagine what it would be like if your five senses—sight, hearing, smell, taste, and touch—were completely independent from one another. You would not be a creature that wakes or sleeps, because your senses would not all be operating in the state of waking and all be resting in the state of sleep. Rather, each sense would operate for some time and then take a snooze, so that you would spend a greater part of your life in an erratic state, neither fully awake nor entirely asleep. Moreover, you would not be able to tell that a piece of Camembert cheese is white and smelly, because you would have no means of relating what you see to what you smell. Each sense would create a phenomenal world of its own, and there would be nothing to mesh these worlds. What is worse, if you lived long enough with your senses cut off from one another, there would not be a 'you' in the first place, because each sense would have its own subject of experience, oblivious of the others. Your body would be housing five yous, a visual you, an auditory you, an olfactory you, and so forth.

Should your perceptual abilities be accompanied by other capacities, such as imagination and memory, these capacities would be bereft of their unity. The visual you would have only visual images and visual memories, the auditory you would have only auditory images and auditory memories, and so forth. Each you would be enriched only within its own narrow confines, locked away from the other yous. Should your perceptions give rise to desires, they would be distributed among the subjects of different senses. The visual you might find a piece of Camembert cheese pleasant and tell your body to take it, while the olfactory you would find it unpleasant and tell your body to shun it. Thus action would be seriously impeded, in some cases impossible. Your body simply would not be able to serve all yous at once, and there would be no means of reaching an agreement as to which you is going to use the body at what time. In fact, it seems that no you would ever know of the existence of the other yous housed in the same body.

This dire scenario does not come from a best-selling book by Oliver Sacks. Rather, it is developed from a suggestion made by Plato in his dialogue *Theaetetus*, almost two-and-a-half millennia ago. Fortunately, the suggestion was followed by Plato's proposal how to avoid the scenario. I suppose many readers would find his proposal congenial, since it consists of postulating a conscious subject which uses the senses and thinks about their reports. Aristotle proposed to avoid this scenario differently, by postulating a perceptual power over and above the five senses which monitors their states and co-ordinates their reports. This perceptual power is known as the 'common sense' (κοινὴ αἴσθησις, *sensus communis*), and it is the topic of this book. To see why Aristotle decided to avoid the described scenario in this particular way, rather than in the way proposed by his master, let us take a closer look at Plato's *Theaetetus*.

In this dialogue Socrates looks for a definition of knowledge with a talented young mathematician called Theaetetus. The first and longest part of the dialogue is devoted to Theaetetus' first reply that knowledge is perception. In order to show that perception cannot amount to knowledge, towards the end of the first part of the dialogue Plato gives an account of the senses. The aim of his account is to reduce perception to passive reception of basic sensible qualities (e.g. white, salty, hot) by means of the senses. This in turn results in an expansion of the active process in which the so-called 'common features' (τὰ κοινά) are grasped. These are the features that characterize, among other things, different basic sensible qualities, and they include 'being', 'difference', 'sameness', 'likeness', and 'unlikeness'. Plato insists that the soul engages in this active process by means of its own resources, unaided by the senses and the bodily parts in which the senses reside. Since knowledge requires a grasp of the common features, knowledge can only be found in this activity in which the soul engages by its own means. Hence, not only can knowledge not be identified with perception, but no case of perception as such can ever constitute a case of knowledge.

So there are two essentially different cognitive processes, according to Plato. Perception is the passive process of grasping a limited number of features, namely basic sensible qualities. The grasp of one kind of basic sensible quality is achieved by means of one sense only, and this grasp is available to human beings as well as to other animals from their birth. By contrast, there is the activity of grasping an entirely different sort of feature, namely the common features. This is achieved by the soul's own means, without any reliance on the senses, and it requires development through experience and education. It seems that Plato conceives of this latter activity as some sort of thinking.[1]

It is important to note Plato's insistence that the subject of both of these kinds of cognitive process is one and the same. More precisely, Plato thinks that it is the soul that does both of them, only by different means. It perceives by means of certain bodily parts, namely the sense organs, whereas it thinks by means of its own resources. Myles Burnyeat rightly acclaims this as 'the first unambiguous statement in the history of philosophy of the difficult but undoubtedly important idea of the unity of consciousness'.[2]

Let us now look more closely at the first part of Plato's argument, the part in which he establishes the soul as the proper subject of perceiving, as opposed to the sense organs. At 184c5 and following, Plato's Socrates asks Theaetetus whether it is more correct to say that we see with (τῷ) the eyes, or by means of (διὰ τοῦ) the eyes. This grammatical contrast points to a philosophical contrast between two importantly different views of the subject of perception. To say that we see *with* the eyes is to say that it is our eyes that do the seeing. To say that we see *by means of* the eyes is to say that we, or our soul, use the eyes as the instrument of seeing. Theaetetus decides that it is more correct to say that we perceive by means of the eyes, and Socrates commends his answer:

> Indeed, young man, for it would surely be strange if several different senses were sitting in us as in wooden horses, rather than there being some one form, the soul or whatever one ought to call it, in which all those converged and with which we perceive perceptible things by means of those as instruments. (*Theaetetus* 184d1–5)

There are several unclear details in this short passage, but the following is beyond doubt. The idiom of seeing with the eyes implies the unacceptable situation metaphorically described as 'the senses sitting in us as in wooden horses'. The tacit assumption seems to be that the senses are localized in different parts of the body, namely the sense organs.[3] If perception were achieved by each sense organ individually,

[1] I infer that the activity of grasping the common features is a sort of thinking from the vocabulary of διανοεῖν (185a4, 9, b7), ἀναλογίζεσθαι (186a10, c3), and συλλογισμός (186d3). At 187a2–8 Theaetetus proposes to call this process δοξάζειν, forming of judgement or opinion.

[2] Burnyeat (1990: 58).

[3] For instance, at 185c3 Plato speaks of the sense of taste as 'the capacity by means of the tongue' (ἡ διὰ τῆς γλώττης δύναμις).

the implication would be that the spatially separate senses, each being localized in a different part of the body, would remain also functionally separate. Each sense would do its own work with respect to one kind of basic sensible quality, and there would be nothing to use the senses. The preferred idiom of seeing by means of the eyes, on the other hand, suggests that there is some one thing—Plato proposes to call it 'soul'—in which the senses are integrated.[4] And because they are integrated in the soul, they can be used to perceive whatever is there to be perceived, to compare or discriminate perceived things, and so forth.

How should we understand the metaphor of the senses sitting in us as in wooden horses? The later scholiast on this passage, Arethas of Caesarea (tenth century AD), suggests that Plato had in mind the Trojan horse in the trunk of which the Achaeans hid their best warriors in order to sneak them into the besieged city.[5] This interpretation is accepted by several commentators, and it is very attractive. However, while agreeing that the wooden horse in which the senses are sitting is the Trojan horse, and hence that Plato likens the senses to the men ensconced inside the Trojan horse, further exegesis is needed.

The metaphor can be interpreted as conveying three closely related yet distinct ideas. First, it conveys the idea of the autonomy of each sense. In the depicted situation, each sense minds its own business within the realm of one kind of basic sensible quality, without any co-ordination with the other senses. Second, the metaphor conveys the idea of something that contains the senses, but cannot use them. In the depicted situation the senses are found within something unconscious, like the wooden trunk of the Trojan horse. The wooden horse is just a container in which the senses sit, not the sort of thing that could make use of the senses. Third, even if the wooden horse could make use of the senses, that would be of no avail, since the wooden horse is not the sort of thing that takes nourishment, perceives objects, desires them, and moves accordingly. Having the senses and being able to use them is just one part of what it is to be a certain sort of thing, namely an animal,

[4] What Plato proposes to call the 'soul' (ψυχή) in *Theaetetus* 184d3 may correspond to what he calls the φρόνιμον in *Timaeus* 64b5, as Lautner (2005: 250–1) suggests. If we assume with Lautner that the φρόνιμον, to which bodily affections have to be transmitted in order to be perceived, is or belongs to the rational part of the soul, then the picture of the integration of the senses in the *Timaeus* conforms to the picture we find in the *Theaetetus*.

[5] See the scholium on *Theaetetus* 184d (*Scholia Platonica*, 440–1 Greene).

which includes having various other capacities and a suitable body in which these capacities are realized. Clearly, the wooden horse is no such thing.

All three unacceptable consequences of the situation depicted in the metaphor go against our experience of perceiving, and they are circumvented by the alternative implied in the idiom of seeing by means of the eyes. To perceive by means of the eyes suggests that there is a subject that uses the sense of sight localized in the eyes. Indeed, it is the same subject that uses all the other senses, each couched in a different part of the body. Plato calls this subject 'soul', and he says that the senses, each located in one sense organ, stretch from there and converge (*συντείνειν*) in the soul. By converging in the soul, which is taken to be something conscious and active, the senses are integrated. And because they are integrated in the soul, they can be used by it.

The soul uses the senses primarily in such a way as to receive impressions of the basic sensible qualities. That is precisely what it means to perceive (*αἰσθάνεσθαι*) in Plato's theory. However, the soul also operates 'itself by itself', in addition to using the senses to perceive. For instance, the soul applies common features such as 'sameness' and 'difference' to the impressions received through the senses and thus discriminates them. When the soul applies the common features to impressions received by means of the senses, the soul is not just perceiving, but also thinking about what it perceives. What I am getting at is that co-ordination of the senses seems to involve the active process of thinking—or whatever it is that the soul does when it operates 'itself by itself'—and this process is essentially different from perceiving, the passive process of receiving basic sensible qualities. To put it differently, in Plato's view the senses are not integrated at the level of perception, but at the level of thought. Thus it is not unfair to say that Plato expands the scope of thought at the expense of perception in his project of dissociating knowledge from perception.

Now Aristotle's discussion of perception belongs to a different project, with different premisses and aims. Speaking very generally, Aristotle's project is to give a systematic account of animals. Such an account ought to explain, among other things, the behaviour of animals which is often stunningly complex. This can be explained within Plato's framework—provided one is prepared to attribute some level of thought to non-human animals. Plato seems to be prepared to do so,[6] but not Aristotle. One of his fundamental premisses is that non-human animals *cannot* think or form opinions.[7] If non-human animals cannot think or form opinions, it would be difficult to adhere to Plato's framework and explain how they can survive, let alone behave intelligently. Their survival depends on their ability to find food, for instance, and finding food depends on their ability to pick out something warm, soft, and moist from the environment which is cold, hard, and dry. This ability in turn depends, at least partly, on the ability to differentiate these sensible qualities, and this latter ability is construed by Plato in terms of the soul applying the common features 'same' and 'different' to these sensible qualities, and that is some sort of thinking.

Aristotle's project thus requires a different, we might say less anthropocentric, notion of the soul which can explain behaviour of animals without recourse to thought. This urges Aristotle to do exactly the opposite of what Plato has done, namely to expand the scope of perception at the expense of thought. That is to say, what is required for Aristotle's project is a notion of the soul in which co-ordination of the senses does not involve thinking, but is achieved entirely at the level of perception. For this purpose, and in line with the basic premisses of his philosophy, Aristotle proposes a significantly different picture of the soul and its relation to the senses.

Despite the fundamental disagreement between Plato and Aristotle due to their different philosophical projects, there can be little doubt that Aristotle was impressed by the metaphor of the wooden horse. He must have thought that a satisfactory theory of perception should avoid the consequences implied in the situation depicted by the metaphor. He agreed with Plato that the senses must be integrated in some single thing, and that this allows them to be used in various ways. He disagreed, however, about the nature and power of that which integrates the senses, and consequently, about the way the senses are co-ordinated. In Aristotle's theory, the senses are not integrated at the level of something that is the subject of both perceiving and thinking. Rather, the senses are integrated by the common sense. Thus integrated, co-ordination of the senses is achieved perceptually, and it can be attributed to non-rational

[6] See *Timaeus* 41d4–42e4 and 90e1–92c3, *Phaedo* 81b1–82b8, *Phaedrus* 249b1–5, *Republic* X 619e6–620d5, *Laws* XII 961d1–10, *Statesman* 263d3–8; cf. Diogenes Laertius III.15.

[7] The far-reaching consequences of this premiss have been rightly emphasized by Sorabji (1992: 196; 1993: 7–20).

animals. With his notion of the common sense, then, Aristotle avoids not only the unpalatable situation depicted by the metaphor of the wooden horse, but also the particular way Plato has dealt with it, which is incompatible with Aristotle's project and fundamental assumptions.

Both philosophers had some ideas about the physiological basis of the integration of the senses, and it is very likely that in developing these ideas they relied on ancient medical theories which postulated a central organ of awareness. There had been an intense and long-lasting debate among physicians as to which organ that was. However, they agreed that the central organ is connected with the rest of the body through a network of channels, and that the substances running through the channels carried perceptual impulses from the periphery to the central organ. Various mental occurrences, especially disturbances and pathological conditions, were explained with reference to the state of the central organ. It is usually assumed by historians of ancient medicine that theories associated with the medical schools of Cnidus and Sicily maintained that the heart was the central organ of awareness, and that they assigned a prominent role to blood. Adherents of the medical school which flourished on the island of Cos, by contrast, took the view that the brain was the seat of awareness, and they emphasized the role of air.[8]

Plato's ideas were stated in his monumental dialogue *Timaeus*, where he leans towards the views of the Coan school. Plato located the rational soul, which seems to be the subject of sensory experience, in the head, and he attached special importance to the marrow of which the brain is made. Aristotle, by contrast, sided with the other school and located the common sense in the heart. One of the main reasons for Aristotle's choice of organ was his conviction, supported by his empirical research, that the heart is connected in one way or another with all the sense organs, whereas the brain is not. Hence, he thought that the heart is the central or master sense organ, and the seat of the common sense. Another reason, also based on Aristotle's empirical research, is his view

[8] The cardiocentric view is manifest in some Hippocratic writings, most notably *On Diseases, On Places in Man*, and *On the Heart*. It has been endorsed by Aristotle, Diocles of Carystus, Praxagoras of Cos, and the Stoics. The encephalocentric view is found in the Hippocratic *On the Sacred Disease* and *On the Nature of Man*, and some version of it has been advocated by Alcmaeon of Croton, Philolaus, Diogenes of Apollonia, possibly by Anaxagoras and Democritus, by Plato in the *Timaeus*, and the Peripatetic Strato of Lampsacus. The discovery of the nervous system by Alexandrian doctors in the early 3rd century BC gave support to the latter view, which won the day by late antiquity. For a selection from the vast literature on this subject, see Van der Eijk (2005: 124 n. 13).

that the heart is connected in one way or another with all the other vital activities, whereas the brain is not. The heart is where the crucial stage of the nutritive process takes place, namely the production of blood, where desires and aversions arise, and where impulses to locomotion come from. Hence, Aristotle thought of the heart as the central or master organ *toto caelo*, very much like we think of the brain.

We know that Aristotle got his physiology all wrong. There is a complex nervous system with a number of hierarchically organized perceptual sub-systems integrated in the brain. Moreover, we think that integration of the senses must be a part of a larger story—a story of consciousness—which ought to explain not only the integration of the senses but of all our cognitive, emotional, and conative abilities. Finally, we do not think that the senses are integrated by another sense. To be sure, some philosophers, such as Kant or Armstrong, would be prepared to argue that the senses, together with the other mental abilities, are integrated by an 'inner sense', but that is only a figure of speech, not a 'sense' properly speaking. Given our knowledge of neurophysiology and our intuitions about consciousness, it is natural to raise the question why we should study the Aristotelian notion of the common sense. I have three reasons to offer.

First, this notion is philosophically interesting. Some scholars have found in it rudiments of a theory of consciousness.[9] I would say, more cautiously, that it can be fruitfully related to several facets of current discussions about consciousness.[10] One set of current discussions is devoted to perceptual consciousness, which is mainly awareness of what is going on in one's environment by means of the five senses. It is often claimed that one of the central features of perceptual consciousness is its unity. Of course, there are various ways in which perceptual consciousness is unified, and not all of them are addressed by Aristotle. However, some ways are addressed, and they are addressed with the notion of the common sense. For instance, one way in which perceptual consciousness is unified is that it enables integration of sensible properties accessed through different sense modalities into coherent wholes, for example when we perceive white and sweet as

[9] Kahn (1966), Modrak (1981*a*; 1987: 133–54); cf. Hardie (1976), Caston (2002).

[10] It seems to me that there is very little or nothing in Aristotle that can be plausibly related to the so-called 'phenomenal consciousness' and 'access consciousness' (introduced by Block 1995) which are at the centre of current discussions of consciousness in the philosophy of mind; cf. Caston (2002) and Johansen (2006).

bound together, as different properties of the same object. We shall see that Aristotle recognizes the importance of this phenomenon and that he gives it an interesting explanation which relies on a particular notion of simultaneity.

On the other hand, Aristotle addresses some issues that are on the periphery of modern research on the unity of perceptual consciousness. For instance, perceptual consciousness is unified in such a way that it is not disrupted by occasional incapacitation of one or more senses, but by periodical incapacitation of all the senses in sleep. Aristotle's notion of the common sense is introduced to explain, among other things, why that is so.

Another set of current discussions is devoted to consciousness understood as awareness of what is going on in one's mind. There is a long and distinguished tradition of philosophers, from Locke and Kant to Armstrong and Lycan, who argue that we are aware of what is going on in our minds in a way which resembles the way we are aware of what is going on in our environment, that is, by some sort of perception. Hence they take consciousness to be a matter of reflection, inner sense, monitoring, or second-order perception of our own mental states and activities. Aristotle's notion of the common sense seems to be a precursor of that tradition, since he argues that the awareness of our perceptual states is of perceptual sort, for it is achieved by a perceptual power, namely the common sense. Although the common sense provides us with access to our perceptual states only, thus capturing only a segment of the relevant notion of consciousness, what Aristotle has to say about this function of the common sense is, I think, rather stimulating. What follows from his account, for instance, is that awareness of our perceptual states should be regarded as an aspect, possibly the most important aspect, of the unity of perceptual consciousness. That is to say, part of what it is to have one's perceptual consciousness unified, according to Aristotle, is to be aware of one's perceptual states. I shall offer some thoughts as to why the awareness of one's perceptual states is important for an animal. Moreover, Aristotle observes that the common sense enables us to be aware not only of our perceptions of colours and sounds, but also of our failures to perceive, as when we find ourselves surrounded with darkness and silence. This observation, I shall argue, has far-reaching consequences which have gone unnoticed in recent discussions.

The second reason for studying Aristotle's notion of the common sense is its historical importance. To illustrate this, let me quote a critical remark written in the mid-seventeenth century, almost two millennia after Aristotle: 'Some say the Senses receive the Species of things, and deliver them to the Common Sense; and the Common Sense delivers them over to the Fancy, and the Fancy to the Memory, and the Memory to the Judgement, like handling of things from one to another, with many words making nothing understood' (Thomas Hobbes, *Leviathan*, I.2.8). What Hobbes is criticizing in this passage is the medieval theory of the so-called 'internal senses'. Medieval philosophers argued that human beings share with higher animals a certain number of capacities, called 'internal senses', which are located in the three Galenic ventricles of the brain. There was some disagreement as to how many capacities there are and how they are arranged in the ventricles. All major medieval philosophers agreed, however, that one of these capacities is the 'common sense' and that it is located in the anterior ventricle of the brain, right where all the sensory nerves were believed to end up. The common sense receives perceptible forms (*species*) from the external senses, it compares the received forms, differentiates them, and unifies them. Thus processed, perceptible forms are passed on to the other internal senses.

The next internal sense is imagination. Imagination collects and manipulates the forms. Some medieval philosophers distinguished between imagination proper and fantasy as two distinct internal senses, with slightly different functions. Roughly speaking, imagination retains and collects the processed forms, whereas fantasy divides them and combines them into representations of things that were not perceived. Next, medieval philosophers recognized the existence of a capacity which enables the animal to extract vital information about its environment from the form processed by the common sense and imagination, and to perform intelligent actions on that basis, such as avoiding harmful things like predators, pursuing beneficial things like food and medicinal substances, making provisions of food, and building complex structures such as webs or nests. This capacity is called the 'cogitative' or 'estimative' capacity, and it was located in the middle ventricle of the brain. In all variants of the theory, the last capacity in the series, located in the posterior ventricle of the brain, is the capacity of storing the entirely processed perceptible forms, that is, memory.[11]

[11] Thomas Aquinas and John of Jandun recognized four internal senses: the common sense, imagination, *vis cogitativa*, and memory. Avicenna, followed by Robert Grosseteste, Albert the Great, and Roger Bacon, argued for five internal senses: the common sense,

This theory provided a complete description of animal cognition, but only a partial description of human cognition. The medieval philosophers believed that human beings are endowed also with reason which enables them to acquire, manipulate, and express concepts, as well as to extract universals from particulars and thus attain scientific understanding of things. Assuming that reason is not located in any bodily organ, they believed it to be immortal. Since the medieval philosophers baulked at overcrowding heaven with the souls of beasts, they needed a theory which explains complex behaviour of animals without recourse to reason. The theory of the internal senses satisfied the need in a robust way: it was cogent and logically consistent, and it was in agreement with both philosophical tradition and medical knowledge of the day. And apart from providing an account of cognition and behaviour of animals, it gave an account of non-rational cognitive abilities of human beings, it could explain failures of human cognitive functioning following head injuries and fevers, and it was often invoked in explanations of mental disorders and paranormal phenomena.

The father of modern anatomy, Andreas Vesalius, undermined the physiological basis of the theory of the internal senses by his detailed anatomical study of the human brain in the sixteenth century. He showed, among other things, that there is no direct connection between the anterior ventricle of the brain and any of the sensory nerves, and that the arrangement of ventricles is not as simple and clear-cut as the medieval descriptions suggested. However, the theory of the internal senses was far too deeply entrenched to be abandoned in the light of Vesalius's findings; rather, attempts were made to preserve the theory by providing it with a more suitable physiological basis.

In a letter to Mersenne of 21 April 1641, Descartes wrote: 'It is also certain that the seat of the common sense has to be very mobile in order to receive all impressions that arrive from the senses.'[12] Famously, Descartes located the seat of the common sense in the pineal gland. The renowned Oxford physician and anatomist Thomas Willis, whose lectures were attended by John Locke, argued that the sensory nerves are connected to the medulla oblongata, that the common sense is located

imagination, fantasy, *vis aestimativa*, and memory. A somewhat dated but still useful account of the chequered history of the internal senses in Latin, Arabic, and Hebrew medieval philosophy can be found in Wolfson (1935).

[12] *Oeuvres de Descartes*, III.362; cf. III.263 (Adam and Tannery).

in the adjacent corpus striatum, that images were projected on the neighbouring corpus callosum, and that in the end they are retained in the cortex, which is also the seat of the rational soul in human beings.[13]

It is unclear to me if, and to what extent, Hobbes's criticism of the theory of the internal senses was influenced by anatomical considerations. What is clear, however, is that his criticism was motivated by his conscious opposition to the medieval philosophical tradition. He refused to recognize the existence of immaterial entities such as perceptible forms, as suggested by the quoted passage. Instead, Hobbes advocated a materialist view of the world and proposed a unified mechanistic explanation of cognition and behaviour—of animals and humans alike—in terms of motions and inclinations. Descartes also rejected the medieval philosophical tradition and heralded mechanistic explanations as far as the physical world went. However, he still found use for the theory of the internal senses, as is illustrated by the following passage: 'But before I speak in greater detail about sleep and dreams, I ask you to consider what is most noteworthy about the brain during the time of waking: namely, how ideas of objects are formed in the place assigned to the imagination and to the common sense, how these ideas are retained in the memory, and how they cause the movement of all the bodily parts' (Descartes, *Treatise on Man*).[14] This passage clearly shows that the Aristotelian notion of the common sense has survived, at least in some form and for some time, even the wholesale rejection of the Aristotelian medieval tradition to which this notion had belonged. I want to stress this fact because it shows that the notion of the common sense, which originates with Aristotle, was one of the most successful and resilient of Aristotelian notions. As we have seen, throughout its history it has been bolstered by physiological considerations, but it was not dependent on them; it grew out of Aristotelian philosophy, but it did not hang upon it. The reason for abandoning this notion in the late seventeenth and eighteenth centuries was not that the problems it addressed were recognized as false or unimportant, but that they were

[13] Cf. Kemp and Fletcher (1993: 567), Bennet and Hacker (2003: 30–3), and Molnár (2004: 334). Willis was the first person to locate the rational faculties in the cerebral cortex. His view was based on comparative anatomical research which revealed that human beings have a proportionally larger cortex with a greater number of convolutions than other animals, and that persons suffering from congenital idiocy have a less developed cortex than healthy human beings.

[14] *Oeuvres de Descartes*, XI.174, trans. S. Gaukroger in Descartes (1998: 146). For other references to the common sense in Descartes, see *Oeuvres de Descartes*, XI.175–7 and 227, V.313, VIIIB.344 and 356–7, X.414.

addressed more convincingly and comprehensively within new theories of the mind and cognition, such as Locke's or Kant's.

The third reason for studying Aristotle's notion of the common sense is that, after centuries of interpretative efforts, it is still a subject of controversy. The divergence as to what the common sense in Aristotle is, what its functions are, and how they are discharged is so wide that one would be hard pressed to find two scholars who agree on all substantive points.

An attempt to summarize uncontroversial points concerning Aristotle's notion of the common sense yields a disappointingly short list. First, it is a perceptual power distinct from the five ordinary senses. Second, it is a perceptual power of a different type and order from the five senses. Third, it allows Aristotle to say that the five senses are not mutually independent capacities, but form some sort of unity. Fourth, it is closely connected with Aristotle's idea that the heart is the central sense organ. Fifth, it is in charge of certain functions that, in Aristotle's view, go beyond the five senses taken individually. Every further point or specification is likely to be controversial.

We would like to know how Aristotle arrives at his notion of the common sense, what sort of unity the senses form, and how this gives rise to a distinct perceptual power. Moreover, we would like to know what are the functions of this power, and exactly how they are discharged. A number of modern scholars have tackled these questions, sometimes with considerable plausibility and ingenuity, but rarely without controversy. Let me illustrate the intensity of the controversy by briefly surveying various suggestions of eminent scholars as to what the common sense is and what its functions are.

Sir David Ross gives the following account: 'The phrase *κοινὴ αἴσθησις* is rare in Aristotle, but conveniently sums up a whole mass of doctrine, provided it be interpreted not as being another sense over and above the five, but as the common nature inherent in them all. We must think of sense as a single faculty which discharges certain functions in virtue of its generic nature but is also specified into the five senses.'[15] It is far from clear what the 'common nature' inherent in all five senses is supposed to be, or what it means for something to discharge functions 'in virtue of its generic nature'. Ross does not explain this, and he hardly spells out the 'whole mass of doctrine' summed up in the phrase *κοινὴ αἴσθησις*. Charles Kahn criticizes Ross for giving 'a misleading account

[15] Ross ((ed.)1955: 35); cf. Ross ((ed.)1961: 33 and 1949: 140).

of the *sensus communis*'.[16] He thinks that the *De Anima* and *Parva Naturalia* form a continuous and progressive exposition of one single unified faculty of perception, and the failure to recognize this fact results in 'the concept of the *sensus communis* (which) is merely a truncated form of this Aristotelian doctrine of the unified faculty of perception'. On the other hand, Deborah Modrak claims that the common sense is 'simply the capacity for joint activity by the five senses'.[17] Stephen Everson retorts that the point about the common sense 'is not that it is possessed by the special senses *jointly*, but precisely that it is possessed in common by those senses and so it is not specific to any'.[18] He maintains that the common sense 'is something which each sense possesses but not *as that sense*: it is a capacity it has in virtue of being part of the perceptual capacity as a whole and not of being that particular sense.' Obviously, there is substantial disagreement among scholars as to what the common sense is.

Let us take a look at the functions that modern scholars ascribe to the common sense. Ross writes:

> The functions in which the perceptive faculty operates in this unspecialized way are the following: (1) the perception of the 'common sensibles'; (2) the perception of the 'incidental sensibles'; (3) the perception that we are perceiving; (4) discrimination between the objects of different senses. (5) Finally, Aristotle argues that the inactivity of all the senses which is found in sleep cannot be a mere coincidence but must be due to the inactivity of the central perceptive faculty of which they are differentiations.[19]

In contrast to Ross, Irving Block thinks that perception of the common sensibles—features perceived through more than one sense, such as shape, magnitude, or change—is the work of nothing other than the individual senses.[20] David Hamlyn, on the contrary, argues that the phrase 'common sense' names a specialized perceptual power whose one and only function is to perceive the common sensibles.[21] Kahn excludes function (2) from Ross's list on account of the fact that it 'belongs to the sense faculty only *incidentally*'.[22] However, he adds to Ross's list: (6) the sense of time; (7) the capacity for imagination; (8) the capacity for memory; and (9) the capacity for dreaming. Richard Sorabji provides

16 Kahn (1966: 63).
17 Modrak (1981*b*: 406; cf. 1987: 62–71).
18 Everson (1997: 155 n. 26).
19 Ross ((ed.)1955: 35); cf. Ross ((ed.)1961: 33–6 and 1949: 140–2).
20 Block (1988: 244–5, 247–8 n. 10; cf. 1961*b*: 62).
21 Hamlyn (1968: 204–6; (ed.)1968: 128–9).
22 Kahn (1966: 64).

a list which agrees with Kahn's except that it expands it with another three functions: (10) perceiving simultaneously different sense objects; (11) perceiving that they belong to one thing; and (12) perceiving proper objects of one sense by another sense, for example perceiving sweet by sight.[23] Block adds yet another function to the common sense, and that is: (13) to objectify perceptions, that is, to give their contents objective reference.[24] This suffices to show how wide the disagreement concerning the functions of the common sense is among contemporary scholars.

The illustrated disagreements are generated by real difficulties in the subject-matter. I think that there are three main sources of difficulties surrounding Aristotle's notion of the common sense. First, the notion emerges from Aristotle's philosophical project and method, which are not only far removed from ours, but may inspire modern readers with disbelief. Second, Aristotle is rather inconsistent in his use of terminology, which complicates the matter greatly. Third, passages in which Aristotle explains the functions that belong to the common sense are often compressed and textually problematic, and as a result it is hard to make sense of them. The last two sources of difficulties frustrated ancient as well as modern interpreters, so they can be only of partial help in bring us closer to an understanding of Aristotle's notion of the common sense.

Dealing with these sources of difficulties in an appropriate way ought to remove at least the most acute difficulties and thus make Aristotle's notion of the common sense clearer. This is what I hope to achieve in this book. Most of my efforts will be directed at fathoming and elucidating Aristotle's views, rather than to their evaluation or placement in the context of contemporary debates. Hence, this book is primarily intended for specialists in ancient philosophy, especially those interested in Aristotle's psychology and theory of perception. Other scholars might wish to consult my interpretations of individual passages in Aristotle, many of which are well known and widely debated. However, I will occasionally engage in identifying parallels and dissonances between Aristotle's and contemporary theories in the philosophy of mind and psychology, so my discussion, especially in

[23] Sorabji (1972: 75–6). The list of Bennett and Hacker (2003) corresponds to that of Kahn, to which they add function (11) listed by Sorabji.

[24] Block (1960: 98–9). This view goes back to Zeller (1921: 544), and it has been advocated more recently by Van der Eijk ((ed.)1994: 50, 76; 2000: 65).

Part III, might be of some interest to readers primarily involved with contemporary theories.

Part I presents the philosophical framework within which the notion of the common sense appears. An exposition of Aristotle's programme and method will inform us how he arrives at this notion, how the common sense is related to the individual senses and other cognitive capacities, what sort of unity is at work there, and how the common sense is related to a system of bodily parts with the heart at its centre. This Part will provide us with a conceptual apparatus used in the following chapters and necessary for the success of the whole endeavour.

Part II offers a detailed treatment of all the passages in which the phrase 'common sense' occurs in Aristotle's extant works. This will show that the phrase 'common sense' occurs more often than is acknowledged in the contemporary literature, and also that it is used in different ways and for different things. One consequence of the findings in this Part is that some functions attributed to something called 'common sense' do not really belong to the common sense, but to other cognitive capacities. I will suggest what these capacities are, and how they might discharge these functions. Another consequence is that it is necessary to look at passages which do not explicitly use the phrase 'common sense' to find out what the functions of the common sense are, and how they are supposed to work.

The relevant passages are examined in detail in Part III, and each function of the common sense is explained at length. It will often be necessary to delve into Aristotle's obscure analogies, or to relate his discussions to Plato's views on particular issues, in order to get clearer about Aristotle's position. Nevertheless, these examinations will yield novel interpretations of the functions of the common sense, and I hope that at least some of these interpretations will show Aristotle's views to be sensible and interesting.

PART I

THE FRAMEWORK

It becomes, therefore, no inconsiderable part of science barely to know the different operations of the mind, to separate them from each other, to class them under their proper heads, and to correct all that seeming disorder, in which they lie involved, when made the object of reflection and enquiry. (. . .) And if we can go no farther than this mental geography, or delineation of the distinct parts and powers of the mind, it is at least a satisfaction to go so far.

David Hume, *An Enquiry concerning Human Understanding*

1

Aristotle's Project and Method

It is well known that Aristotle's philosophy of nature, or physics, studies natural substances by analysing them into form and matter. Matter is the substrate of form, the stuff in which form is realized. Form, on the other hand, is the structure imposed on a chunk of matter, that which organizes some stuff in such a way that the compound has the shape that objects of this kind typically have. But form is not only the organization of a chunk of matter, it is also an irreducible capacity, or a set of capacities, which enables the compound to function and behave in ways characteristic of objects of that kind. It is imperative for an Aristotelian philosopher of nature to study both form and matter because natural substances are composites of both. However, it is also imperative to study form first and foremost, because form is prior to matter. For matter to exist actually, it must have some form or other. It is the form which unifies a piece of matter, organizes it in a particular way, endows the compound with function, and thus makes it the sort of thing it is. Hence, when an Aristotelian philosopher of nature studies a natural substance, he must first provide an account of its form to be in a position to give an account of its matter.

According to Aristotle, living beings constitute one large class of natural substances. Consequently, they are studied by physics in such a way that they are analysed into form and matter. Forms of living beings (τὰ ἔμψυχα) are their souls (ψυχαί), whereas their natural instrumental bodies (σώματα φυσικὰ ὀργανικά), that is, natural bodies equipped for doing whatever living beings of a given sort typically do, are their matter. Scientific study of living beings, therefore, requires first of all an account of the soul. Such an account is supplied in the treatise *De Anima.*

In the beginning of the very first chapter of this treatise (*DA* I.1 402^a10–22), Aristotle indicates a methodological difficulty: how should one study the soul? I take it that he is not wondering about the correct method of discovery, but rather about the correct method of exposition—how one should proceed if one wants to give an adequate account of the soul.

On the one hand, the soul has to be explained in such a way that its essence is expounded as well as its main attributes (*DA* I.1 402^{b}16–403^{a}2). An account of the soul should clarify not only what the soul is, but also what it does, or rather what it is that a living being does in virtue of its soul. Specifying the essence of the soul without saying anything about taking nourishment, growing, reproducing, perceiving, moving about, and thinking would be uninformative.

On the other hand, an account of the soul should not be concerned, at least not primarily, with the soul in general, because the soul in general does not exist in reality.[1] What exists in reality are souls of different kinds of living beings, the soul in general being only a generic concept applicable to all existent souls. It is quite obvious that plants have one sort of soul and animals another, since animals do many things that plants do not, and they all do these things in virtue of their souls. Likewise, different species of animals have different souls. For instance, rational animals have different souls from non-rational animals. Rational animals think, and since they think in virtue of the soul they have, their souls must be importantly different from the souls of non-rational animals. Therefore, an adequate account of the soul should be concerned with souls that exist in reality, that is, the souls of plants, animals, and human beings.

One obvious way to satisfy both requirements is to give separate accounts of different sorts of soul and explain the vital activities that they make possible. However, that task would involve unnecessary repetition.[2] An account of the soul of plants would tell us about the principle which enables plants to do what they typically do, namely to take nourishment, grow, and reproduce. Since animals also take nourishment, grow, and reproduce, an account of the soul of animals would have to repeat the same things already set out in the account of the soul of plants. And when one comes to give an account of the soul of human beings, one would have to repeat the same things already set out in the account of the soul of higher animals, since human beings do the main things that higher animals do—perceive, desire, move about—and they think in addition to all that.

A more economic strategy is to give separate accounts of different capacities of the soul, each capacity being the principle of one activity

1 *DA* I.1 402^{b}1–8, II.3 414^{b}20–415^{a}13.

2 *PA* I.1 639^{a}15–29, 5 645^{b}10–13.

of living beings. But how does Aristotle decide what counts as a distinct capacity of the soul? Since the soul is that which enables all activities of living beings, and there are indefinitely many activities manifested by an enormous variety of living beings, if each activity is due to one capacity of the soul it seems that there will be indefinitely many capacities of the soul (*DA* III.9 432^{a}22–4).

Aristotle observes that there is a group of closely related activities which is present in all living beings, namely taking nourishment, growing, and reproducing. The peculiarity of this group of activities is that in one kind of living beings (plants) it is found to exist without any other activity, since they do not engage in any activity other than taking nourishment, growing, and reproducing. No other kind of salient activity of living beings is found to exist without at least one other kind of activity.[3] Perception is not found to exist without taking nourishment, growing, and reproducing, since all living beings that can perceive (animals) invariably take nourishment, grow, and reproduce. In fact, animals use their senses precisely in order to detect food and to locate potential mates. Moreover, moving about is not found to exist apart from perceiving, taking nourishment, growing, and reproducing, since all living beings that can move about (mobile animals) invariably perceive, take nourishment, grow, and reproduce. Again, with the ability to move about animals are more efficient in finding food and mates, and in this they rely on the distal senses in particular. Finally, thinking is not found to exist without all the aforementioned activities—at least not in the sublunary sphere—because living beings that think (humans) invariably move about, perceive, take nourishment, grow, and reproduce. In fact, thinking enables human beings to perform all these activities not only more efficiently, but in a way which contributes to their well-being. All this shows that there is an order of ontological priority among the salient activities or groups of closely related activities of living beings, such that the presence of a higher activity in every case involves the presence of the lower

[3] Another exception may be thinking; cf. *DA* I.1 403^{a}8–10, 4 408^{b}18–25, II.2 413^{b}24–6, III.4 429^{a}24–7, 5 430^{a}16–18, 22–5; *GA* II.3 736^{b}27–9. Aristotle's position on the thinking capacity of the soul is highly controversial. I shall not attempt to do it justice in this brief overview, as that would complicate matters without contributing significantly to my endeavour. The reader may wish to consult a sample of recent publications from the vast literature on the subject: Modrak (1991), Kahn (1992), Kosman (1992), Frede (1996*b*), Van der Eijk (1997), Sisko (1999), Caston (1999; 2000), Gerson (2004).

ones.[4] This order equips Aristotle with a reliable criterion for deciding what counts as a capacity of the soul. Namely, one capacity of the soul is the principle of one of these ordered salient activities of living beings.

The same order which holds among salient activities of living beings clearly holds among the capacities of the soul. The nutritive capacity of the soul is unique in that it is the only capacity found to exist apart from any other, namely in plants. Aristotle would say that it is separable (χωριστόν) from the other capacities of the soul. This is not the case with any other capacity of the soul, save perhaps with the intellect. The perceptual capacity is not separable from the nutritive, the locomotory capacity from the perceptual and the nutritive, and the thinking capacity from the other three. 'The situation with the soul is similar to that concerning geometrical figures,' writes Aristotle in *DA* II.3 414^b28–32, 'for in the case of both figures and living beings that which is prior is always potentially present in what follows in order, for instance the triangle in the quadrangle, and the nutritive capacity in the perceptual one.'

This ontological order of capacities of the soul reflects the differences that exist among salient kinds of living beings, namely plants, animals, among animals those that are mobile, and among mobile animals those that are rational.[5] Hence, upon completing his detailed accounts of each capacity of the soul, Aristotle is entitled to conclude that his study of the soul deals with souls that exist in reality. Since living beings of different kinds have different souls, that is, souls with different capacities, successive accounts of the capacities of the soul, following their ontological order, constitute an economic strategy of explaining souls that exist in reality, namely the souls of living beings of different kinds.

We can now appreciate why Aristotle thinks that the division of the soul into the rational and non-rational part, or Plato's division of the soul into the rational, spirited, and appetitive part, are inadequate for scientific study of the soul.[6] Such divisions overlook other important

[4] The notion of ontological priority is explained in *Cat.* 12 14^a30–5 and *Met.* V.11 1019^a2–5.

[5] Aristotle recognizes borderline cases that cannot be unqualifiedly subsumed under any one of these salient kinds, but they do not seem to upset Aristotle's framework; cf. Lloyd (1996: ch. 3).

[6] Cf. *DA* III.9 432^a24–6. For the purpose of ethical investigation the division of the soul into the rational and non-rational part is both acceptable and appropriate; cf.

activities of living beings. And there is no easy or informative way of accommodating the omitted activities in the earlier divisions. For instance, should one associate perception with the rational or with the non-rational part of the soul? In the case of lower animals perception belongs to the non-rational part of the soul, whereas in the case of humans it seems to belong to the rational part of the soul, since our perceptions can be and usually are informed by our thoughts and concepts. Scientific study of the soul requires division along 'natural joints', to borrow a Platonic expression. As we have seen, the analysis of the soul into distinct capacities following their natural order does the trick.

This strategy of explaining the soul is evident from the structure of the main books of *DA*, books two and three. In *DA* II.1–2 Aristotle gives an account of the soul in general, with his much-debated definition of the soul as 'the primary actuality of the natural instrumental body'.[7] In *DA* II.3 he shows that there is an order of ontological priority among the capacities of the soul, and that the best way to study the soul is to give successive accounts of each one of them. From *DA* II.4 we learn that, in order to explain a capacity, one must explain the relevant activity, and in order to explain the activity, one must first explain the object of that activity.[8] In the second part of the same chapter Aristotle gives a (regrettably) brief account of the most fundamental, nutritive capacity of the soul. The rest of book two, chapters 5–12, and the first two chapters of book three are devoted to the next capacity in the order of priority, which is the perceptual capacity of the soul. The following chapter discusses imagination as something closely related to both perception and thought, whereas *DA* III.4–8 deal with the thinking capacity of the soul. Chapters 9–11 provide a treatment of the desiderative and locomotory capacities of the soul.[9] Finally, chapters 12 and 13 discuss

EN I.13 1102^{a}26–32 and *EE* II.1 1219^{b}32–5. For interpretations of the relationship among different divisions of the soul mentioned by Aristotle, see Fortenbaugh (1970), and Vander Waerdt (1985; 1987).

[7] *DA* II.1 412^{b}5–6. Notable discussions of Aristotle's definition of the soul can be found in Owens (1971*a*), Ackrill (1972/3), Bolton (1978), Charlton (1980), Ward (1996), Menn (2002), and Bos (2003).

[8] *DA* I.1 402^{b}10–16, II.4 415^{a}14–22.

[9] One might wonder why Aristotle reverses the order and discusses the desiderative and locomotory capacities *after* discussing the thinking capacity. One probable reason is that an account of thinking naturally comes after accounts of perception and imagination, so that it made good sense to give a continuous exposition of the cognitive capacities. The other reason is that, having provided an adequate treatment of the non-rational

certain points that put perception in a teleological perspective, linking it with survival and nourishment.

Now that we understand Aristotle's overall strategy, we should pause to consider the nature of Aristotle's division of the soul. Aristotle insists that the capacities into which he divides the soul are not spatially separable parts of the soul, but only its conceptually distinct parts. It is important to understand what this means and why Aristotle insists on this point.

We have seen that a higher capacity of the soul is not found to exist apart from the lower ones. This has two implications. One is that the capacities of the soul are not parts into which the soul can be actually divided. Physical objects, for example a lump of clay, can be broken up into chunks, and each chunk carries on existing independently of the others. The soul is a form, by contrast, and hence not the sort of thing that can be divided in such a way that its parts exist separately from one another. The other implication is that the soul is not an aggregate of its capacities. The capacities of the soul cannot come together to make up a soul, whereas smaller chunks of clay can be put together to produce a single lump of clay. An aggregate like a lump of clay is a weak sort of unity generated simply by adjoining its parts. The soul, on the other hand, is the strongest sort of unity which does not admit of parts into which it can disintegrate, or from which it can be generated.

Nevertheless, capacities of the soul can be distinguished from one another with reference to different activities that living beings display in virtue of their souls. Having distinguished different capacities of the soul, we have divided it conceptually—'in account' (λόγῳ), or 'in being' (τῷ εἶναι), as Aristotle would say. Each vital activity, or set of closely related activities, of living beings is assigned to one capacity of the soul, and hence the capacities differ 'in being': what it is to be this capacity is different from what it is to be that capacity, since this capacity is responsible for one activity, and that capacity is responsible for another activity. And since the account of each capacity must specify the activity for which this capacity is responsible, capacities of the soul will accordingly differ from each other 'in account'.

Resulting from a conceptual division of the soul, the capacities can be regarded as parts of the soul, but only in a weak sense of the word 'part'. The capacities of the soul are thus conceptual, or logical parts

and rational cognitive capacities, Aristotle was then able to give an account of both non-rational and rational motivation.

of the soul. Indeed, Aristotle often talks of the capacities of the soul as its parts, but he seems to do so only for convenience, without ever implying that they are parts in the strong sense of spatially separable parts.[10] His very concept of soul as the form of the living body rules out the possibility that the soul can be chopped up into separately existing parts. Due to this particular bit of Aristotle's theory, the distinction between parts and capacities of the soul will come to play a significant role in the subsequent theorizing about the soul.[11]

One of the advantages of Aristotle's idea that the soul is only conceptually divisible is that it allows him to avoid problems which he detected in Plato. In the *Timaeus*, Plato argues that the rational part of the soul is located in the head, the spirited in the chest, and the appetitive in the abdomen.[12] If the soul is actually divided into the three parts located in three different parts of the body, what keeps the soul together? Surely it cannot be the body, because it is the soul that keeps the body together, not vice versa.[13] Furthermore, the spatial division of the soul seems to imply that the three parts of the body, each housing one part of the soul, could exist separately from one another, and hence that the body is a unity of a weak sort, not unlike an aggregate.[14]

These problems do not arise for Aristotle. Conceptual division of the soul threatens neither (i) the unity of the soul, nor (ii) the unity of the living body.

[10] Cf. *DA* II.2 413^{b}27–32, III.9 432^{a}19–32; *EN* I.13 1102^{a}28–32; *EE* II.1 1219^{b}32–5.

[11] In his lost work *On Capacities of the Soul*, of which fragments are preserved in Stobaeus (I.49.24–6 Wachsmuth = Porphyry frs. 251–4 Smith), Porphyry writes: 'The ancients are divided . . . also about the parts of the soul, and in general what a part is and what a capacity, and wherein their difference lies' (Stobaeus I.49.25a = Porphyry fr. 253 Smith). There is also a fragment of Iamblichus' text of the same title (Stobaeus I.49.33) and a short piece ascribed to Plutarch under the title *Whether That Which Enables Emotions is a Part or a Capacity of the Human Soul*.

[12] *Timaeus* 69d6 ff. For a lucid recent discussion of the tripartite soul in the *Timaeus*, see Johansen (2000; and 2004: ch. 7).

[13] Cf. *DA* I.5 411^{b}5–9. Aristotle's view that it is the soul that keeps the body together is based on the insight that the body disintegrates when the soul perishes, i.e. when the living being dies. This fact, however, did not prevent the Epicureans from maintaining that it is the body which keeps the soul together; cf. Annas (1992: 123–56, esp. 147–8).

[14] Consider, for example, Plato's description of the head in *Timaeus* 44d3–45a3. The rest of the body is said to be attached to the head in order to supply it with a means of transportation over uneven terrain. This suggests that if the terrain were smooth, without any protrusions or hollows, the head would have no need of the rest of the body, which means that it could, in principle, exist separately from the rest of the body.

(i) Each particular soul is, for Aristotle, one single entity responsible for all activities of the living being whose soul it is. The fact that we can analyse the soul into distinct capacities, so that each capacity is responsible for one activity or set of closely related activities, by no means compromises the soul's unity. To say that an animal perceives on account of the perceptual capacity of its soul and moves about on account of the locomotory capacity of its soul does not entail that the soul is a mere aggregate of such capacities, or that it can be broken up into these capacities. This is proved by the fact that when some animals are actually divided, various capacities of the soul are preserved by both parts, rather than being parcelled out between them. For instance, each part of a divided centipede remains sensitive to touch and wiggles for some time, which means that each part has the abilities to perceive and move about—'and if it has perception,' Aristotle infers, 'it also has imagination and desire'.[15]

(ii) Each particular soul, being a unity, renders the living body that it informs a unity. Of course, one can specify different sets of bodily parts that a living body must have if it is to be informed by a soul with certain capacities. For instance, there must be a set of bodily parts constituting something like a digestive system if a living being is to have the nutritive capacity of the soul. Or there must be something like a system of bones, muscles, and tendons if an animal is to have the locomotory capacity of the soul. Although the digestive system may be spatially distinct from the locomotory system, the living body as a whole is not an aggregate of such systems, and hence cannot be actually divided into them. The digestive system cannot be severed from the rest of the body, because even if one was skilful enough to remove it from the body without damaging its integrity, this severed system would nonetheless lose its form and function, and thus cease to be a digestive system. The living body as a whole is informed by the soul as a whole, and we distinguish parts of the living body with reference to their functions, for example the digestive system with reference to digestion, the locomotory system with reference to locomotion, and so on. But the living body with

[15] *DA* II.2 413^b16–24. Sprague (1989) offers a lucid discussion of Aristotle's uses of divided living beings. In a nutshell, the higher a living being is on the scale of nature, the greater degree of unity it has, and hence the less able it is to live when divided; cf. *DJS* 2 468^a28–$^b12$ and *IA* 7 707^b1–3 in particular.

such parts cannot be actually divided so that these parts retain their functions. When actually divided, these parts lose their functions and become fundamentally different things from what they were prior to being divided.[16]

We have seen that the soul allows only for a conceptual division, and such a division guarantees both the unity of the soul and the unity of the living body. Now the same sort of division can be applied at a lower level, that is, on the capacities of the soul themselves. When Aristotle comes to the perceptual capacity of the soul, it turns out to be itself conceptually divisible into capacities of a lower order, namely the individual senses, which exhibit the same sort of order which holds among the main capacities of the soul. There are some animals with the sense of touch only, some with several other senses in addition, and still others with all five senses. It follows that the sense of touch is ontologically prior to the other senses in that it is found to exist without the other senses, for certain kinds of animal were thought to possess only the sense of touch,[17] while the other senses are not found to exist without the sense of touch.

In *DA* II.7–11 Aristotle gives successive accounts of the five senses. Curiously, however, he does not follow their natural order. Quite the opposite, he starts with sight and ends with touch. This may have something to do with the fact that touch is the most complex of all the senses, as we shall explain in the next chapter. Sight, on the other hand, is in a way the paradigmatic sense,[18] and Aristotle might have intended to facilitate the understanding of his accounts of the other senses by first offering an account of sight. Finally, in *DA* III.1–2 Aristotle deals with certain issues concerning perception in such a way that it becomes clear that the perceptual capacity of the soul is not an aggregate of the individual senses, but a unified whole.

[16] Cf. *DA* II.1 412^{b}18–22; *PA* I.1 640^{b}35–641^{a}5; *GA* I.19 726^{b}22–4; *Met.* VII.10 1035^{b}16–18, 16 1040^{b}6–8.

[17] e.g. sponges and ascidians; cf. *HA* VIII(IX).1 588^{b}4–22; *PA* IV.5 681^{a}10–^{b}13.

[18] Cf. *DA* III.3 429^{a}2–4 and Stigen (1961).

2
The Perceptual Capacity of the Soul

A quick glance at the summary of the *De Anima* suffices to establish that Aristotle's account of the perceptual capacity of the soul is considerably longer and more worked out than his accounts of the other capacities. This is hardly surprising, given the internal complexity of this capacity. I have pointed out that the perceptual capacity is divided into the five senses with a certain order among them, so it is reasonable to expect that an account of that capacity will be extensive. Perhaps Aristotle's special attention to the perceptual capacity of the soul can also be explained with reference to the importance he attaches to perception. Perception is what distinguishes animals from plants.[1] It is necessary not only for mere preservation of animals, but also for their well-being.[2] Perception is the fundamental cognitive capacity in the sense that all other cognitive capacities and dispositions that an animal might have are ultimately based on perception, including rational capacities.[3] For all these reasons it is crucial for Aristotle to give an appropriately detailed account of the perceptual capacity of the soul.

The perceptual capacity of the soul is the subject of *DA* II.5–III.2. In II.5 Aristotle provides preliminary remarks about perception in general. II.6 introduces a classification of objects of perception. II.7–11 deal consecutively with matters concerning sight, hearing, smell, taste, and touch. Having dealt with these matters, in II.12 Aristotle summarizes his discussion with a set of general remarks about the senses. The first two chapters of the third book present a series of discussions of specific issues. III.1 discusses how many senses there are, and why there is more than one sense. III.2 discusses the awareness of perceiving, the relation

1 *DA* II.2 $413^{b}3$–4, 3 $414^{b}3$; *DS* 1 $436^{b}10$–12; *DSV* 1 $454^{b}23$–4; *PA* II.5 $651^{b}3$–4, 8 $653^{b}22$–3, III.4 $666^{a}34$; *GA* I.23 $731^{b}4$–5, II.1 $732^{a}12$–13, 3 $736^{a}30$, 5 $741^{a}9$.

2 *DA* III.12 $434^{b}21$–7, 13 $435^{b}13$–24; *DS* 1 $436^{b}10$–$437^{a}3$.

3 Cf. *APo.* II.19 $99^{b}31$–$100^{b}5$; *Met.* I.1 $980^{a}27$–$981^{a}12$; cf. M. Frede (1996*a*), Gregoric and Grgic (2006).

between the sense and its object, and perceptual discrimination. Some of the discussions in *DA* III.1–2 are crucial for our enterprise and will receive detailed examination in Parts II and III.

I have already mentioned Aristotle's methodological rule that, in order to explain a capacity, one must explain the relevant activity, and in order to explain the activity, one must first of all explain the objects of that activity. In Aristotle's view, objects of perception are crucial for understanding perception, so let us first say something general about them.

Aristotle's word for an object of perception is *τὸ αἰσθητόν*, literally 'that which can be (or is) perceived', or 'the perceptible'.[4] With a stronger connotation of objectivity and availability, it can also be rendered as 'that which is there to be perceived'. Aristotle divides perceptibles into two large classes: those that are perceived in themselves (*καθ' αὑτό*), and those that are perceived accidentally (*κατὰ συμβεβηκός*). This distinction requires some explanation.

Features that are perceived in themselves are causes of perception in virtue of being what they are. For instance, colour is the type of feature that activates the sense of sight. If certain conditions are satisfied, for example if there is a transparent medium which is lit and a healthy animal with functional eyes in the proximity, there is nothing additional that a colour requires in order to activate the animal's sense of sight and be seen. On the other hand, features that are perceived accidentally do not activate the senses in virtue of being what they are. Rather, they are perceived in virtue of their accidental unity with features which *are* perceived in themselves. For example, I look at a particular physical object and I see Socrates. However, this object does not affect my sight insofar as it is Socrates, but insofar as it happens to be, among other things, coloured. It is this object's colour that activates my sight, and, provided that certain conditions are met, it is because this coloured object is accidentally Socrates that I see Socrates. Socrates is thus an accidental perceptible.

The class of features perceptible in themselves is further divided into two: the special perceptibles (*τὰ ἴδια αἰσθητά*), and the common perceptibles (*τὰ κοινὰ αἰσθητά*). The special perceptibles are features

[4] The standard English translation of *τὸ αἰσθητόν* is 'sensible'. However, I shall henceforth use the rendering 'perceptible', for two reasons. One is that the word 'sensible' may be taken to reflect the distinction between sensing and perceiving, which is a distinction Aristotle did not make. The other reason is that in some contexts it is useful to keep the etymological link between the Greek verb *αἰσθάνεσθαι* ('to perceive') and the substantive *τὸ αἰσθητόν* ('the perceptible').

of physical objects, or produced by physical objects, which are available to one sense and one sense only. For instance, colour is the special perceptible of sight, sound is the special perceptible of hearing, and so on. Each kind of special perceptible is the type of feature that determines the essence of one sense. For instance, the essence of hearing is determined by sounds, for hearing is defined as the capacity to perceive sounds. However, the fact that hearing is defined with reference to sound does not imply that sound is the only type of feature that can be perceived by the sense of hearing. What it implies, rather, is that all other types of feature in some way depend on sound for their being perceived by hearing. To understand what hearing is, therefore, one must understand first of all what sound is. This is, I take it, why features such as sounds and colours are said to be perceptibles 'in the strict sense' (κυρίως, *DA* II.6 418^{a}24–5).

Because the essence of each sense is determined with reference to one kind of special perceptible, the senses are infallible with respect to their special perceptibles.[5] Given that the sense of sight, for instance, is essentially the capacity to perceive colours, the idea that nature would furnish animals, in particular the most perfect ones, with a capacity which does not afford correct perception of colours in normal circumstances is repulsive to Aristotle's teleological view of nature. It has to be noted, however, that in one passage Aristotle says that 'perception of the special perceptibles is true or contains falsity in the minimum degree' (*DA* III.3 428^{b}18–19). I understand this qualification with reference to the possibility of some disorder in the sense organ or the rest of the body, commotion in the medium, or disturbance in the soul, all of which may prevent a sense from perceiving its special perceptible correctly.[6] In principle, however, the senses do perceive their corresponding special perceptibles correctly.[7] This is what enables Aristotle to build the whole edifice of knowledge on the foundation of perception.

[5] *DA* II.6 418^{a}11–16, III.3 427^{b}12, 428^{a}11, 6 430^{b}29; *DS* 4 442^{b}8; *Met.* IV.5 1010^{b}2, ^{b}23–5.

[6] This interpretation of Aristotle's qualification has been defended by various scholars, e.g. Block (1961*a*), Gaukroger (1981), and more recently Charles (2000: 118–24).

[7] Perhaps I should note in passing that it would be more correct to say, according to Aristotle, that the *animal* perceives by means of its senses, rather than that the senses perceive; cf. *DA* I.4 408^{b}11–15, II.2 414^{a}5–14. However, Aristotle often speaks of the senses perceiving and other capacities of the soul doing their respective activities, probably because in most cases that is a simpler idiom which can be easily translated into the more correct one.

There are five kinds of special perceptible, each kind being a spectrum of qualities ranging between a positive and a negative extreme. Each kind of special perceptible is accessible to one sense only: colour is the special perceptible of sight, sound of hearing, odour of smell, flavour of taste, whereas three ranges of tactile qualities (warm–cold, wet–dry, and soft–hard) are the special perceptibles of touch.[8] Although the special perceptibles largely correspond to the modern secondary properties, it is important to bear in mind that for Aristotle the special perceptibles are fully real and causally efficacious features of physical objects, not merely their phenomenological effects. For Aristotle, colours and sounds are out there to be seen and heard by any sentient being endowed with the senses of sight and hearing respectively.[9]

The other kind of feature perceived in itself is the common perceptible. The common perceptibles are change, rest, shape, magnitude, number, and one,[10] according to the most comprehensive list supplied in *DA* III.1 425^{a}16.[11] These are the features of physical objects which

[8] What unites the three ranges of tactile qualities is that they are perceptible properties of the body as such. This in turn secures the unity of the sense of touch; cf. *DA* II.11 422^{b}17–33, 423^{b}27–31.

[9] This is emphasized by Broadie (1993) and used by Burnyeat (1992; 1995) in support of his claim that perception involves no material processes. Broackes (1999) shows that the reality and causal efficacy of special perceptibles does not necessarily support Burnyeat's controversial claim, which I will address below. Aristotle's perceptual realism is discussed also by Silverman (1989) and Esfeld (2000).

[10] The reason why Aristotle's list in almost all manuscripts and modern editions (a notable exception is Ross's *editio maior* from 1961) contains both 'number' *and* 'one' is that Aristotle, like Plato, does not consider one as being properly a number. For Aristotle, one is the building-block or principle of numbers, so that number is a 'multitude of ones' (*Met.* X.1 1053^{a}30; *Phy.* III.7 207^{b}7; cf. *Met.* XIV.1 1088^{a}6–8). The same idea is found in Euclid's definition of number in *Elements* VII, *def.* 2. The first philosopher who seems to have made an attempt to bring one into the conception of number was Speusippus; cf. Tarán (1981: 32–8, 276–7).

[11] Many interpreters would think that this list is not exhaustive. In *DS* 4 442^{b}5–6 Aristotle mentions rough and smooth, and sharp and blunt as common perceptibles, along with magnitude and shape. However, these can be treated as species of shape, although I admit that it is not entirely clear that Aristotle has treated them so; cf. *DS* 4 442^{b}11–12; *Cat.* 8 10^{a}11–24; *GC* I.2 329^{b}18–20, 32–4. Some interpreters would include time as a common perceptible, or perhaps subsume it under number. I will argue in Part II, Ch. 4 that this position is untenable and that time is *not* a common perceptible. Furthermore, Theophrastus seems to think that distance is a common perceptible, since he mentions it along with change and shape in his *De Sensu*, §§ 36 and 54. The view that distance is a common perceptible is shared by Alexander (1901: 84.10–13, 85.14–16) and recorded by Aëtius (*Placita* IV.8.6 Diels). However, distance can be easily subsumed under magnitude. So perhaps one could argue that the list of the common perceptibles in *DA* III.1 425^{a}16 is exhaustive.

are available to more than one sense, at least to sight and touch, which is why they are called 'common'. The common perceptibles largely overlap with the modern primary properties, although in Aristotle's account they are found to be associated with special perceptibles more often than with physical objects.[12] This is because the common and the special perceptibles, as Aristotle puts it, 'always follow upon each other'.[13] For instance, colours and tangible qualities always come in certain shapes and magnitudes, just as shapes and magnitudes always come with colours and tangible qualities.

I suppose that the common and the special perceptibles always follow upon each other because the common perceptibles are, generally speaking, features of physical objects and their parts which externally determine the special perceptibles inherent in, or produced by, these physical objects and their parts. I say that the common perceptibles determine the special perceptibles *externally*, because they do not affect the colour that an object has, for instance, but they pack it into a single stationary patch of a round shape of a particular magnitude. Every special perceptible is thus determined by at least some common perceptibles. More precisely, each special perceptible is either one or many, either changing or resting, and some special perceptibles, notably colours and tangible qualities, are always also of some shape and magnitude. Although the common perceptibles cannot be perceived independently of the special perceptibles, they affect the senses in virtue of being the features that necessarily accompany the special perceptibles, and that is, I take it, what motivates Aristotle's classification of the common perceptibles as 'objects perceived in themselves'.[14]

In *DA* III.3 428^{b}22–5 Aristotle says that of the three kinds of perceptibles, perception of the common perceptibles is the most fallible. This probably has something to do with the fact that the common perceptibles are not perceived by a special sense designed for that

[12] In fact, the only place where common perceptibles are explicitly associated with physical objects is *DA* III.3 428^{b}22–3. Their association with special perceptibles is asserted in *DA* III.1 425^{a}16–19 and ^{b}5–11, and probably implied in *DA* III.12 435^{a}7 and *DS* 1 437^{b}5–9.

[13] *DA* III.1 425^{b}8–9; cf. Graeser (1978: 79–81) and Brunschwig (1996: 194–5, 214–18).

[14] This classification is not unproblematic, not least because Aristotle seems to say in *DA* III.1 425^{a}14–15 that the common perceptibles are perceived accidentally. I shall deal with this passage in Part II, Ch. 2. For discussions of Aristotle's classification of the common perceptibles as καθ' αὑτὰ αἰσθητά, see Graeser (1978), Owens (1982), Brunschwig (1996), and Everson (1997: 141–57).

purpose, but rather by several individual senses designed to perceive their respective special perceptibles, as Aristotle suggests in *DS* 4 442^b6–9. Of course, the accidental perceptibles can also be perceived by several senses, for one can both see and hear Socrates, but the point is that our sensitivity to the common perceptibles depends on our using several senses and comparing their reports. This circumstance, about which I will have more to say in Part II, Chapter 2, and Part III, Chapter 5, seems to make perception of the common perceptibles particularly prone to error.

At this point I should like to pause and make two observations in connection with Aristotle's classification of the objects of perception. First, having said what kinds of objects of perception there are, Aristotle has already committed himself to a view as to what perception is. For him, as for Plato, perceiving has to do in the first place with basic sensible qualities such as colours, sounds, odours, flavours, and tactile qualities. But it also has to do with shapes, magnitudes, instances of change and rest, pluralities and unities. In addition, perception has to do with things accidentally united with colours and sounds, shapes and magnitudes, and so on. This indicates Aristotle's wide divergence from Plato. We have seen in the Introduction that for Plato perceiving is nothing in addition to seeing colours, hearing sounds, smelling odours, tasting flavours, and feeling tactile qualities. Aristotle's classification of objects of perception indicates a significant expansion of the cognitive scope of perception. In fact, Aristotle expands the scope of perception far beyond perceiving special, common, and accidental perceptibles, because there are still other things that are grasped by perception. This brings me to the second point.

We have seen that colours and sounds, shapes and magnitudes, and things accidentally associated with these are all things that can be perceived. They were said to be 'perceptibles' (αἰσθητά). However, Aristotle maintains that many other things can be perceived, such as the difference between a colour and a sound, or the very activities of seeing or hearing. Yet Aristotle never refers to these as 'perceptibles'. This suggests that Aristotle's classification of objects of perception in *DA* II.6 is not intended to be an exhaustive categorization of *everything* that falls under the scope of perception, but only of objective features, features out there to be perceived. In other words, Aristotle's classification is a result of an analysis of the ways in which the physical world presents itself to sentient beings. Other things that fall under the scope of perception, such as differences between special perceptibles of different kinds, or the activity of perceiving, require further explanation. Perception of such things cannot be explained with reference to the individual senses only, which is why Aristotle needs an additional perceptual power. This additional perceptual power is what the present work aims to clarify.

Now that we understand what the objects of perception are, let us turn to the corresponding activity, perceiving. Aristotle received the view that perceiving consists in some sort of being affected and changed by the object of perception.[15] However, he insists that it is not a standard sort of change. In the standard sort of change there is a process whereby the patient gradually becomes like the agent. For instance, water heated by fire gradually becomes hot. This process takes time, and it is terminated when the quality of the patient at the beginning of the process is replaced by another quality of the same kind at the end of the process. What happens in perception is nothing like that; it is being affected or changed only in an extended sense.

We must remember that the senses, according to Aristotle, are conceptually distinct parts or aspects of the soul, and the soul is an organized set of fully developed capacities ready to make the living being take nourishment, reproduce, perceive, or move about whenever the relevant conditions obtain. The senses are members of this organized set, that is, they are fully developed capacities ready to be exercised with respect to their objects. Now the exercise of a sense is not the standard sort of change, because it is not a process whereby one quality gets replaced by another. There is no end result in which the activity terminates. When a sense is changed by the object of perception, it is brought to perfection in that it actually does what it is the capacity for doing. In short, the sense is not really changed, but realized or activated. This activity of course occurs in time, but it does not take time for it to occur. It is not that we have to look for some time in order to see at the end; rather, we see at each and every moment for as long as we look. So, while it is true that in perception the senses are affected and changed by the objects, this is a special sort of change.

Aristotle's distinction between the standard sort of change and the special sort of change involved in the exercise of a fully developed capacity should be viewed in the light of his strategy to explain perception first and foremost in terms of form. He agrees with his predecessors that perception involves two things, one that acts and the other that is affected. He also agrees that these two things are material substances,

15 *DA* I.5 410^{a}25–6, II.5 416^{b}33–5.

but he disagrees that perception can be explained with reference to their material interaction, which is the standard sort of change. Aristotle believes that perception should be explained primarily with reference to the 'interaction' of their forms, which constitutes a special sort of change. The relevant form of the thing that acts (physical object) is a special perceptible, and the relevant form of the thing that is affected (animal) is the sense. When the former acts on the latter, the sense is exercised with respect to this special perceptible: it is turned from potentially to actually perceiving it. And fundamentally that is what it is to perceive: it is for a sense to be affected by a special perceptible of the relevant kind.

Accordingly, in *DA* II.12 424^{a}18–19 Aristotle defines the sense as that which is capable of receiving perceptible forms without matter.[16] To receive the form of an object without matter is to become like it in form, but not in matter. It is to take on the form of an object without taking on its matter. When the sense is said to receive perceptible forms, or to become like them, I take it that this amounts to perceiving perceptible forms. The sense is essentially the capacity to receive perceptible forms. And we must not ask why, or in virtue of what, the sense is the capacity to receive perceptible forms. This is just what the sense is. It is not something to be further explained, but something that explains other things.

Assuming that this is only the formal part of Aristotle's explanation of perceiving, it is reasonable to suppose that there is also a corresponding material part. However, the *DA* does not have much to say about material processes involved in perceiving. This is not surprising, given that the work is devoted to the formal aspect of living beings. However, some scholars have a different explanation. In his famous paper 'Is Aristotelian Philosophy of Mind Still Credible?', Myles Burnyeat argues that acts of perception involve no material processes whatsoever, thus launching a controversy which lasts to this day. I am indebted to this and other of Burnyeat's papers on the subject for the light they shed on the formal part of Aristotle's explanation, but I am not satisfied

[16] My interpretation of this particular characterization is essentially that of Burnyeat (1992; 1995), although I do not accept the consequence that he draws from it, namely that perception involves no material processes. This aligns my understanding of perception in Aristotle closer to that of Lear (1988: 101–16), Ward (1988), Silverman (1989), Bradshow (1997), and Caston (2005). A different interpretation of the quoted characterization of the sense is advocated by Slakey (1961), Sorabji (1971; 1974; 1992), Cohen (1992), Sisko (1996), and Everson (1997).

with what they tell us (or fail to tell us) about a certain number of passages in the *DA*—not to mention other biological works—which suggest that perception does involve material processes. For instance, in *DA* II.12 424^{a}28–32 Aristotle claims that too intense perceptibles destroy sense organs, 'for if the change is stronger than the sense organ, it ruins the *logos*—that is, the sense—just as the consonance and pitch of the strings are destroyed when plucked violently'. Unless perception involves material processes, how could perceptibles have this deleterious effect on the sense organ? Moreover, how would perception differ from thinking, given that thinking is said to be improved by intense objects of thought due to its independence of the body?[17] Finally, what would correspond to violent plucking of strings in Aristotle's analogy? To give a different example, in III.2 425^{b}23–5 the sense organs are said to receive the relevant perceptibles without matter, which is why, 'even when the perceptibles are gone, there are perceptions and images in the sense organs'. Aristotle's explanation of the phenomenon of retention is much easier to understand under the assumption that reception of perceptibles involves material processes which persist inside the sense organs after the perceptibles are no longer causally efficient. In fact, in *DI* 2 459^{a}23–^{b}7 Aristotle himself evokes the standard sort of change in his explanation of the phenomenon.[18]

What these material processes amount to in the case of each sense, and whether they transmit information by encoding perceptible objects in some way or by exemplifying them, are difficult and much-debated questions into discussion of which I need not enter here. I will only say this much: given what Aristotle claims in the whole body of his biological works, there are good reasons to suppose that perception does involve material processes. These processes do not, and indeed, from Aristotle's point of view, cannot *explain* what perception essentially is (which is why they do not loom large in the *DA*), but they do have a prominent role in Aristotle's explanations of various things closely related to perception, for example temporary or permanent loss of the ability to perceive, after-images, imagination, and the like.[19]

Let us resume our exposition of Aristotle's account of the perceptual capacity of the soul. Aristotle does not think that it is sufficient for an

[17] *DA* III.4 429^{a}31–^{b}5; cf. Lear (1988: 112) and Sisko (1996).

[18] Other passages in the *DA* which seem to imply that perception involves material processes are e.g. I.1 403^{a}3–8, 16–19, II.8 420^{a}3–19, 30–^{b}4, and 11 424^{a}1–10. Caston (2005) offers a valuable discussion of some of these passages.

[19] Cf. Van der Eijk (1997: 228–30), and Caston (2005: 290–2).

adequate account of the senses to specify only what their corresponding special perceptibles are. It is also necessary to specify the conditions for each kind of the special perceptible to be actually perceived. This refers, first of all, to the medium. The role of the medium is evident from the way the distal senses work. Given that colours, for instance, do not, and indeed could not, affect sight through contact between the coloured object and the eye, there must be something between them that enables colours to affect sight. In analogy with the distal senses, Aristotle concluded that the contact senses also have a medium, only their medium is not external, but internal to the body. It turns out that the internal medium of the contact senses is the flesh and the tongue, whereas their proper sense organ is the heart. I shall say more about this in the next chapter.

For something to be a medium, it must have a particular quality which enables it to mediate perceptible qualities. This quality can be generally characterized as neutral, or mean, with respect to one range of qualities that figure as one type of special perceptible. For instance, air and water serve as the media of colour because air and water are transparent. Transparency is the neutral quality with respect to the range of colours, and that is what enables air and water to be changed by colours. But again, the medium is not changed by colours in the standard sense: if we look at a red object through a glass of water, water is not changed by the red colour in the same way in which it would change if we poured red ink in the water. The medium is changed by colours in the sense that it makes them manifest, available to potential perceivers.

It is crucial to see that here too Aristotle is giving an explanation in terms of form. Transparency is the quality a substance must have in order to be able to mediate colours, and we should think of the ability to mediate colours as the form of transparent substances. A substance must have a particular quality—the ancient commentators called it 'transsonance'—in order to be able to mediate sounds, and similarly for the other kinds of special perceptibles. Again, there is the question of material processes involved in mediation of the special perceptibles. The situation concerning this question is very similar to that concerning the question of material processes involved in perception; in fact, these two questions are tied together and have a common answer. Material processes in the media of some senses, such as touch and hearing, are acknowledged more explicitly than in the case of others, but they seem to be admitted even in the case of sight, the least corporeal of the senses, as when Aristotle says that 'the air made the eye-jelly such and such, and the eye-jelly in turn something else . . .'.[20]

Once we understand what the special perceptibles of a sense are, how they are produced, what their medium is like, which conditions need to be satisfied for mediation to take place (e.g. the transparent substance has to be lit), and what the sense organ in contact with the medium is like, we have a complete understanding of what this sense is and what it is to exercise it, that is, what it is to see, hear, and so on. Indeed, if we look carefully at *DA* II.7–11, where successive accounts of the individual senses are explicitly said to be given,[21] we see that Aristotle's main effort in fact goes into describing the special perceptibles, the media, and the conditions for the production and mediation of the special perceptibles, with very little further explanation as to what the senses are and what it takes for them to be exercised.

So far we have seen that in *DA* II.5–12 Aristotle makes some general observations about the senses, and he gives accounts of the issues necessary for understanding each individual sense. It is only when he comes to discuss particular questions in the first two chapters of the third book that we find out that the five senses are not mutually independent capacities, but form a unity. Towards the end of *DA* III.1, at 425^a31, we hear about the senses accidentally perceiving each other's special perceptibles 'not as themselves [viz. not as this or that individual sense], but as one'. At the end of *DA* III.2, at 427^a9–14, that which discriminates between different special perceptibles is compared to a geometrical point, and in certain cases it acts as the relevant individual senses and, at the same time, as one single thing. This analogy will be explored in detail in Part III, Chapter 2, but already at this stage we can see that Aristotle was committed to the view that the senses form a unity. In fact, it has to be the sort of unity which will enable integration and co-ordination of the individual senses.

In line with my exegesis in the previous chapter, I submit that the unity of the perceptual capacity of the soul is achieved in the same way in which the unity of the soul is achieved. We have seen that the soul is one single thing divided only conceptually, in the sense that we can analyse it into different parts or aspects according to the most salient activities of living beings, such that each part or aspect of the soul is responsible for one vital activity. However, in reality there is only one soul in each case, which is what ensures integration and co-operation of

[20] *DA* III.7 431^a17–19; cf. Lear (1988: 112–14).
[21] Cf. *DA* II.11 424^a15–16.

various parts or aspects of the soul, as when perception helps an animal to take nourishment or to move about. Thus the soul is responsible for all the activities that a living being with this soul manifests. Likewise, only at a lower level, the perceptual capacity of the soul is one single thing divided only conceptually, in the sense that we can analyse it into different senses according to different kinds of the special perceptible, such that each sense is responsible for perceiving the special perceptibles of one kind only. However, there is really one single perceptual capacity of the soul, which ensures that it can operate not only as this or that individual sense, but also as one. This allows Aristotle to explain certain complex perceptual activities which cannot be explained in terms of the individual senses taken severally. I shall return to this crucial point in Chapter 4.

Having completed the exposition of Aristotle's account of the relevant part or aspect of the form, that is, the perceptual capacity of the soul, let us now turn to his account of the relevant matter, namely the system of parts that a living body must have if it is to be informed by a soul with a perceptual capacity.

3

The Sensory Apparatus

Before we turn to Aristotle's material account of perception, some preliminary methodological remarks are in order. First, there is no account of the living body exactly parallel to the account of the soul. That is to say, Aristotle does not study the living body by supplying successive accounts of bodily parts, or systems of bodily parts, each corresponding to one part of the soul treated in the *De Anima*. Aristotle's approach to animal bodies in the treatise *De Partibus Animalium* is much more systematic than that. In this treatise he starts with basic parts at a lower level of organization, and then moves on to more complex parts at higher levels of organization, treating separately of internal and of external complex parts, first of blooded and then of bloodless animals. Hence, we have to extract his views about the bodily parts and processes involved in perception from the account provided in the *PA*. Also, we find many useful passages in other biological works, chiefly in the *Parva Naturalia*. This is a collection of shorter treatises devoted to various salient activities and affections of living beings, such as perceiving, remembering, sleeping and waking, dreaming, ageing, or breathing. The treatise devoted to perception, *De Sensu et Sensibilibus*, presupposes the account in the *DA* and discusses special topics related to perception which were merely skimmed or left untouched in the *DA*. As for the other treatises, since their topics could not be adequately discussed in the *DA* without disrupting its programme to study the soul by treating each one of its main capacities, Aristotle explores these issues in separate works.[1] And because they are explored in separate works, Aristotle is able to discuss them with reference to matter as well as form, which is why these discussions have a different character from those found in the *DA*. Parts of the *PN* will turn out to be of

[1] This view of the place and scope of *PN* in Aristotle's biological works is essentially that of G. R. T. Ross ((ed.) 1906: 1); cf. Van der Eijk ((ed.) 1994: 68–72; and 1997: 209 n. 14).

key importance for the purpose of the present chapter and my entire project.

Second, in considering Aristotle's material account of perception, we must bear in mind the role of matter in Aristotle's explanations. We have seen that Aristotle insists on explaining matter with reference to form. An adequate account of the matter of a natural substance consists in showing that it is necessary for substances of that sort to have the material constitution that they have, if they are to have their form and function. This is known as 'hypothetical necessity'.[2] Thus, once the form of animals is explained, the task of the material account is to show that the body an animal characteristically has is necessary, or ideally suited, for animals to have the specified form. Consequently, the constitution and processes in the relevant parts of the body do not explain the senses and their operation, but rather the senses and their operation—as specified in the formal account—explain the constitution and processes in the relevant parts of the body. Since the place of the material account in Aristotle's programme is fundamentally different from that in ours, his explorations of the living body are less extensive and meticulous than we would like them to be, so we should not expect too much from his material account of perception.

What must a body be like, then, if it is to be an animal's body, that is, of a living being capable of perceiving? Clearly, it has to be such that a soul with a perceptual capacity can be realized in it. We have seen that the perceptual capacity of the soul is a unity with some internal complexity. So the animal body must be composed of such parts and structured in such a way as to accommodate both the unity and the complexity of the perceptual capacity of the soul. Let us first see what these parts are like and how they are structured.

At a lower level of organization, the living body consists of the so-called 'uniform' or 'homoeomerous' parts. They are made of a single element, or of a mixture of elements, and they are called 'uniform' because each piece of it is the same as the whole, for example any piece of flesh is flesh, any piece of blood is blood. Aristotle says that there are fluid and soft uniform parts, such as blood, flesh, marrow, semen, gall, milk, and so on, and solid and hard uniform parts, such as channels, blood-vessels, skin, bone, sinew, and so on.[3] At a higher

[2] Notable discussions of this notion include Cooper (1985; 1987), Balme (1987*b*), and Charles (1988; 1991).

[3] *HA* I.1 487^{a}1–10; *PA* II.2 647^{b}10–20.

level of organization, uniform parts combine into non-uniform or anomoeomerous parts, such as hand, trunk, or head.

Perception takes place only in parts that are uniform, the reason being that only uniform parts are receptive of perceptibles.[4] Only uniform parts are receptive of perceptibles—and I assume Aristotle means the special perceptibles—because only uniform parts have the particular neutral quality, shared with the media, which allows them to be affected by perceptibles in the relevant way. We have seen that the medium of colours, for instance, has to be transparent, because transparency is the quality which enables the medium to be affected by colours so as to make them manifest. Similarly, the sense organ of colours, the eye-jelly (κόρη), is made of water because water is transparent, and transparency is the quality which enables the eye to be affected by colours so as to see them. Or, to put it more precisely, transparency is the quality which enables the eye to house the sense of sight which can be activated by colours so as to make the animal see them. It follows that transparency is the quality a material substance must have in order to be able to mediate colours, if it is inanimate, and to perceive them, if it is animate, that is, if it belongs to a living body with a soul that has a perceptual capacity. In other words, transparency is hypothetically necessary both for the medium's ability to manifest colours, and for the sense organ's ability to see colours.

The peripheral sense organs of the distal senses are uniform parts made of one element, water or air. The sense organ of sight is the water in the eye, because water is transparent and, unlike air, it is easily encapsulated in the eyeball. The sense organ of hearing is the air sitting still in a chamber inside the ear, because motionless air can receive any sound. Aristotle says very little about the sense organ of smell, but it seems to be the air in the nostrils or nasal channels of land animals, or the water in the gills or blowhole in water animals; air and water are potentially dry, and hence the sort of substances that can receive any odour.[5] The peripheral sense organs of the contact senses, or rather their connate media, are mixtures of elements. The flesh cannot receive just any tangible quality because it is itself a body with some tangible qualities. Naturally, a thing cannot receive those qualities that it already

[4] *PA* II.1 647^{a}5–8; cf. *HA* I.4 489^{a}23–6; *PA* II.1 647^{a}22–3; *DA* III.1 425^{a}3–9; *DS* 2 438^{b}16–439^{a}5. Of the uniform parts, I take it, those classified as solid and hard are not receptive of perceptibles in the relevant way.

[5] For a discussion of the sense organ of smell, see Johansen (1998: 226–51).

has. However, the flesh is made of the right mixture of elements, so that it has the mean quality in each spectrum of tangible qualities, which makes it equally receptive of qualities on both sides of each spectrum.

The flesh and tongue are the connate media of touch and taste, according to Aristotle, whereas the proper sense organ of touch and taste is the heart. The way Aristotle arrives at this conclusion is rather complicated, based on weak arguments and slack empirical evidence.[6] The heart is connected with their connate media on the surface of the body by a network of blood-vessels. Two major blood-vessels, the 'great blood-vessel' (*vena cava*) and the aorta, originate in the heart, and the further they go the more they branch into smaller and smaller blood-vessels, thus supplying every corner of the body with blood, including all of the flesh and the tongue.

The peripheral sense organs of the distal senses are also connected with the heart. These sense organs are set upon channels which terminate in small blood-vessels around the brain. These small blood-vessels are connected with larger blood-vessels in the neck that ultimately terminate in the heart.[7] Aristotle says that the nasal and aural passages are full of connate *pneuma* (*GA* II.6 743^{b}35–744^{a}5). Presumably, the same is the case with the passages which lead from the eyes to the small blood-vessels around the brain.[8] The subject of *pneuma* is controversial and I shall not attempt to discuss it here. It will suffice to note that *pneuma* is said to be warm air inside the body of blooded and at least some bloodless animals. And it is connate (σύμφυτον) because it is not drawn from the outside, but generated together with, and maintained inside, the body. I shall proceed on the assumption that *pneuma*, being a uniform part of the right sort (air), is capable of receiving perceptibles of the three distal senses located in the head. I share this assumption with a large group of interpreters, but I disagree with those in that group who deny that blood is also receptive of perceptibles.[9]

[6] Cf. *DS* 2 438^{b}30–439^{a}2; *DJS* 3 469^{a}10–23; *PA* II.10 656^{a}27–^{b}6. Aristotle's evidence for this view is discussed by Lloyd (1978: 222–3).

[7] Of course, this applies only to blooded animals. Bloodless animals have 'analogous' bodily structures.

[8] These passages are usually identified as the optic nerves, although Aristotle could not have know them under that description; cf. Solmsen (1961).

[9] Beare (1906: 333–6), Peck (1942; 1953), Solmsen (1961: 171–4), Lloyd (1978: 222–3), Verbeke (1978), Webb (1982), G. Freudenthal (1995), Johansen (1998: 92); cf. n. 17 below.

Blood is an all-important uniform part. It is nourishment in the ultimate form.[10] Blood is produced in the heart, from where it pours into the blood-vessels. Aristotle was ignorant of the circulation of blood, but he did not think that blood sits still inside the body. Motion of blood is part of the digestive cycle, which looks roughly as follows. Ingested food is concocted in the stomach, concocted food passes into the vascular system where it mixes with blood. Concocted food carried with blood ends up in the heart, where it is transformed into blood. When this process is complete, replenished blood is dispatched back to the periphery, supplying it with nourishment.[11] But it is not only nourishment and growth that depend on blood, it is also perception.

Properties of blood are said to determine the animal's ability to perceive. Blood can be thinner or thicker, purer or more turbid, colder or warmer. Properties of blood are determined by its composition, and they vary in different parts of the body. The more earthy stuff in blood, the thicker and more turbid it is. The more watery stuff, the thinner and purer it is. Also, blood around the brain is colder because the brain is cold, whereas blood in the chest and abdomen is hot because the heart and the stomach are hot. So blood has different properties in different places of the same animal. Properties of blood change over the years in the same individual. Individuals of different sex in the same species are said to have slightly different blood, whereas different species have significantly different blood.[12] All this accounts for variations in perceptual abilities and, consequently, in other cognitive abilities.[13]

Thin, pure, and cold blood is said to be conducive to perception.[14] That is why the sense organs of the distal senses, which are supposed to be particularly sharp, are located in the head. Blood in that area is thinnest, purest, and coldest.[15] Aristotle does not explain why such blood should be more conducive to perception than that of the opposite properties, but the most plausible answer is that blood with such

[10] *DJS* 3 469^{a}1–2; *PA* II.3 650^{a}34–5, 4 651^{a}14–15, IV.3 678^{a}6–9; *GA* I.19 726^{b}1–5, II.4 740^{a}21.

[11] Digestive process is closely related to sleep, and I shall say more about it in Part III, Ch. 3.

[12] *PA* II.2 647^{b}34–5; *HA* III.19 521^{a}2–6.

[13] This is discussed in some detail by Van der Eijk (1997).

[14] *PA* II.2 647^{b}29–648^{a}13, 4 650^{b}22–4, 651^{a}15–19.

[15] *DSV* 3 458^{a}13–14; *PA* II.7 652^{b}32–3, 10 656^{b}2–5, IV.10 686^{a}9–11.

properties is more receptive of perceptibles of the distal senses located in the head. In fact, Aristotle seems to think that appropriate distribution of blood in the body is necessary for perception. Until thin and pure blood is separated off from thicker and more turbid in the final stage of the digestive process, and until the former ends up in the upper parts and the latter in the lower parts of the body, the animal is asleep and its senses incapacitated.[16]

It is not difficult to find some support for the view that blood is receptive of perceptibles. For instance, the heart is said to be receptive of all kinds of perceptibles (*PA* II.1 647^{a}25–30), and since the heart is made of the same sort of stuff as blood (^{a}32–^{b}8), it is natural to suppose that blood also is receptive of all kinds of perceptibles. Furthermore, one could argue that blood is receptive of some perceptibles (e.g. tangible qualities) due to the solid earthy element in its composition, and of others (e.g. colours) due to the transparent watery element. Consequently, blood in the head is more watery and thin in order to be more receptive of the perceptibles of the distal senses located in the head, whereas blood in the lower parts of the body is more earthy and thick in order to be more receptive of tangibles. So there are reasons to think—although Aristotle does not explicitly say so—that blood is a uniform part of a particular composition in order to be receptive of all kinds of the special perceptible.[17]

The heart is another, if rather unusual, uniform part. What is unusual about the heart is that it qualifies at the same time as a uniform and as a non-uniform part. Aristotle believes that the heart is the principle of animal locomotion, and since only non-uniform parts can initiate action, the heart is non-uniform 'in shape and form', while being uniform 'in composition' (*PA* II.1 647^{a}31–3). The heart is uniform in composition, I take it, precisely in order to be able to receive all perceptibles. The composition of the heart crucially determines perceptual abilities of blooded animals. In one place Aristotle says that animals with hard and thick hearts have poor perception, whereas animals with softer hearts have good perception (*PA* III.4 667^{a}9–14). This passage will be discussed in greater detail in Part II, Chapter 3, where we shall learn

16 *DSV* 3 458^{a}10–25; cf. Part III, Ch. 3.

17 The role of blood in perception is a controversial matter. Assuming that there must be some substance in the body that connects the periphery with the central sense organ, many scholars find *pneuma* a more likely candidate. However, Modrak (1987: 73–5) has convincingly argued that this position involves even greater difficulties; cf. Van der Eijk ((ed.)1994: 81–7; 1997; and 2000).

that it is the preponderance of earthy stuff that makes the heart, or any other part of the body, hard and thick.

In the Introduction I have mentioned the debate between those ancients who thought that the heart is the central sense organ, and those who thought that it is the brain. A number of philosophical considerations led Aristotle to side with the former.[18] First, he thinks that the heart is the first part to develop in an embryo, and the first to have blood in it.[19] As soon as the heart is formed, it governs the development of the individual animal. It is also the part whose destruction marks the destruction of the whole animal.[20] Second, the heart is an indispensable part for the material realization of all capacities of the soul. Apart from playing a crucial role in nourishment, and in close connection with its role in perception, Aristotle maintains that the heart is the part where pleasure and pain occur (*PA* III.4 666^{a}11–13), hence the place where desire arises, typically the desire to go for what is pleasant and to avoid what is painful. It is also the part in which locomotion originates. Aristotle believes, to put it very simply, that perception gives rise to desire, and desire triggers locomotion. His explanation of animal locomotion in the *De Motu Animalium* clearly requires that the heart is the common part of the systems of bodily parts in which these parts of the soul—the perceptual, the desiderative, and the locomotory—are realized.[21] Third, the heart occupies the central position in the body.[22] This enables the heart to be maximally efficient in producing effects in the periphery, and in receiving information from it. Fourth, the heart or its analogue—in contrast with the brain, for instance—is said to be present in all animals without exception.[23] This ensures that all animals have, among other things, a central sense organ. There are still other considerations which led Aristotle to believe that the heart is the central sense organ, and he conducted some anatomical

[18] For Aristotle's arguments against the view that the brain is the central sense organ, see *PA* II.10 656^{a}13 ff.

[19] *DR* 20 480^{a}6–8; *HA* III.19 521^{a}9–10; *PA* III.4 666^{a}7–11, ^{a}34–^{b}1; *GA* II.4 740^{b}2–5.

[20] *DJS* 3 468^{b}28–31; *PA* III.4 667^{a}34–^{b}3; *GA* II.5 741^{b}18–22, 6 743^{b}25–6.

[21] *MA* 7 701^{b}16–32, 9 702^{b}12–28, 11 703^{b}24–9; cf. *DJS* 1 467^{b}15–27, 3 469^{a}5–7, 4 469^{a}23–7; *PA* II.1 647^{a}24–31.

[22] *DJS* 1 467^{b}28–468^{a}1, 4 469^{a}23–32; *MA* 9 702^{b}25–8, 10 703^{a}4–14; cf. *PA* III. 4 665^{b}18–21, 666^{a}15–16, 7 670^{a}24–6. The argument for the central position of the heart is, quite rightly, challenged by Galen, *On the Doctrines of Hippocrates and Plato* II.4.15–16 (De Lacy).

[23] *PA* III.4 665^{b}9–10; *GA* IV.4 771^{a}3.

research in support of this view. However, his anatomical observations are crass, unclear, and inconsistent.[24] Geoffrey Lloyd has shown that Aristotle was interested in anatomy only to the extent that it enabled him to identify bodily structures that can plausibly be said to constitute the right sort of matter for the form which has already been set out, and such a procedure is unlikely to yield correct empirical results.[25]

We have seen that the heart is connected with the relevant uniform parts at the surface of the body through *pneuma* in the channels, and through blood in the network of blood-vessels. Those uniform parts at the surface which receive perceptibles through external media are continuous with *pneuma*, which is also receptive of these perceptibles. *Pneuma* is in turn continuous with blood, which seems to be receptive of all kinds of perceptibles, if in different degrees relative to its composition in different parts of the body. The uniform parts on the surface which receive perceptibles through direct contact are continuous only with blood, and all blood ends up in the heart, which is explicitly said to be receptive of all kinds of perceptibles. So, there seems to be a continuous system of uniform parts which can receive perceptibles, and which extends from different points on the surface of the body, terminating in the same place, the heart. This is, I take it, why the heart is said to be 'the sense organ common to all peripheral sense organs',[26] and 'the master sense organ to which all sense organs lead' (*DSV* 2 455^{a}33–4).

This continuous system of uniform parts receptive of the special perceptibles, stretching from the surface of the body and terminating in one single central sense organ, is what I shall henceforth call the 'sensory apparatus'. Now, if a living being is to have a soul with a perceptual capacity, which is itself a unity of some internal complexity, it must have a body equipped with a sensory apparatus, and the apparatus must be of the sort of composition and structure that we have outlined. First, the sensory apparatus must be composed of uniform parts of a particular sort, because only such parts can receive perceptibles. Of course, they can receive perceptibles in the relevant way only if they are part of a

[24] Aristotle's observations about the heart in particular are discussed in detail by Huxley (1879), Ogle ((ed.)1882: 193–200), Platt (1921), Shaw (1972), Harris (1973: 121–34), and Lloyd (1978).

[25] See Lloyd (1978; and 1996: 136): 'he (viz. Aristotle) discusses some topics in a cursory, even a minimalist, fashion—as for example the nature of the connections between the senses and the heart, where, once he can propose some link, the matter is not pursued further.'

[26] *DJS* 1 467^{b}28; cf. *DSV* 2 455^{a}19–20.

living body informed with a soul that has a perceptual capacity, but the point is that without these uniform parts the living body could never be thus informed.

Second, the sensory apparatus must be internally continuous to ensure that perceptibles received by various uniform parts on the surface of the body are received also by the central sense organ inside the body. If this continuity is interrupted at any point, there can be no perception. Aristotle illustrates this by observing that soldiers go blind when the channels behind their eyes are severed by a blow to the temple.[27]

Third, the sensory apparatus must be sufficiently complex to provide for the complexity of the perceptual capacity of the soul. Taking into account the findings from Chapter 2, the complexity of the perceptual capacity of the soul has two distinct facets. One facet has to do with the number of individual senses, which are conceptually distinct parts or aspects of the perceptual capacity of the soul. This facet of the perceptual capacity's complexity requires a sensory apparatus which comprises appropriate uniform parts—the peripheral sense organs—in appropriate places. That is to say, for an animal to have a soul with a perceptual capacity which will enable the animal to see, hear, and so on, the animal's body must be equipped with a sensory apparatus that comprises water in the eyes, air in the ears, and so on. The other facet of the perceptual capacity's complexity has to do with its ability to discharge certain perceptual functions that go beyond the individual senses—for example, to perceive differences between colours and sounds, or to perceive the activities of seeing or hearing—on account of its being a single thing. Now this facet of the complexity of the perceptual capacity of the soul seems to require a sensory apparatus with a central sense organ receptive of all perceptibles.

Let me clarify the relevance of all this. If the sensory apparatus were not composed of the peripheral sense organs connected with a central sense organ, it would not be able to sustain a perceptual capacity with both its unity and its complexity. Without its unity, Aristotle would find himself in the unacceptable situation depicted by Plato's simile of the wooden horse. Without its complexity, on the other hand, Aristotle would be unable to avoid the wooden horse situation in the particular way required by his programme, namely by integrating the senses at the level of perception (as opposed to Plato, who integrates them at the level of thought).

[27] *DS* 2 438^{b}12–16. For a detailed discussion of this passage, see Johansen (1998: 67–95).

What follows from this picture of the sensory apparatus is that perception does not really take place in the peripheral sense organs, but in the central sense organ. I suppose that is part of the reason why the heart is called 'the primary sense organ'.[28] The role of the peripheral sense organs is to receive perceptibles from the external media and to transduce them to the central sense organ through a network of channels filled with *pneuma* and blood. Although Aristotle seems to think that there is no significant gap between the reception of perceptibles by the peripheral and by the central sense organ, it nevertheless seems correct to say that perception occurs only when perceptibles mediated by the peripheral sense organs are received by the central sense organ.[29]

However, if the peripheral sense organs function simply as media, why did nature equip animals with peripheral sense organs in the first place? Instead of the eyes, would it not be more economical to have holes filled with the external air which is transparent anyway? Johansen has argued persuasively that the advantage of the sense organs is that they, unlike the external media, are always receptive of the relevant perceptibles, and in some cases the sense organs also compensate for the deficiencies of the external medium and improve the mediation.[30] One further, no less notable, reason for having peripheral sense organs is that perceptions can linger in them for some time, which explains phenomena such as after-images, images, and dreams.

Aristotle maintains that perceptibles in acts of perception set up 'changes' (κινήσεις) in the peripheral sense organs: 'Perceptibles corresponding to each sense organ produce perception in us, and the affection (πάθος) which comes about from them is present in the sense organs not only while the perceptions are active, but also when they are gone.'[31] This affection has to reach the central sense organ to be registered, and that is when the animal experiences images. However, the affection need not arrive at the central sense organ immediately, but often remains dormant in the peripheral sense organ. How long the affection remains

28 *DSV* 2 456^{a}21, 3 458^{a}28, 29.

29 I cannot agree with Van der Eijk ((ed.)1994: 80), who claims that 'relative autonomy in the execution of perception cannot be denied to the peripheral sense organs', and that the role of the central sense organ comes to the fore only 'when the particular perceptions are used, (i.e. when they are compared or co-ordinated with other perceptions, or when their correctness is judged)'. If so, why do the soldiers wounded in the temple go blind, rather than becoming incapable merely of comparing and co-ordinating visual with perceptions of other kinds?

30 See Johansen (1998: 288).

31 *DI* 2 459^{a}24–8; cf. *DA* III.2 425^{b}23–5; *DI* 2 460^{b}2–3, 3 461^{a}26–7, ^{b}21–3.

dormant depends largely on the composition of the sensory apparatus. It is unclear what sets off the affection toward the central sense organ, but at least in some cases this is caused by the recession of blood in the digestive cycle. On its way to the central sense organ the affection may be dispersed or skewed by digestive processes in the blood-vessels, which explains respectively non-occurrence and distortion of dream-images. Aristotle explains various memory failures in a similar fashion, with reference to the state and processes in the sensory apparatus.[32]

There are many acute problems with Aristotle's account of imagination and its exact relation to perception.[33] However, there is no need to deal with these problems here, or to engage any further with the subject of imagination. I suppose many scholars will find it surprising that I should say so, because it is the standard view that imagination is a function of the common sense. I will presently show that this is a mistake, so I hope I will be excused for thinking that the preceding remarks on imagination suffice.

To conclude. The sensory apparatus is an organized system of parts which supplies material conditions for the perceptual capacity of the soul. This system of parts must be continuous and it must include a central sense organ receptive of all special perceptibles in order to accommodate the unity and the complexity of the perceptual capacity of the soul. The material composition of the sensory apparatus determines how many perceptibles an animal can perceive, that is, how many senses it has and how accurately it can perceive them. Perceptions also leave traces in the sensory apparatus, and under certain conditions these traces produce images. Hence, in addition to supplying material conditions for the perceptual capacity of the soul, the sensory apparatus also supplies material conditions for the imaginative capacity of the soul.

On the assumption that I have now given an adequate outline of the sensory apparatus, my presentation of Aristotle's explanation of perception is complete. In the preceding chapter we have learnt about the relevant form, that is, the perceptual capacity of the soul, and the conditions of its being exercised. In this chapter we have learnt about the matter which is required for the relevant form to be realized, that is, the sensory apparatus. If we understand the relevant form and matter,

[32] Cf. *DM* 1 450^{a}32–^{b}11, 2 453^{a}14–^{b}7, and Part II, Ch. 4.

[33] For some notable discussions of *phantasia* in Aristotle, see Schofield (1978), Nussbaum ((ed.)1978: 221–69), Watson (1982), Modrak (1986; 1987: 81–110), Wedin (1988: 23–99), D. Frede (1992), Caston (1996), Turnbull (1996), Everson (1997: 157–228), and Osborne (2000).

we understand what perception is and what it takes for perception to occur. On the one hand, it takes external objects with certain properties, material substances with certain qualities that allow for the mediation of these properties, and in some cases certain further conditions of the mediation; on the other hand, it takes a living being with a soul that has a perceptual capacity and a body with a sensory apparatus. When all these things come together, nothing further is needed for perception to occur. At any rate, that is the bottom line of Aristotle's explanatory strategy.

4

The Common Sense and the Related Capacities

I have argued in Chapter 2 that the most convenient way to present a substantive account of the soul, according to Aristotle, is to divide it into capacities responsible for the most salient activities of living beings, and then to discuss these capacities successively in their natural order. It has been pointed out that the conceptual division of the soul into capacities does not threaten the unity of the soul. Being only conceptually divided, each particular soul remains one single entity which is responsible for all activities characteristic of the living being with that soul.

It is important to understand that the conceptual division of the soul enables Aristotle not only to proceed systematically by explaining one capacity of the soul after another, and thus to provide a substantive account of the soul as we find it in the *DA*. It also enables him to divide the soul along different joints, and thus to account for other, more complex, activities of animals. This is exactly what he does in some treatises from the *Parva Naturalia*. When the soul is conceptually redivided for such purposes, new and previously unmentioned capacities of the soul emerge. None of this need involve inconsistency. Since each particular soul is really one single thing responsible for all activities characteristic of the living beings with that kind of soul, there is nothing problematic about making new conceptual divisions which will bring out parts or aspects of the soul suited to explain other or more complex activities.

Let me give an example of this practice. Some of Aristotle's remarks about thinking clearly require that the thinking capacity of the soul has access to objects of the perceptual capacity of the soul. Now if the thinking capacity has access to objects of the perceptual capacity of the soul, there cannot be a sharp divide between the two capacities.[1] This is clear from Aristotle's statement that one of the capacities which defines the soul of animals is 'that concerned with discrimination (τὸ κριτικόν), which is the work of thought and perception' (III.9 432^{a}15–16). At another point (III.4 429^{b}10–18) he explains that we apprehend compound substances and their essences either by different capacities or by the same capacity 'differently disposed' (ἄλλως ἔχοντι).[2] The latter alternative suggests that the capacities of perception and thought are two dispositions of the same capacity of the soul.[3] So, in some contexts, or for some purposes, Aristotle seems to believe that there is one single cognitive part or capacity of the soul, which comprises both the perceptual and the thinking capacity.[4] And because this cognitive capacity of the soul is one single thing, it can combine the proper activities of both the perceptual and the thinking capacity, so that a human being can have thoughts about objects of perception and perceptions informed by thoughts.

There is a better-documented example of the same practice which will introduce us to some concepts important for the success of our entire project.[5] We have seen that Aristotle concludes his account of the perceptual capacity of the soul in *DA* III.2. In the next chapter he

[1] So, for instance, Kahn (1966: 78–9) and Modrak (1987: 117–24).

[2] Earlier interpretations of this passage are surveyed by Hicks ((ed.)1907: 489–91). It contains two peculiarities, which can be briefly noted. First, the thinking capacity is related to the perceptual capacity 'as a bent line is related to itself when straightened out' (^{b}16–17). I am not sure that I fully understand the gist of this comparison, and consequently whether it implies that these two capacities are related in a significantly different way than the capacities described as being 'one in number but different in being'. Second, Aristotle admits the possibility that the thinking capacity may be separate from the perceptual capacity. This may be motivated by his wish to allow for the case of active intellect in *DA* III.5. I am indebted to David Sedley for drawing my attention to these two points.

[3] Cf. Hamlyn ((ed.)1968: 137–8), Modrak (1987: 117–24; 1991: 758–9), and Whiting (2002: 195–6).

[4] This is how Alexander of Aphrodisias read Aristotle (1887*a*: 78.6–21; 1887*b*: 119.11–13). The same view is ascribed to an Aristo by Porphyry in the lost work *On Capacities of the Soul* (Stobaeus I.49.24 = Porphyry fr. 251 Smith). My hunch is that this is the 3rd-century BC Peripatetic Aristo of Ceos, rather than the Stoic Aristo of Cos, or the 1st-century Peripatetic Aristo of Alexandria. I hope to substantiate my hunch in a future study on the reception of Aristotle's notion of the common sense in the Peripatetic tradition from Theophrastus to Alexander.

[5] Another example can be found in Aristotle's discussion of the locomotory capacity of the soul in *DA* III.9–10. For an extensive interpretation of this capacity, which bears marked parallels with the picture I am painting here, see Whiting (2002).

considers imagination. In the course of a fairly involved discussion, he makes imagination different from perception, yet causally dependent on it.[6] Although it is quite clear that imagination is a capacity which depends on perception, Aristotle does not venture a statement as to the precise relationship between the perceptual capacity of the soul (*τὸ αἰσθητικόν*) and the imaginative capacity of the soul (*τὸ φανταστικόν*).[7] But when Aristotle comes to discuss memory in *DM* 1, at one point his argument requires joint activity of perception and imagination.[8] For that purpose he introduces a capacity of the soul which comprises both the perceptual capacity discussed in *DA* II.5–III.2, and the imaginative capacity indicated in *DA* III.3. The soul is now conceptually divided in such a way that we have a more general capacity which is itself conceptually divided into the perceptual and the imaginative capacity. Because this more general capacity comprises both the perceptual and the imaginative capacity as its conceptually distinct parts or aspects, it can discharge activities of the perceptual as well as of the imaginative capacity; more to the point, because the more general capacity is really a single thing only conceptually divided, it can discharge certain complex activities on account of its unity. These complex activities discharged on account of its unity combine the proper activities of the two constituent parts, namely perception and imagination. To put it differently, Aristotle explains complex activities that combine perception and imagination by positing a more general capacity of the soul. This more general capacity of the soul is one single thing whose conceptually distinct parts or aspects are the perceptual and the imaginative capacity of the soul. Note that Aristotle does not have to worry about the material basis of this more general capacity of the soul, since there is one single system of bodily parts—the sensory apparatus—which, as we have seen, supplies material conditions for both perception and imagination.

Aristotle refers to this more general capacity of the soul as 'the primary perceptual capacity' (*τὸ πρῶτον αἰσθητικόν*), apparently to distinguish it from the perceptual capacity narrowly conceived and treated in *DA* II.5–III.2.[9] That this primary perceptual capacity is indeed in charge

6 Cf. *DA* III.3 428^{a}5–16, 428^{b}10–429^{a}2.

7 Cf. *DA* III.9 432^{a}30–^{b}3.

8 That is, at any rate, how I understand Aristotle's argument in *DM* 1 449^{b}30–450^{a}14. I provide a detailed interpretation of the argument in Part II, Ch. 4.

9 *DM* 1 450^{a}11, 14, 451^{a}16; *DSV* 1 454^{a}22–4.

of both perception and imagination follows from Aristotle's statement that sleeping and being awake are 'both affections related to *perception* of the primary perceptual capacity'.[10] Unless the primary perceptual capacity was also in charge of something other than perception, notably of imagination which is active during sleep, it would be rather difficult to explain the qualification 'related to perception' (περὶ αἴσθησιν) in the quoted sentence.[11] Sometimes again Aristotle refers to this more general part of the soul simply as 'the perceptual part' (τὸ αἰσθητικόν), omitting the adjective 'primary'. This is probably because he thought that the referent is sufficiently determined by the context. This is the case, for instance, with Aristotle's statement that 'dreaming is the work of the perceptual capacity, and of that capacity *qua* imaginative' (*DI* 1 459ᵃ21–2).

There are good reasons to call this more general capacity of the soul αἰσθητικόν, 'perceptual'. First of all, we must remember that the Greek word αἴσθησις and its cognates have wider connotations than the English word 'perception' and its cognates. The word αἴσθησις can, and in Aristotle often does, refer not only to the awareness of objects and properties out there, but also to the awareness of subjective states, such as feelings of pleasure and pain, being asleep, having sense-impressions, or being aware of time.[12] Because the Greek word αἴσθησις and its cognates have such a wide application, we can see why Aristotle should like to call the more general capacity of the soul αἰσθητικόν. We can also see that the rendering 'perceptual', which I have used consistently in this book, is inappropriately constrictive in this particular case. But even with the constrictive connotations of the English word 'perception', it is not entirely inappropriate to call this more general capacity 'perceptual', after its more fundamental part or aspect. Perception is more fundamental in the sense that imagination causally depends on perception, which explains the character of images.[13] Perception is more fundamental also in the sense that Aristotle leaves room for the possibility that some

[10] ἄμφω γάρ ἐστι τὰ πάθη ταῦτα περὶ αἴσθησιν τοῦ πρώτου αἰσθητικοῦ (*DSV* 1 454ᵃ22–4).

[11] One might object that 'the primary perceptual part' here refers to the primary sense organ, i.e. the heart. This may be grammatically possible, but one glance at the whole passage will suffice to show that Aristotle is in fact talking about parts or capacities of the soul. In particular, see the opening sentence of the passage at 454ᵃ11 ff.

[12] Cf. *PA* II.17 661ᵃ6–8, III.4 666ᵃ11–13; *Pol.* I.1 1253ᵃ12–14; *DI* 3 462ᵃ3; *DI* 2 460ᵇ2–3; *DM* 1 449ᵇ29–30, 450ᵃ18–19.

[13] e.g. *DM* 1 449ᵇ30–450ᵃ7, 450ᵇ17 ff.; *DI* 2 459ᵃ24–8, 459ᵇ5 ff., 3 461ᵃ16–22, 25–ᵇ5, 7–30; *DDS* 1 463ᵇ8.

animals have perception but no imagination, although this is somewhat controversial.[14]

On the other hand, qualifying the more general capacity as 'primary' (πρῶτον), in contrast with the perceptual capacity narrowly conceived, may not be an unfortunate choice of words either, as it might be intended to indicate that the former is of a higher rank or level of generality than the latter.[15] Although Aristotle's Greek name for this more general capacity of the soul is quite appropriate, and its English translation not entirely inappropriate, in order to prevent the confusion between this more general capacity and the perceptual capacity of the soul strictly speaking, I shall henceforth call it, for want of a better name, 'the sensory capacity of the soul'.

It turns out that we have to distinguish between two items, the sensory capacity and the perceptual capacity of the soul. The sensory capacity of the soul emerges from Aristotle's discussions of memory and dreaming in *DM* and *DI*. Aristotle's account of the perceptual capacity of the soul is supplied in *DA* II.5–III.2, and we have dealt with it in Chapter 2. Now if my interpretation is correct, these two items stand in a certain relationship, namely the sensory capacity comprises the perceptual capacity as one of its conceptually distinct parts or aspects (the other part or aspect being the imaginative capacity). And just as the sensory capacity is conceptually divided into the perceptual and the imaginative capacity, the perceptual capacity is in turn itself conceptually divided into the particular senses. We can represent this by the diagram in Fig. 1.[16]

Because the sensory capacity of the soul is conceptually divided into these two parts or aspects, it can discharge activities of either of its parts. When it operates as the perceptual capacity, it enables the animal to

[14] In *DA* III.3 428^{a}9–11 Aristotle seems to deny imagination to some lower animals. In III.11 434^{a}4–5, on the other hand, he seems to allow such animals to have imagination in some indeterminate way.

[15] By the same reasoning, it can be objected, there is a sense in which the entire soul is the πρῶτον αἰσθητικόν. I have no qualms with that, except that introducing the entire soul in this particular context would be misplaced. It seems to me that the qualification πρῶτον is introduced to distinguish this more general capacity from the perceptual capacity narrowly construed.

[16] Admittedly, the imaginative capacity of the soul is also itself conceptually divided into parts or aspects, e.g. the part responsible for memory, the part responsible for dreaming, etc. It would take an extensive exploration to determine how many parts or aspects of the imaginative capacity Aristotle would admit, first in non-rational and then in rational animals. My diagram does not indicate the conceptually distinct parts of the imaginative capacity of the soul.

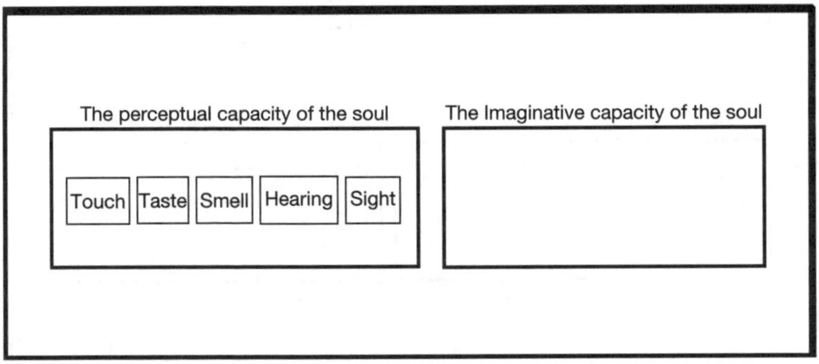

Figure 1. The sensory capacity of the soul

perceive various things; when it operates as the imaginative capacity, it enables the animal to experience images. Likewise, the perceptual capacity of the soul is conceptually divided into five parts or aspects, namely the five particular senses, and hence it can discharge activities of each one of its parts. When it operates as sight it enables the animal to see, when it operates as hearing it enables the animal to hear, and so forth.

On the other hand, the sensory capacity of the soul is in fact a single thing which is only conceptually divided. Hence, it can discharge certain activities that go beyond either of its two conceptually distinct parts taken separately. That is to say, on account of being a unified whole, the sensory capacity can discharge complex non-rational activities that combine perception and imagination, such as 'experience' (ἐμπειρία).[17] This allows us to speak of a higher-order cognitive power emerging from the unity of the sensory capacity of the soul, and this power is in charge of the complex non-rational activities.[18] Likewise, the perceptual capacity of the soul is a single thing which is only conceptually divided. Hence, it can discharge certain activities that go beyond any of its five conceptually distinct parts taken separately. In other words, on account of being a unified whole, the perceptual capacity can discharge

[17] At least the sort of experience accessible to some non-rational animals; cf. *Met.* I.1 980^{b}26–7 and Gregoric and Grgic (2006). Other examples of such complex activities will be suggested in Part II, Ch. 3–5.

[18] This higher-order cognitive power emerging from the unity of the sensory capacity of the soul, I submit, is the cognitive pinnacle of non-rational animals, and it ultimately explains their feats of intelligence; cf. Part II, Ch. 3, pp. 94–5 with n. 28.

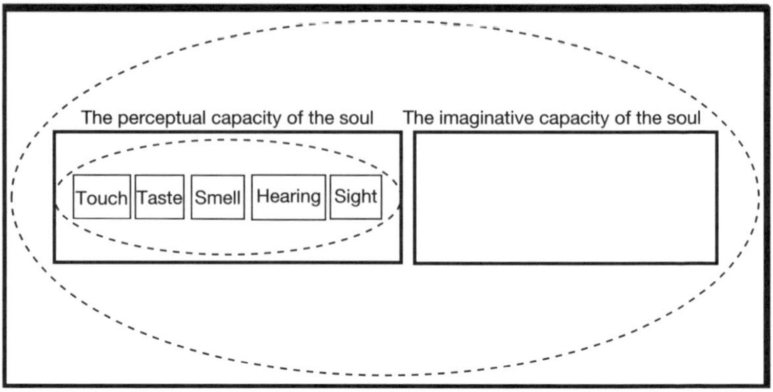

Figure 2. The sensory capacity of the soul

complex perceptual activities that involve two or more senses, such as simultaneous perception or perceptual discrimination, but also other activities that no individual sense can achieve on its own, such as perceiving that we see and hear. Thus we can speak of a higher-order perceptual power emerging from the unity of the perceptual capacity of the soul, which is in charge of such complex perceptual activities. The modified diagram (Fig. 2) indicates the two higher-order powers, one emerging from the unity of the sensory capacity, and the other emerging from the unity of the perceptual capacity.

This is the framework which equips us to deal with our subject adequately, and I shall draw on it extensively in the rest of this work. Now to the heart of the matter.

We shall see in Part II, Chapters 3 and 4, that Aristotle occasionally refers to the sensory part of the soul as the 'common sense'. He does so in the course of discussions which will be shown to require the notion of a more general capacity of the soul which encompasses both perception and imagination. However, there is a number of passages where he also uses the phrase 'common sense' differently, with reference to other things, and that, of course, easily leads to confusion. What these other things are will be clarified in Part II.

To add to the confusion, in one passage of the *DSV*, to be discussed thoroughly in Part III, Chapter 3, Aristotle mentions a 'common power accompanying all the senses'.[19] With the adjective 'common',

[19] *κοινὴ δύναμις ἀκολουθοῦσα πάσαις* [sc. *ταῖς αἰσθήσεσι*], (*DSV* 2 455ᵃ16).

this phrase is highly reminiscent of the phrase 'common sense' (ἡ κοινὴ αἴσθησις). However, the context makes it quite clear that the phrase 'common power' in *DSV* 2 does not refer to the sensory capacity of the soul, but rather to the higher-order perceptual power emerging from the unity of the perceptual part of the soul (the smaller ellipse in the diagram). Also, there are other passages which discuss this perceptual power, referring to it in different ways. All these passages will be extensively examined in Part III.

Leaving scattered and relatively unclear discussions of difficult issues concerning closely connected things without a consistent terminology is a perfect recipe for creating confusion. In this particular case, the confusion prevents the reader from distinguishing slightly different items set out in the framework above, in particular the sensory capacity of the soul and the higher-order perceptual power emerging from the unity of the perceptual capacity of the soul. The result is the idea that there is only one item there, a 'common sense', which is in charge of functions that in fact belong to two different items, the sensory capacity of the soul and the higher-order perceptual power which emerges from the unity of the perceptual capacity of the soul. It is hardly surprising, therefore, that interpreters disagree as to how many functions belong to the common sense and how exactly these functions are supposed to work. Indeed, many interpreters of Aristotle, ancient and modern, were taken in by the confusion and thus failed to get things right.

Given that Aristotle does occasionally refer to the sensory capacity of the soul as the 'common sense', one might expect an account of this capacity in the rest of this book. However, my aim is much more modest. In the rest of the book I shall focus solely on the higher-order perceptual power emerging from the unity of the perceptual capacity of the soul, that is, the power represented by the smaller ellipse in the diagram above. I shall do so not only because this perceptual power and its functions are complicated and interesting enough to receive close scrutiny, but also because the 'common sense' is traditionally taken as a strictly perceptual power, often in clear contradistinction to the imaginative capacity of the soul. This use is found in the ancient Peripatetics, some Arabic commentators, Latin scholastic philosophers, and early modern philosophers like Hobbes and Descartes.[20]

Since many philosophers in the tradition employ the phrase 'common sense' in that way, perhaps it is not illegitimate to set aside Aristotle's

[20] Cf. Introduction, pp. 10–13.

own use of that phrase with reference to the more general capacity—the sensory capacity of the soul—which includes imagination in addition to perception. This divergence from Aristotle's own use of the phrase finds additional justification in Part II, where I show that Aristotle's use varies in different contexts, which suggests that this particular bit of terminology has not been fixed in his mind.

Having justified my divergence from Aristotle's use, I should hasten to add that the way I use the term 'common sense' in the rest of this book does not correspond entirely to the use prevalent in philosophical tradition, because the latter vacillates between the perceptual capacity of the soul per se and the higher-order perceptual power that emerges from it, often without recognizing a clear distinction between the two. In order to avoid even the slightest confusion, I should note that from this point onward I shall employ the phrase 'common sense' solely with reference to the higher-order perceptual power emerging from the unity of the perceptual capacity of the soul.

Before I put the proposed framework to work, I would like to address an objection that might be raised against it. One could say that Aristotle did not draw the boundaries between various capacities in the way I have suggested. In particular, it may be the case that he held the view that the imaginative capacity of the soul is a subordinate aspect of the perceptual capacity of the soul, so that he did not need a more general capacity which comprises them both.[21] I admit that this is a possibility. This possibility would probably appeal to interpreters like Martha Nussbaum, who argue that imagination is in some way constitutive of perception, so that every act of perception involves an act of imagination.[22] However, it seems to me that Aristotle took the view that there are acts of perception which do not involve imagination, just as there are acts of imagination which do not involve perception.[23] So he must have conceived of them as two distinct capacities. Of course, accepting that Aristotle conceived of perception and imagination as two distinct capacities does not necessarily commit one to accepting the proposed framework. But if one does accept that Aristotle conceived of perception and imagination as two distinct capacities of the soul, one should not find the proposed framework objectionable. On the contrary, one should find it useful at least for heuristic purposes.

[21] This objection was suggested to me by David Sedley.
[22] Nussbaum ((ed.)1978: 255–61).
[23] Cf. *DA* III.3 428^{a}5–16 and Everson (1997: 157–86).

Let us suppose that Aristotle indeed viewed the imaginative capacity of the soul as a subordinate aspect of the perceptual capacity of the soul, although he conceived of perception and imagination as two distinct capacities of the soul. In that case we must assume that he made a distinction between the role of the perceptual capacity in perceiving and its role in experiencing images. Now if we think that Aristotle allowed also for joint work of perception and imagination, as I think he did, then we should also assume that he distinguished the third role of the perceptual capacity of the soul, namely its role in combining perception and imagination. Whereas it is difficult to keep these three roles distinct if they are ascribed to the same thing, it is easy to do so if they are ascribed to three slightly different things. In the framework that I have proposed, these three roles are ascribed, respectively, to the perceptual capacity of the soul, to the imaginative capacity of the soul, and to the sensory capacity of the soul; the sensory capacity of the soul comprises the former two capacities as its conceptually distinct parts and it is therefore capable of combining their operations. The heuristic value of the proposed framework should be obvious.

Quite generally, then, my last line of defence of the outlined framework, should I be forced to make it, would be to say that even if Aristotle did not draw the boundaries in every detail as I have suggested, it is helpful to draw them so in our attempt to come to grips with his mental geography.

PART II

THE TERMINOLOGY

Everything had a name, but although every name was nothing without the thing named, the thing cared nothing for its name, had no need of a name, and was itself only.

John Banville, *Doctor Copernicus*

1

Overlooked Occurrences of the Phrase 'Common Sense'

It has often been claimed that the phrase *κοινὴ αἴσθησις*, usually translated as 'common sense', occurs only three or four times in the Aristotelian corpus. Three occurrences are recognized by all contemporary scholars: *DA* III.1 425^{a}27, *DM* 1 450^{a}10, and *PA* IV.10 686^{a}31. Some scholars recognize also an incomplete occurrence in *DA* III.7 431^{b}5, which is difficult both on textual and exegetic grounds, and which will be discussed thoroughly in Chapter 5 of this Part. However, the phrase 'common sense' can also be found in *HA* I.3 489^{a}17 and *Met.* I.1 981^{b}14. To my knowledge, these two occurrences have never been treated, or even mentioned, by any scholar dealing with, or only touching upon, Aristotle's notion of the common sense. Let us first review these two overlooked occurrences and see what the phrase 'common sense' means there.

In *HA* I.3 489^{a}17 Aristotle says: 'Only one sense is common to all animals, touch' (*πᾶσι δὲ τοῖς ζῴοις αἴσθησις μία ὑπάρχει κοινὴ μόνη, ἡ ἁφή*). In the *DA* Aristotle emphasizes the fundamental importance of touch as the sense which is indispensable for the preservation of animals.[1] The sense of touch is said to be the only sense common to all animals because it is necessary for each and every animal to possess it. Without the sense of touch, no animal could survive.

The same idea is found in *EN* III.10 1118^{b}1, where Aristotle concludes that the sense with which self-indulgence is connected is 'the most common of the senses' (*κοινοτάτη τῶν αἰσθήσεων*), referring again to the sense of touch.[2] Being the only sense which is found in each

[1] Cf. *DA* II.2 413^{b}4–9, III.12 434^{b}11–18.

[2] Assuming that the sense of touch is inseparable from the sense of taste, Sisko (2003) argues that the superlative of the adjective 'common' in *EN* III.10 is used precisely in order to demarcate touch from taste, as Aristotle's argument concerning self-indulgence

and every individual animal, touch is inevitably the most common of all the individual senses. The fact that touch is the *most* common sense clearly does not imply that the other senses are not common, but only that they are *less* common than touch. In other words, the senses other than touch are not found in animals of every species; however, they are found in animals of different species, which suffices to call them the 'common senses', if *less* so than touch. Thus even the least common sense, whichever it may be, is still a common sense. It is a common sense because it is found in animals of different species, and what makes it the least common is that it is found in the comparatively smallest number of animals of different species.

It seems safe to make the following generalization. A sense is called 'common' if it is found in a number of individual animals not all of which belong to the same species. The senses which are found in a larger number of individual animals across different species are consequently *more* common, and those that are found in a smaller number are *less* common. It follows that the five individual senses are common in different degrees, but each one of them must nevertheless be regarded as a common sense, because each one of them is found in a number of individual animals not all of which belong to the same species.

This is confirmed by a passage in *Met.* I.1 981^{b}13–15. The translators tend to misinterpret this passage precisely because they misunderstand the crucial expression. The text goes as follows: *τὸ μὲν οὖν πρῶτον εἰκὸς τὸν ὁποιανοῦν εὑρόντα τέχνην παρὰ τὰς κοινὰς αἰσθήσεις θαυμάζεσθαι ὑπὸ τῶν ἀνθρώπων κτλ.* Ross translates it: 'At first he who invented any art that went beyond the common perceptions of man was naturally admired by men, etc.'[3] Similarly, Tredennick translates: 'It is therefore probable that at first the inventor of any art which went further than the ordinary sensations was admired by his fellow men.'[4] Realizing that *τὰς κοινὰς αἰσθήσεις* in this passage cannot refer to a plurality of some unspecialized perceptual capacities accompanying the individual senses, as the common sense is usually understood, the translators found themselves in a difficulty which they hoped to solve by taking the notoriously equivocal term *αἴσθησις* not as a *capacity* of perception, but as an *act* of perception. Thus they translate *τὰς*

requires. Sisko does not take into consideration the *HA* I.3 passage in which touch is explicitly said to be the one and *only* sense common to all animals.

[3] Ross ((ed.)1928: ad loc.); also in Barnes ((ed.)1985: II.1553).

[4] Tredennick ((ed.)1933: 7).

κοινὰς αἰσθήσεις as 'common perceptions' or 'ordinary sensations'.[5] Presumably, such acts of perception are labelled 'common' because they are shared by all human beings—as in Ross's translation, which restricts such acts to 'men' without direct textual support—or otherwise because they are shared by human beings *and* other animals.

One look at what immediately precedes suffices to show that this is not what Aristotle has in mind. At 981^{b}10–13 he says that the senses are the most reliable source of cognition of the particulars, but since they are unable to disclose the causes, there is no wisdom in them. Art, on the other hand, does disclose the causes, and hence there is wisdom in it. What is being compared here are not *acts* of perception and *acts* of art, but rather the senses and art as *capacities* or *dispositions* of different cognitive import. Therefore, in the quoted passage Aristotle is in fact saying that the person who first transcended the limited cognitive capacities of the five senses to invent an art, which is a higher cognitive disposition, was naturally admired and considered very wise. Hence the correct translation of the sentence is: 'At first he who invented any art that went beyond the common senses was naturally admired by men'—observing that the phrase 'common senses' refers to the five individual senses.

Why does Aristotle choose to refer to the five individual senses using the phrase 'common sense' in the context of *Met.* I.1? Aristotle's choice of words seems to be guided by the contrast drawn between the senses as a set of lower cognitive capacities shared by all human beings and many other animals, and art as a higher sort of cognitive capacity shared only by the few human beings who have managed to acquire it through experience. Therefore, all human beings and other animals are aware of certain things (perceptibles) in virtue of the five senses they are born with, whereas few human beings are aware of certain other things (causes in a certain domain) in virtue of the art that they have acquired. The five senses are thus characterized as the 'common senses' in order to bring out the fact that they are shared by all human beings and many animals, in contrast with art, which is uncommon and rare, for it is shared only by a minority of human beings.

There are three important points emerging from the present discussion. First, we have seen that the phrase 'common sense' occurs five or six times in Aristotle (six or seven times, if we include the superlative in *EN* III.10 1118^{b}1), rather than three or four times, as claimed by

[5] Another suggestion is Taylor's ((ed.)1949: 71), 'common sense-perceptions'.

contemporary scholarship. Second, we have learnt that in the overlooked occurrences the phrase 'common sense' refers to the individual senses, to the sense of touch in particular, or to the five individual senses indiscriminately. Third, we have seen that in the three analysed passages the phrase 'common sense' is not a proper name for any particular perceptual capacity, but rather a description applicable to the individual senses in certain contexts. In *HA* I.3 489^{a}17, and similarly in *EN* III.10 1118^{b}1, it is a description of the sense of touch, whereas in *Met.* I.1 981^{b}14 it is a description of all the five individual senses. The reason why Aristotle describes the individual senses as 'common' in these three passages is to bring out the fact that they are shared by animals of different species.

Bearing this in mind, let us turn to the occurrence of the phrase 'common sense' in *DA* III.1, which is, I think, the main source of confusion concerning Aristotle's views on the common sense.

2

De Anima III.1 425^a27

The primary purpose of *DA* III.1 is to show that there can be no sense in addition to the five individual senses, that is, sight, hearing, smell, taste, and touch. Having shown in the first part of the chapter (424^b22–425^a13) that there can be no additional sense for the special perceptibles, in the second part (425^a14–29) Aristotle argues that there can be no special sense for the common perceptibles either. Aristotle's argument in the second part of *DA* III.1 is both dense and textually uncertain, which is why it must be read very carefully. I translate the whole Greek passage as it is presented in the Appendix, with minimal interpretation.

> Nor again can there be a special sense organ for the common perceptibles, which we perceive by each sense accidentally—e.g. change, rest, shape, magnitude, number, one—for all of these we perceive by change (e.g. [we perceive] magnitude by change and hence also shape, for shape is a kind of magnitude; what is at rest by not changing, and number by negation of continuity) and with special perceptibles, for each sense perceives one. Hence it is clear that it is impossible that there should be a special sense for any one of these, e.g. for change. In that case it would be as we now perceive sweet by sight; and this [we perceive] because we happen to have a perception of both of them, by which, if they concur, we grasp them simultaneously. If not, we would perceive them in no other way than accidentally, as [we perceive] the son of Cleon, not because he is the son of Cleon, but because he is white, and to this [sc. the white] it accidentally belongs to be the son of Cleon. However, for the common perceptibles we in fact have a common sense, not accidentally. Therefore, there is no special [sense for the common perceptibles]; for we would perceive them in no other way than as stated. (*DA* III.1 425^a14–29; see Appendix (a))

The first problem with this passage is the claim in the opening clause that the common perceptibles are perceived by each sense accidentally (κατὰ συμβεβηκός). This appears to be in flat contradiction with Aristotle's classification of objects of perception in *DA* II.6, where the common perceptibles are said to be perceived in themselves (καθ' αὑτά).

The literature offers three principal ways of resolving this inconsistency, all of them essentially denying that at 425^{a}15 Aristotle maintains that the common perceptibles are perceived accidentally by the individual senses, in the strict sense of 'perceiving accidentally' exemplified by the perception of the son of Cleon, or by the perception of sweet by sight.

The three solutions of the inconsistency are thoroughly discussed by Owens, and we may review them briefly.[1] The first solution is simply to insert the negation before the words *κατὰ συμβεβηκός* at 425^{a}15, with support from three late manuscripts and William of Moerbeke's Latin translation.[2] This is a rather drastic solution which has impressed few scholars.

The second solution is to assume that the expression 'accidental' at 425^{a}15 is used in a looser sense than the usual one. In this loose sense the expression captures the fact that the common perceptibles are not properly perceived, but only relayed by the individual senses. The idea is this: since the common perceptibles affect the individual senses together with the special perceptibles, they are classified as objects perceived in themselves; but since they are not properly speaking *perceived* by the individual senses, they are said to be perceived 'accidentally' by each individual sense, and thus the contradiction is avoided. Although this solution seems plausible and enjoys popularity among the interpreters,[3] it is beset with serious problems. It implies that the expression *κατὰ συμβεβηκός* is used in two very different senses in the same argument (it is certainly used in the strict, technical sense at 425^{a}24, and most probably at ^{a}27). What is more, given that Aristotle is usually quick to point out equivocations, we would expect him to mark this verbal shift had it been there. Finally, it is doubtful whether Aristotle would permit the claim that a perceptible affects a sense yet not so as to be perceived by that sense. In other words, it is questionable whether the suggested loose sense of the expression *κατὰ συμβεβηκός* is permitted.

The third solution is to interpret the line in which the individual senses are said to perceive the common perceptibles accidentally as a part of the hypothesis which Aristotle is rejecting. Thus, 425^{a}14–15 is essentially

[1] Owens (1982); cf. Brunschwig (1996: 208–18).

[2] Torstrik ((ed.)1862), followed by Neuhaeuser (1878: 35), Biehl ((ed.)1884: 69), Susemihl (1884: 42 n. 52), and Block (1988: 248 n. 10).

[3] Its advocates include Zeller (1921: 542–3), Kampe (1870: 104–5 n. 5), Trendelenburg ((ed.)1877: 427–30), Wallace ((ed.)1882: 252–4), Beare (1906: 284–5), Hicks ((ed.)1907: 426–31), De Corte (1932: 190–6), Siwek ((ed.)1933: 302–3), Ross ((ed.)1961: 270), Hamlyn ((ed.)1968: 117), Graeser (1978: 81–6), Maudlin (1986: 64–5), Modrak (1987: 64), Everson (1997: 156).

saying that if there were a special organ for the common perceptibles, each individual sense would perceive them accidentally, and that is what Aristotle wants to refute. Admittedly, this is not a straightforward reading of the text at ^{a}14–15, with the verb *αἰσθανόμεθα* in the indicative.[4] However, allowing that it is not unusual for Aristotle to put things in such a hasty way, this seems to be the least problematic solution, and it is favoured by the ancient as well as some modern commentators.[5]

All three solutions are committed to the view that the common perceptibles are more intimately related to the individual senses than the accidental perceptibles and the special perceptibles of one sense to another sense. It follows that the individual senses play a significant role in the perception of the common perceptibles, and the question is just how extensive this role is. Those who opt for the second solution think that the individual senses alone do not suffice for the perception of the common perceptibles, so that an additional perceptual capacity is required, and the phrase 'common sense' introduces just that. Given that many scholars subscribe to this solution,[6] I propose to regard it as the standard view. Those who opt for the first or third solution, on the other hand, are led to think that the individual senses do suffice for the perception of the common perceptibles, in which case another interpretation of the phrase 'common sense' is needed. For, if the common perceptibles are perceived by the individual senses, how does the 'common sense' come in? This question will be addressed in the second half of the present chapter.

Let us consider the standard view first. According to this view, the individual senses alone cannot perceive the common perceptibles, which is why an additional perceptual capacity is introduced. The additional perceptual capacity is not a sixth sense on a par with the five individual senses, but a higher-order perceptual power which accompanies the individual senses and accomplishes tasks that they cannot accomplish

[4] Theiler ((ed.)1959: 131) has proposed to read *αἰσθανοίμεθ' ἂν* instead of *αἰσθανόμεθα* in line 15, which is attractive. But perhaps Greek grammar allows us to read the second clause in its received form as expressing the consequence of the idea introduced in the first clause, so that we can translate: 'Nor again can there be a special sense organ of the common perceptibles, which we then perceive by each sense accidentally.'

[5] So Themistius (1899: 81.18–82.37), Philoponus (1887: 454.2–5, 457.10–23), Simplicius (1882: 182.38–183.4), Rodier ((ed.)1900: II.353), Tricot ((ed.)1934: 148), Theiler ((ed.)1959: 131), Kahn (1966: 53 n. 24), Owens (1982: 235–6), Lories (1991: 414–15), Brunschwig (1996: 218).

[6] See n. 7 below.

severally. It is assumed that this higher-order perceptual power is here called the 'common sense'.

An adherent of the standard view has to complete two tasks. First, he has to explain the specific role of the individual senses in the perception of the common perceptibles. That is, he has to show that the individual senses are engaged in the perception of the common perceptibles to the extent which is, on the one hand, sufficient to classify the common perceptibles as things perceived in themselves, and on the other hand, insufficient to assert that the common perceptibles are thereby actually perceived by the individual senses, since the crucial role in the perception of the common perceptibles is taken to belong to the common sense. Second, an adherent of the standard view must explain the specific role of the common sense in the perception of the common perceptibles. That is, the common sense should be engaged in a way which compensates for the insufficiency of the individual senses in perceiving the common perceptibles. This would warrant Aristotle's claim at 425^a27 that for the common perceptibles we have a 'common sense', which presumably perceives them 'not accidentally'.

These two tasks require a good deal of speculation, since Aristotle's texts offer little evidence. The speculation usually proceeds along the following lines. The common perceptibles are classified as things perceived in themselves because they do affect the individual senses by virtue of what they are, but they cannot be actually *grasped* by the individual senses, because the individual senses discriminate only their corresponding special perceptibles. For the common perceptibles to be actually grasped, then, a higher-order perceptual power is required to extract the relevant information from what the individual senses supply. So the common perceptibles are perceived in themselves, because, unlike the accidental perceptibles, they do affect the individual senses; however, they are not actually *perceived* by the individual senses, but only by the higher-order perceptual power which grasps them non-accidentally.[7] The reason why this power is called the 'common sense',

[7] I believe this captures the essence of the interpretations offered by Alexander of Aphrodisias (1887*a*: 65.8–21), Kampe (1870: 104–5 n. 5), Baeumker (1877: 64–6), Wallace ((ed.)1882: pp. lxxix–lxxx, 252–4), Beare (1906: 282–90), Hicks ((ed.)1907: 427), De Corte (1932: 189–90), Siwek ((ed.)1933: 302–3), Ross (1949: 140; (ed.)1961: 33), Graeser (1978: 81–6), Modrak (1981*a*; 1981*b*; 1987: 62–71), and Everson (1997: 148–57).

some interpreters seem to infer from this passage, is precisely because it perceives the common perceptibles non-accidentally.[8]

In itself, the standard view is not unreasonable, and it makes tolerable sense of the whole passage. However, it is subject to the following six difficulties. First, it is built on tenuous textual evidence. The only place in the entire body of Aristotle's works where the common perceptibles seem to be unambiguously associated with anything other than the individual senses is the passage currently under consideration.

Second, in *DA* III.1 425^b4–11 Aristotle considers the question why there are several individual senses rather than only one. His answer is this: in order that the common perceptibles are 'less likely to escape our notice' (ὅπως ἧττον λανθάνῃ). This formulation implies only that it would be *harder* to perceive the common perceptibles if we had a single sense, not that it would be impossible to perceive them. The passage seems to suggest that some common perceptibles could be detected, at least to some extent, by an individual sense, without the activity of a higher-order perceptual power.[9] And if one insists that the activity of a higher-order perceptual power has to be present, assuming that it plays an essential (non-accidental) role in the perception of the common perceptibles, then one has to explain why should the number of individual senses make any difference to the way in which the common perceptibles are perceived. That is, if we have the common sense for the common perceptibles, shouldn't its coupling with only a single individual sense, such as touch or sight, allow us to perceive the common perceptibles as sharply as they possibly can be perceived?

Third, if we have a higher-order perceptual capacity which perceives the common perceptibles in a proper, non-accidental fashion, it would be rather difficult to explain why the perception of the common perceptibles is particularly prone to error, as Aristotle claims in *DA* III.3 428^b22–5.[10]

Fourth, in *DSV* 2 455^a14–$^b2$ Aristotle says that each individual sense has some special and some common functions, and he supplies examples. The special function of sight is seeing, whereas the common

[8] Kahn (1966: 52) writes: 'The systematic use of the same term "common" for both object and faculty tends inevitably to suggest a one-to-one relationship between the two, whereas in fact nothing could be more misleading.' I agree with Kahn, but wonder where he finds the 'systematic use' of the term 'common' for faculty in Aristotle.

[9] This passage is discussed in greater detail in Part III, Ch. 5.1.

[10] Cf. Part I, Ch. 2, pp. 32–3, where this claim receives a relatively simple explanation under the assumption that the common perceptibles are perceived by the individual senses.

functions, such as perceiving that one sees or discriminating sweet from white, are assigned to a 'common power which accompanies all the senses'. The perception of the common perceptibles is not mentioned as one of the common functions assigned to the 'common power'. This is not conclusive, of course, but it is reinforced by other passages which suggest that for Aristotle seeing does not consist only in grasping colours, but also in grasping the common and accidental perceptibles.[11]

Fifth, unlike all the other occurrences of the phrase 'common sense' in Aristotle, in *DA* III.1 425^{a}27 it is not preceded by the article. Even if the phrase preceded by the article does refer to a perceptual power distinct from the individual senses, the omission of the article in this place seems to indicate that the phrase might be used in a peculiar way. This problem has been noted by some scholars, but not explained.[12]

Sixth, unlike the other occurrences of the same phrase, in *DA* III.1 425^{a}27 the word order is reversed, which may be another indication that the phrase is used in a peculiar way. This reversal has not been noted in the literature, as far as I know, let alone explained.

I suppose that an interpretation of Aristotle's argument which avoids the outlined problems, or offers acceptable solutions, is preferable to the standard one which proceeds on the assumption that the common perceptibles are perceived by a higher-order perceptual power accompanying the individual senses. Such an interpretation is available—if one abandons the view that the phrase 'common sense' at 425^{a}27 refers to a higher-order perceptual power. The preceding chapter should make us amenable to this move, since we have seen that the phrase 'common sense' is sometimes used as a context-dependent description applicable to the individual senses. So let us try an alternative interpretation.

First a glance at the logic of Aristotle's argument. It is a *reductio ad absurdum* argument intended to prove that there is no special sense for the common perceptibles by showing that the existence of such a sense would have unacceptable consequences. The argument goes as follows. If we suppose that there is a special sense for the common perceptibles (the hypothesis, *p*), we would have to perceive the common perceptibles either accidentally in the way in which we perceive sweet by sight (the first disjunct, *q*), or accidentally in the way in which we perceive the son of Cleon (the second disjunct, *r*). Apparently, it is tacitly presumed that there is no other way in which we could perceive

11 Cf. *DA* III.1 425^{a}29–30, 12 435^{a}5–10; *DI* 1 458^{b}4–9.

12 Cf. Hamlyn ((ed.)1968: 119), Graeser (1978: 79).

the common perceptibles, given the hypothesis. Since we perceive the common perceptibles neither in the way we perceive sweet by sight ($-q$), nor in the way we perceive the son of Cleon ($-r$) it follows that there is no special sense for the common perceptibles ($-p$).[13]

Several things should be noted here. First, the argument relies all along on the matter-of-fact presumption that we perceive the common perceptibles by the individual senses. That is to say, Aristotle is considering what it would be like to perceive the common perceptibles *by the individual senses*, if there were a special sense for the common perceptibles. He maintains that, if there were a special sense for the common perceptibles, we would perceive them *by the individual senses* either in the way we perceive sweet by sight or in the way we perceive the son of Cleon. Second, the whole argument seems to appeal to the intuition that we perceive the common perceptibles in a more immediate way than the way we perceive special perceptibles of one sense by another sense, or the way we perceive the accidental perceptibles. So, what secures the conclusion $-p$ is that disjuncts q and r are counterintuitive. Presumably, the claim at 425^a27 that 'for the common perceptibles we actually have a common sense, not accidentally' also controverts q and r, but we shall come to that later.

Given the logic of Aristotle's argument, we would like to interpret the phrase 'common sense' so that, on the one hand, it is something that we have for the common perceptibles, and on the other hand, that we perceive the common perceptibles with the individual senses. This requires that the 'common sense' be something confined to the individual senses, rather than a perceptual capacity in addition to the individual senses. However, there is more than one way to construe this.

In the following pages I shall first present an interpretation which simply identifies the 'common sense' with the individual senses. This interpretation avoids or solves some of the problems we have shown to undermine the standard view, and to that extent it is preferable to the standard view. However, I shall argue that this interpretation is

13 The argument takes the following logical form:

$$\begin{array}{l} p \rightarrow (q \vee r) \\ -q \\ -r \\ \hline -p \end{array}$$

not itself free from difficulties. Hence, I will offer yet another, slightly more complex, interpretation. This final interpretation will be shown to avoid or solve all the problems for the standard view, without suffering any further difficulties, which makes it, I think, the best available interpretation of the phrase 'common sense' in *DA* III.1 425^{a}27.

Let us first consider the possibility that the 'common sense' refers simply to the individual senses. We have seen in the preceding chapter that the phrase 'common sense' can have that reference, and hence it is not unreasonable to entertain the possibility that this is how the phrase is used in *DA* III.1 425^{a}27. This reading of the phrase 'common sense' is supported by one of the most prominent ancient interpreters of Aristotle, John Philoponus, who gives the succinct comment on line 425^{a}27: 'By the "common sense" Aristotle does not mean the common sense which he discusses in what follows, but he calls the five senses "common sense".'[14] Also, some contemporary interpreters have suggested that the common perceptibles are perceived by nothing other than the individual senses, although they do not explain how to square this with the text.[15]

There is one immediate problem for this reading of the phrase 'common sense', though. If Aristotle indeed wants to say that for the common perceptibles we have the five individual senses, why does he use the phrase 'common sense' in the singular instead of in the plural? Had he put it in the plural, as he did in *Met.* I.1 981^{b}14, he would minimize the chance of being misunderstood.

Perhaps there is a way round this problem. It is not unreasonable to suppose that Aristotle's choice of words has something to do with the way he introduces the hypothetical sense for the common perceptibles. In lines ^{a}21 and ^{a}28 Aristotle speaks of a 'special sense' (*ἰδία αἴσθησις*) for the common perceptibles, and in both lines the phrase 'special sense' lacks the article. In contrast with a special sense for the common perceptibles, Aristotle posits a common sense, also without the article. The omitted article could perhaps be explained as indicating indeterminacy.[16] Instead of *a* special sense for the common perceptibles, we have *a* common sense, that is, *any* one of the common senses. If we accept this explanation, which hinges on grammatical subtleties, we could agree that the point of employing the adjective 'common' in this context is to

[14] Philoponus (1887: 460.17–19). The authorship of this commentary is disputed; cf. Lautner (1992).

[15] Block (1961*a*: 1 n. 2); Cashdollar (1973: 164).

[16] See Schwyzer (1950: 23).

bring out the contrast between the hypothetical 'special' sense for the common perceptibles, and the factual sense which is 'common' in the sense of being 'ordinary' or 'regular'.

It seems to me that this interpretation is preferable to the standard one which refers to the higher-order perceptual power which accompanies the individual senses. However, this interpretation has two weaknesses in addition to stretching the grammar of the sentence. First, it implies that the adjective 'common' is used in two slightly different senses within a single clause, once for the perceptibles which are *shared* by different senses, and once for a perceptual capacity which is *ordinary*. Second, this interpretation cannot explain the reversed word order in the phrase 'common sense' at $425^{a}27$.

I believe that there is an interpretation which avoids all these difficulties. But before I set it out, I would like to make a preliminary point. Suppose a philosopher claimed that there is such a thing as sensitivity to certain features in the world which cuts across the individual senses, for example sensitivity to apples. We are certainly able to detect apples by sight, smell, and touch, and if, for some reason, the philosopher wanted to capture this ability of sight, smell, and touch to detect apples, we would have no reason to object to his talk of sensitivity to apples. We would not be tempted to assume that he is talking about a *sense* for apples in addition to sight, smell, and touch. Nor would it be necessary to assume that his talk implies that there is some distinct capacity for perceiving apples in virtue of which we can detect apples by sight, smell, and touch. The philosopher can very well think that we can detect apples by sight, smell, and touch simply because it is in the nature of these senses to perceive various things, apples among other things, and he can still legitimately talk about sensitivity to apples. And what he effectively does by talking of sensitivity to apples, is that he picks out the ability of sight, smell, and touch to detect specifically *apples*, as opposed to oranges, pears, and other things.

Now, if our philosopher were a native speaker of ancient Greek, how would he say 'sensitivity to apples'? Pretty much the only phrase he could use is *αἴσθησις τῶν μήλων*. Remember that the Greek noun *αἴσθησις* is ambiguous not only in that it can refer both to a capacity and to a corresponding act; it is ambiguous also in that it can refer to different sorts of capacities. Before Plato, for instance, it normally stood for the capacity to become aware of things regardless of what they are and how the awareness is achieved. With Plato, as we have seen, it came to stand principally for the capacity to become aware of basic perceptible qualities, such as colours and sounds, through the sense organs. Aristotle again thinks that there is much more that one can become aware of through the sense organs, and thus the term *αἴσθησις* gets correspondingly expanded. So the noun *αἴσθησις*, even when referring to a capacity, is wide and flexible, much more so than the English noun 'sense'. Hence, we must not always translate *αἴσθησις* as 'sense', and we would be well advised not to do so in *DA* III.1 425^{a}27. Bearing all this in mind, let us return to Aristotle's argument.

Aristotle wants to deny the possibility of a special sense for the common perceptibles, and for this purpose he hypothesizes such a sense for one type of common perceptible, namely change. What is the point of calling the hypothetical sense 'special' (*ἰδία*)? Presumably, it is to capture the idea that change is related to this hypothetical sense in the same way one kind of special perceptible is related to the corresponding individual sense, e.g. colour to sight. In other words, Aristotle is suggesting a perceptual ability whose essence would be defined with reference to change as a type of common perceptible. Thus conceived, this perceptual ability would constitute an extra sense at the same level as the five individual senses, and it would have access to change in the same way as the individual senses have access to their respective special perceptibles. Now if there were such a perceptual ability for change, the individual senses would then access change in the same way as sight accesses flavours, that is, accidentally.[17] However—and this is the crucial point Aristotle is making at 425^{a}27—such access to the common perceptibles is shared by the individual senses.

To put things differently, Aristotle hypothesizes a separate ability to perceive one type of common perceptible. This ability would constitute an individual sense specializing for that type of common perceptible to the exclusion of the other five individual senses, just as each of the five senses is specializing in one kind of special perceptible to the exclusion of the other four. So, the perceptual ability for that type of common perceptible would be separate from the individual senses, just as each individual sense is a perceptual ability separate from the other individual senses. Aristotle denies the existence of a separate perceptual ability for the common perceptibles by saying that for the common perceptibles we in fact have a perceptual ability (*αἴσθησις*) which is shared (*κοινή*) by the individual senses, not accidental to

[17] This is the first disjunct (*q*) in Aristotle's argument proving that there can be no special sense usurping direct, non-accidental access to the common perceptibles.

them (οὐ κατὰ συμβεβηκός)—as a separate perceptual ability for the common perceptibles would be.

According to this interpretation, then, the phrase αἴσθησις κοινή at 425ᵃ27 should be understood as a perceptual ability common to the individual senses. It is not a technical term, but a description of the ability of the individual senses to perceive one set of features in the world, namely the common perceptibles. And it is a perfectly appropriate description. What it describes is indeed an αἴσθησις: it is a perceptual ability, albeit not a separate one entitled to be called a 'sense'. That is why it is crucial for this interpretation to take into account the flexibility of the Greek term αἴσθησις, and refrain from assuming that it refers to a sense. On the other hand, what the phrase describes is indeed κοινή: it is common to the individual senses in that each individual sense has it. Observe that the adjective κοινή has different force here from that in the three occurrences analysed in Chapter 1 of this Part. Here it captures the property of being shared by the individual senses, whereas in *HA* I.3 489ᵃ17 and *Met.* I.1 981ᵇ14 it captures the property of being shared by animals of different species.

With this interpretation none of the outlined problems arises. The passage is entirely in accordance with all the other passages where Aristotle attributes the perception of the common perceptibles to the individual senses. It does not require strenuous exegetical work that lacks confirmation by Aristotle's texts, as is the case with the standard interpretation which makes reference to the higher-order perceptual power in addition to the individual senses. In addition, this interpretation has certain advantages over the interpretation which simply identifies the 'common sense' with the individual senses. First, it provides an explanation of the contrast between the hypothetical 'special' and the factual 'common' ability to perceive common perceptibles without stretching the grammar of Aristotle's sentence. Second, the adjective 'common' is used in the same sense within the same clause, once for the perceptibles which are *shared* by the individual senses, and once for the perceptual ability which is *shared* by the individual senses. Third, it explains the particular word order of the phrase. The present word order emphasizes that for the common perceptibles we have an αἴσθησις which is κοινή. This emphasis would be lost had Aristotle decided to say that for the common perceptibles we actually have a κοινὴ αἴσθησις. Besides, the present word order may have been intended precisely to avoid the confusion with the putative κοινὴ αἴσθησις.

A few additional remarks might prevent possible misunderstanding of the interpretation I am advocating. First, it would be wrong to think that the phrase *αἴσθησις κοινή* in *DA* III.1 425^{a}27 *stands* for the ability of the individual senses to perceive the common perceptibles, as Hamlyn has argued.[18] The phrase is used neither as a proper name, nor as a description necessarily restricted to the ability to perceive the common perceptibles. There is nothing about this description itself which would prevent it from being applied to other perceptual abilities shared by the individual senses. For instance, the ability to perceive the accidental perceptibles is also shared by the individual senses, since we can detect the son of Cleon both by sight and by hearing. Hence, it seems that the ability to perceive the accidental perceptibles could also be described as an *αἴσθησις κοινή*—a sensitivity to certain features in the world shared by the individual senses.

Second, what is described as an *αἴσθησις κοινή* in *DA* III.1 425^{a}27, I take it, is not something that *enables* the individual senses to perceive the common perceptibles. Rather, it is an aspect of the properly functioning individual senses that is picked out and distinguished from the other aspects, for example from their ability to perceive the accidental perceptibles. Recall the idea of sensitivity to apples. Sensitivity to apples is not something that enables sight and smell to perceive apples, but simply an aspect of sight and smell that has to do with perceiving apples as opposed to oranges and peaches. So the perceptual ability for the common perceptibles is just this: the sensitivity to the common perceptibles that cuts across the individual senses.

Third, what is described as *αἴσθησις κοινή* in *DA* III.1 425^{a}27 is not the higher-order perceptual power emerging from the unity of the perceptual capacity of the soul. By saying so, however, I do not wish to claim that the higher-order perceptual power plays no role in the perception of the common perceptibles. Indeed, I will argue in Part III, Chapter 5 that the individual senses would lose much of their sensitivity to the common perceptibles if they were not integrated and accompanied by the higher-order perceptual power. However, it is one thing to investigate what a phrase designates, and quite another to investigate what makes the designated thing possible.

Fourth, I do not wish to deny that there is a manner in which the higher-order perceptual power can be described as an *αἴσθησις κοινή*—a perceptual ability shared by the individual senses. However, it is not an

18 Hamlyn (1968; see also (ed.)1968: 119–20).

ability of the same sort or rank as the ability to perceive the common perceptibles, and consequently, it is not common to the individual senses in the same manner. This is well explained in Simplicius' commentary on *DA* III.1 425ᵃ27.[19] He seems to distinguish very sharply between the ability of the individual senses to perceive the common perceptibles and the higher-order perceptual power accompanying the individual senses. The former, Simplicius explains, is 'common' in the way the property of being biped applies to human beings, whereas the latter is 'common' in the way the property of being five applies to fingers of one hand. Being biped is common to human beings because each particular human being is biped, whereas being five is common to fingers of one hand, not because each particular finger is five, but because five fingers are united in one hand.[20] Thus Simplicius seems to interpret the phrase 'common sense' neither as the individual senses, nor as the higher-order perceptual power accompanying all the individual senses, but precisely as the shared ability of the individual senses to perceive the common perceptibles.

Some such exegesis of the phrase *αἴσθησις κοινή* in *DA* III.1 seems to be pursued by a few modern scholars. I suppose that Kahn had this line of interpretation in mind when he said that 'the common sense described in this passage [sc. *DA* III.1 425ᵃ14–29] is nothing but the *coincidence* of the special senses'.[21] Block thinks that 'the only conception Aristotle had of a "common sense" in the *De anima* is simply that of a facility that the specific senses had of perceiving certain sensibles in common, i.e., the common sensibles'.[22] Brunschwig writes in similar vein that 'common sensibility is considered as a constitutive element of each particular sense'.[23] The main reason why such an exegesis does not enjoy greater popularity among scholars, I think, is the assumption that the phrase is a proper name that cannot refer to anything other than the higher-order perceptual power accompanying the individual senses. Although this assumption has been made by a long and illustrious list of supporters of the standard interpretation of *DA* III.1 425ᵃ14–29, beginning with Alexander of Aphrodisias, it is neither a necessary assumption, nor the one which makes the best sense of Aristotle's text. We have seen that the phrase sometimes functions not as a proper name, but as a context-dependent

[19] Simplicius (1882: 185.7–20). The authorship of this commentary is a matter of controversy; cf. Steel (1997).

[20] Simplicius (1882: 185.16–20). [21] Kahn (1966: 54).

[22] Block (1988: 245). [23] Brunschwig (1991: 470; see also 1996).

description. In this particular context, I have argued, it describes the sensitivity of the individual senses to a particular type of feature in the world, namely the common perceptibles. The proposed exegesis of the phrase paves the way for a more satisfactory interpretation of *DA* III.1.

3

De Partibus Animalium IV.10 686ᵃ31

In *PA* IV.10 Aristotle discusses external non-uniform bodily parts of the highest order of complexity in blooded viviparous animals. He proceeds from the upper to the lower external non-uniform parts. The head, Aristotle says, is for the sake of three things: the brain, the senses, and the organ for the intake of food. The head protects the brain and provides it with a suitable place opposite to the heart which the brain is designed to cool. The head supplies the senses with an environment conducive to their acuity, and furnishes an appropriate location for the organ which ministers the ingestion of food. The neck is for the sake of the windpipe and the oesophagus which it encircles and protects. Next comes the trunk with the front limbs. This immediately calls attention to the difference between human beings and quadruped animals. Namely, quadruped animals have legs with feet for the front limbs, whereas human beings have arms with hands. And this is because the human being is the only erect animal.

The human being is the only erect animal because its nature and essence is divine; the function of the most divine is thinking and being intelligent; and that is not easy when much of the body is pressing from above, for the weight makes thought and the common sense averse to change. Thus, when the weight and the corporeal [constituent] becomes excessive, bodies necessarily incline towards the ground, so that for stability, instead of the arms and hands, nature equipped quadruped animals with forefeet. (*PA* IV.10 686ᵃ27–35)

No interpreter of Aristotle's theory of perception, including those who concentrate on his notion of the common sense, supplies a discussion of this passage. The interpreters are mostly content to remark that Aristotle mentions the common sense in this passage, and they either say nothing further about it, or dismiss it as 'unusual', 'eccentric', or 'curious'.[1] I suspect the reason why the interpreters ignore this passage is that there

[1] Kahn (1966: 60 n. 36), Hamlyn (1968: 195).

is something prima facie perplexing about the statement that 'thought' and the 'common sense' are disposed to change relative to the weight of the upper parts of the body. The problem is that thought and the common sense are supposed to be parts or aspects of the form, rather than material entities that can be affected by the weight of other bodies or by other parts of the same body. It seems particularly odd to say so for thought, given that in Aristotle's view the intellect does not inform any particular part of the body. All of this suggests that Aristotle is speaking quite loosely in this passage, which may have led some interpreters to believe that it is pointless even to try to determine the meaning of the phrase 'common sense' here. While I agree that the text itself allows for different interpretations, I think that pessimism is premature. With a bit of charity we can reach a perfectly cogent reading of the passage which yields a plausible interpretation of the phrase 'common sense', and this interpretation will be confirmed in the following chapters.

To appreciate this passage it is necessary to understand the context of the question Aristotle is addressing. The question is this: why does the human being have erect posture? This question receives a memorable answer in Plato's *Timaeus*. Plato argues that the rational soul is located in the head, the only part of the body which is of a spherical shape required for unimpeded motion of the circles that constitute every rational soul. Because of the natural affinity, or 'kinship', between the rational part of the soul and the heavens, the head is raised towards the heavens, which is what makes the human being erect.[2]

I have argued elsewhere that this natural affinity between the rational soul and the heavens is best understood with reference to sight.[3] The real cause of sight, Plato informs us, is observation of the heavens. By observing motions of stars and planets we grow intellectually and develop a conceptual apparatus by means of which we can discover their cause, the perfectly regular revolutions of the world soul's circles.[4] And once we discover this, we can imitate the world soul in order to perfect our rational part of the soul, control the two irrational parts, and thus lead a rational life. Now to be able to observe the heavens, the sense organ of sight has to be placed in the head mounted on top of an erect body. And since the observation of the heavens is the path to thinking, we can infer that the human being is erect in order to think and live rationally. Observation of the heavens is thus the causal link Plato finds between erect posture and the ability to think.

[2] Cf. *Timaeus* 90a2–b1.

[3] Gregoric (2005).

[4] Cf. *Timaeus* 47b6–c4.

According to Plato, failure to observe the heavens and develop one's intellect in this life results in an appropriate reincarnation in the next life.[5] Depending on the type and magnitude of one's intellectual (and consequently moral) failure in this life, one can be reincarnated, among other creatures, as a quadruped beast, a grovelling reptile, or even worse, as an aquatic creature living in murky depths. Thus Plato proposes a *scala naturae* in which an animal's posture is correlated with its cognitive abilities, so that the more intelligent an animal is the more elevated its body is, and the less intelligent it is the more inclined its body is.[6] The causal link which holds between the human being's erect posture and its superior cognitive abilities seems to be operative throughout the animal kingdom: because lower animals house unintelligent souls, they have no need to observe the heavens, and hence they have inclined postures.

Aristotle fully agrees with Plato that thinking is the most valuable thing of which human beings are capable.[7] He also agrees with Plato that there is a causal link between erect posture of human beings and their ability to think. Moreover, Aristotle subscribes to the idea of a *scala naturae* such that this causal link puts an animal's posture in correlation with its cognitive abilities. Where the two philosophers disagree, however, is in how they explain this causal link.

It is not difficult to see why Aristotle could not embrace Plato's explanation. It is based on a number of premisses incompatible with Aristotle's outlook. To mention only a few, Aristotle could not accept that the soul is spatially divided into different parts of the body, or that it is divided into the rational, the spirited, and the appetitive part. He could not accept Plato's view of the nature and origin of rational souls, or the view that the rational part of the soul is housed in the head. Clearly, Aristotle had to provide a different explanation of the correlation between an animal's posture and its cognitive abilities, one which will be in harmony with his biology.

Aristotle finds his explanation in the notion of bodily proportion, that is, the proportion between the upper parts of the body (the trunk with its

[5] Cf. ibid. 91d6–92c3.

[6] Apart from the posture which determines the distance of an animal's head from the heaven, the shape of the head also plays a role in Plato's theory, cf. ibid. 91e2–92a2.

[7] In 90a9 and c4 Plato calls the rational part of the soul 'the divine' (τὸ θεῖον); cf. Cornford (1937: 353 n. 1). Elsewhere he calls it also 'the most divine' (τὸ θειότατον); cf. 44d5, 45a1, 73a7, 85a6, 88b2. Similarly, in the quoted passage of *PA* IV.10, Aristotle characterizes the human nature and substance as 'divine' (θεία), and adds that thinking and being intelligent is the work of 'the most divine' (τοῦ θειοτάτου).

external and internal parts) and the lower parts (lower extremities with their external and internal parts).[8] There are two main bodily proportions. On the one hand, there is a bodily proportion such that the upper parts are bulkier than the lower parts. This sort of bodily proportion Aristotle calls 'dwarflike' (νανώδης), and it applies to all animals, most perspicuously to the quadrupeds. On the other hand, there is a bodily proportion such that the upper parts of the body are commensurate with the lower parts. Aristotle does not have a special name for this sort of bodily proportion, but we can provisionally call it 'manlike', because it is fully realized in normal grown-up human beings. Manlike bodily proportion enables the erect posture of human beings, which is the most natural posture, according to Aristotle. In this posture the upper parts of the body correspond with the absolute 'up' of the universe, and the lower parts of the body with the absolute 'down' of the universe.[9]

The notion of bodily proportion plays a role in the explanation of various kinds of animal locomotion. In dwarflike beings the upper parts are too heavy to be sustained by the lower parts of the body. This is why quadrupeds use the front limbs to sustain their upper parts, and consequently why they walk on all four feet. As for human beings, 'in order to make their upper parts light and easy to carry, nature took away the corporeal [constituent] from their upper parts for the weight of the lower parts; that is why the buttocks, the thighs, and the calves of the legs are made fleshy'.[10] So the upper parts of grown-up human beings are of such size and weight that they are easily carried by the lower parts of the body.

More importantly, with the notion of bodily proportion Aristotle establishes a causal link between an animal's posture and its intelligence, so that variations in posture—across the species as well as within the same species—reflect variations in intelligence. The more dwarflike an animal is, the heavier its upper parts are, and hence the more it tends to lean forward to sustain the upper parts by the front limbs, and at the same time the less intelligent it is. Non-human blooded

[8] G. Freudenthal (1995: 56–70) argues that Aristotle explains different postures of living beings with reference to different amounts of vital heat inside their bodies. Vital heat indeed plays an important role in some passages explaining the different posture of animals (III.6 669^{b}2–7, IV.10 686^{b}27–31; cf. Lennox ((ed.)2002: 317–18)). It seems that the two explanations of posture, one with reference to vital heat and the other with reference to bodily proportion, are parallel and compatible. However, the explanation with reference to vital heat is of secondary importance for the present purpose, so I refrain from discussing it here.

[9] *PA* II.10 656^{a}7–13; *DR* 13 477^{a}21–3; *HA* I.15 494^{a}26–^{b}1.

[10] *PA* IV.10 689^{b}12–15; cf. *Timaeus* 74e1–75a1.

terrestrial animals are extremely dwarflike in comparison with human beings, which is why they are quadruped and much less intelligent. Infant human beings are more dwarflike compared to grown-up human beings, which is why human infants crawl and are unintelligent.[11] But as they grow, their upper parts gradually become commensurate with the lower parts, and they become erect as their lower parts gain bulk to sustain the upper parts of the body. And as they become erect, they gradually become more intelligent. Pygmies and midgets are not as dwarflike as infants in comparison with normal grown-ups, for they can sustain their upper parts by their lower parts, albeit not without some difficulty. Consequently, Aristotle claims, they do not have as developed intellects as normal human beings.[12]

The virtue of Aristotle's explanation is that the same causal link explains the correlation between posture and intelligence not only across species, but within the same species, and even within the same individual in infancy and maturity. This cannot be said for Plato. He offers several different explanations. First, Plato explains the difference in intelligence between humans and other species with reference to their posture which facilitates or impedes observation of the heavens, but also with reference to the shape of their heads.[13] Variations in intelligence among humans are explained in terms of the proportion between the body and the soul housed in it.[14] Needless to say, the idea that the soul can be disproportionate in relation to the body is unacceptable for Aristotle. Finally, the lack of intelligence in children is explained with reference to the violent process of digestion and reception of external stimuli that obstruct revolutions of the rational soul.[15]

Unlike Plato's, Aristotle's explanation is in tune with his biology, although this requires some elucidation. Let us first outline the physiological theory behind Aristotle's doctrine of bodily proportion by inspecting another, closely related, passage from *PA* IV.10:

The genus of birds and fishes, and the whole [genus] of blooded animals, as I have said, is dwarflike. This is why all animals are less intelligent (*ἀφρονέστερα*)

[11] *DM* 2 453^{b}6–7; *PA* IV.10 686^{b}8–28; *IA* 12 711^{b}12–16.

[12] *PA* IV.10 686^{b}23–6. Cf. *HA* VI.24 577^{b}25–8; Ps.-Aristotle, *Problemata* X.12 892^{a}6–22. An overview of Aristotle's views on dwarfs and pygmies can be found in Dasen (1993: 217–20).

[13] Cf. *Timaeus* 44d3–45a2 and 91d6–92c1.

[14] Cf. ibid. 88a7–b5.

[15] Ibid. 42e5–44b1. A more detailed comparison between Plato's and Aristotle's explanations of the correlation between posture and cognitive abilities can be found in Gregoric (2005).

than human beings. For even among human beings, children in comparison with adults, and those human beings that are in adulthood dwarflike by nature [in comparison with those that are not], even if they possess some other superior capacity, they are deficient in the possession of intellect (τῷ τὸν νοῦν ἔχειν ἐλλείπουσιν). And the cause, as already stated, is that their principle of the soul is indeed very averse to change and corporeal (ἡ τῆς ψυχῆς ἀρχὴ πολλῷ δὴ δυσκίνητός ἐστι καὶ σωματώδης). (*PA* IV.10 686^{b}20–8)

From this passage we learn that other animals, all being dwarflike, are less intelligent than human beings, and that dwarflike human beings are deficient in the possession of intellect in comparison with manlike human beings for the same reason: their 'principle of the soul' is corporeal and averse to change.

What Aristotle calls the 'principle of the soul' is no doubt the heart. At many places the heart is said to be the principle of the nutritive, perceptual, and locomotory capacity of the soul.[16] Nutrition, perception, and locomotion crucially depend on the heart, its structure and composition. The heart has to be like a vessel to receive blood, and it must be hot in order to concoct digested food and produce new blood.[17] It has to be strong and sinewy in order to move the limbs and effect locomotion.[18] Also, the heart must be well jointed or articulated in order to enable good perception (*PA* III.4 667^{a}6–9). More importantly, Aristotle says that animals with hard and thick hearts are said to have poor perception, whereas animals with softer hearts have good perception (*PA* III.4 667^{a}11–14). And this is not just a matter of coincidence, I take it, but of direct causal relation: some animals have poor perception *because* they have hard and thick hearts, whereas others have good perception *because* they have softer hearts.

This might be Aristotle's development of Plato's idea that flesh, which is by nature hard, heavy, and thick, renders the part it envelops insensitive: 'abundant and thick [flesh] tightly packed together, due to its hardness,' writes Plato, 'produces poor perception and thus makes the quarters of thought more forgetful and duller.'[19] Of course, Aristotle

[16] Cf. *DSV* 2 456^{a}5–6; *DJS* 3 469^{a}5–6, 4 469^{a}25–7, ^{b}5–6; *PA* II.1 647^{a}24–6, III.3 665^{a}12–13.

[17] *DJS* 4 469^{b}5–14; *PA* III.4 665^{b}11–16, 34–666^{a}3, 7 670^{a}24–6.

[18] *PA* III.4 666^{b}14–17; cf. II.1 647^{a}31–3.

[19] ἀναισθησίαν ἐμποιοῦσαι [sc. σάρκες], δυσμνημονευτότερα καὶ κωφότερα τὰ περὶ τὴν διάνοιαν ποιοῖεν (*Timaeus* 74e8–10). It seems that Plato here draws a causal connection between perception, memory, and thought. As we shall see shortly, Aristotle does the same.

rejects Plato's view that it is the flesh that renders the part it covers insensitive, since Aristotle regards the flesh as the sense organ, or the connate medium, of touch. However, he accepts the underlying suggestion that a thick, heavy, and hard constitution—of whatever uniform part of the body—renders that part insensitive. And a part is thick, heavy, and hard when there is a lot of earthy stuff in its constitution, that is, when it is 'corporeal'.[20] This is why hair and nails yield no sensation, why hard skin is insensitive, why the eye composed of water polluted with corporeal bits cannot see very well, why the muddy and thick blood is not conducive to perception, and so on.

What Aristotle is saying here, then, is that other blooded animals—all dwarflike by nature—are less intelligent than human beings, and that dwarflike human beings fall behind manlike human beings in the possession of intellect, because their heart is corporeal and averse to change. I read Aristotle as saying that their heart is averse to change *because* it is corporeal. In other words, the heart of dwarflike creatures is thick, hard, and heavy, and as a result it does not undergo change easily. Moreover, I take it that the change in question refers to the processes in the heart that underlie the exercise of the cognitive capacities that depend on the heart.[21] In other words, I understand Aristotle to be saying in the quoted passage that dwarflike creatures have hearts which are corporeal and therefore ill-disposed to undergo the processes which are necessary for more advanced exercise of the cognitive capacities that depend on the heart, that is, the sort of exercise that would render them more intelligent and endow them with intellect.

Now what are the cognitive capacities that depend on the constitution of the heart? I have noted earlier that the fundamental cognitive capacity, namely perception, depends on the heart. But what sort of perception? Since the heart is the proper sense organ of touch and taste, according to Aristotle, it must be the case that the perception of tangible qualities and flavours depends directly on the heart. Moreover, the heart is not only the proper sense organ of touch and taste, but it is also the central sense

[20] For instance, sea water is said to be more corporeal than river water (*GA* III.11 761^b9; *Mete* II.3 359^a15); the sense organ of touch is said to be the most corporeal, or the only corporeal, sense organ (*PA* II.1 $647^a19–21$, 8 $653^b29–30$), blood in the head is said to be thin and pure, and that in the lower parts corporeal, dense, and muddy (*DSV* 3 $458^a10–15$). Cf. *HA* III.20 $521^b26–9$; *PA* III.2 $663^b24–6$, IV.10 $689^b26–8$; *GA* V.2 $781^b19–22$.

[21] For a similar use of the adjective (δυσκίνητος) see *GA* V.1 780^a8. A different interpretation of the adjective in the two passages of *PA* IV.10 is suggested by Van der Eijk (1997: 247).

organ receptive of all special perceptibles. This allows us to conclude that the perception of all types of special perceptibles depends on the heart. Consequently, animals with more corporeal hearts are handicapped to the extent that they do not discriminate as sharply, or as many tokens of a given type of special perceptible, as animals with softer, thinner, and lighter hearts do.

Having weak perception of the special perceptibles seems to suffice for the attenuation of perception of the other kinds of perceptibles. An animal which can discriminate only a modest range of special perceptibles is hardly going to be able to discriminate many common perceptibles, or do so very accurately. For example, an animal which cannot differentiate the colour of some painted patterns against the colour of the background cannot possibly perceive the shape or number of the patterns. Similarly, an animal which is not very sensitive to the common perceptibles is in turn unlikely to be sensitive to many accidental perceptibles. On the other hand, an animal which does not perceive the special perceptibles very well can hardly make extensive employment of the higher-order perceptual power that accompanies the individual senses either. For instance, an animal which perceives few special perceptibles has correspondingly few chances to discriminate between different special perceptibles. It seems, therefore, that all functions of the perceptual capacity of the soul depend on the constitution of the heart.

Furthermore, in order to explain the ability to experience images, which is necessary for his account of memory, Aristotle evokes Plato's famous metaphor of the wax tablet receiving imprints from a signet ring.[22] Just as the quality and duration of imprints depend on the properties of wax, so the constitution of the sensory apparatus determines the quality and duration of the traces left from actual perceptions. If the constitution of the sensory apparatus is too soft and fluid, the traces will be distorted and they will not last long, whereas if the constitution is too hard and solid, no trace will be left at all. In other words, the quality and duration of images depend on the constitution of the sensory apparatus. Although Aristotle does not explicitly mention the heart in this context, it is reasonable to suppose that the constitution of the heart, the central sense organ, determines the quality and duration of images at least as much as the constitution of the rest of the sensory apparatus. If so, it

22 *DM* 1 450^{a}32–^{b}11; cf. *Theaetetus* 191b10 ff.

follows that the imaginative capacity of the soul also depends on the constitution of the heart, and with it also the capacity to store and retrieve things perceived or thought in the past by means of images, that is, memory.

Since both the perceptual and the imaginative capacity of the soul depend on the constitution of the heart, it must affect also those complex cognitive abilities which combine perception and imagination. We have seen in Part I, Chapter 4 that the sensory capacity of the soul is a single thing only conceptually divided into the perceptual and the imaginative capacity, and hence it can operate as a unity and discharge certain activities that combine the proper activities of its two constitutive parts or aspects. For instance, Aristotle thinks that there is a sort of intelligence (φρόνησις) which enables even some non-rational animals to figure out what is good for them in particular situations.[23] I suppose that this sort of intelligence requires joint work of perception and imagination, memory in particular.

Furthermore, it is not only non-rational cognitive capacities that depend on the constitution of the heart. In Aristotle's theory, powerful perception in conjunction with powerful imagination and memory gives rise to experience, and a fair deal of experience is necessary for apprehending those explanatory features which are necessary for understanding, including the self-explanatory features which constitute principles in a given domain.[24] In other words, perception coupled with memory and experience is necessary for the development of various rational cognitive abilities of the thinking capacity of the soul. In addition, continuous exercise of perception and imagination affects the already developed capacities of the thinking capacity of the soul, because fresh data bring about new concepts and consolidate or improve the already existing concepts. So the constitution of the heart has an impact on the thinking capacity of the soul, insofar as it directly determines the sensory capacity of the soul whose non-rational cognitive capacities are necessary for the development and exercise of the thinking capacity of the soul.

We are now able to see that the whole range of cognitive capacities, from perception to thinking, is directly or indirectly related to the composition of the heart. We are now in a position to appreciate the second *PA* passage from which we learn that dwarflike creatures have

[23] I shall say more about this below, pp. 94–5 and n. 28.

[24] *APo.* II.19 99ᵇ36–100ᵇ17; *Met.* I.1 980ª21–982ª2; cf. Gregoric and Grgic (2006).

weaker cognitive capacities because their hearts are corporeal. Such a composition of the heart impedes perception and imagination, which in turn hinders the development and exercise of the higher cognitive capacities. However, in the first of the two cited *PA* passages Aristotle is saying something slightly different. There he speaks about the weight and corporeal constitution of the upper parts of the body, not of the heart in particular. And he is not saying that the heart is averse to change (δυσκίνητος), but that 'thought' and 'common sense' are so. These two points of divergence imply no inconsistency whatsoever. Rather, they are two successive episodes of the same story.

We learn from the first *PA* passage that human beings are erect for the sake of that which is most valuable in them, namely thinking (νοεῖν) and being intelligent (φρονεῖν). This requires a manlike bodily proportion in which some of the corporeal constituent, which otherwise is concentrated in the upper parts of the body, is relegated to the lower parts of the body. Such a distribution of the corporeal constituent makes the lower parts of human beings heavier, and the upper parts lighter. Heavier lower parts are more capable of sustaining the upper parts of the body, and lighter upper parts are more easily carried around by the lower parts. There are two further consequences of such distribution of the corporeal constituent in manlike human beings. One consequence is that the heart, itself being an internal upper part, is less corporeal, which implies that the capacities which depend on it can function better. This is brought out in the second *PA* passage. The other consequence is that the upper parts of the body other than the heart are also less corporeal, which means that they exert less pressure on the heart, so it can function better. This is evinced in the first *PA* passage and in *DM* 2 $453^a31-{}^b4$, where Aristotle says that dwarflike human beings have a weaker memory than manlike human beings 'because a lot of weight rests on the perceptual part'.[25]

To put it in a nutshell, the manlike bodily proportion which makes human beings stand erect is hypothetically necessary for the development and exercise of the higher cognitive capacities, which is the best human beings are capable of. That is, if human beings are to develop and efficiently exercise higher cognitive capacities, then they must have a manlike bodily proportion. If human beings had a dwarflike bodily

[25] διὰ τὸ πολὺ βάρος ἔχειν ἐπὶ τῷ αἰσθητικῷ. I take it that τὸ αἰσθητικὸν here refers to the bodily part involved in perception, rather than to the perceptual capacity of the soul, and that the bodily part in question is or includes the heart.

proportion, their heart would itself be heavier, and, in addition, it would be subjected to a greater pressure exerted by the superincumbent parts. This would make the heart 'averse to change', which is to say that it would be ill-suited to undergo the processes required for more advanced exercise of perception and imagination (including memory). This would, in turn, thwart the development and exercise of the higher cognitive capacities.

Now that we understand the physiological theory behind the first *PA* passage which is of immediate interest to us, let us take a fresh look at it and try to get a clearer picture of the activities and capacities which are specified there. In order to determine what the phrase 'common sense' refers to, we need to see how it is related to 'thinking' and 'being intelligent', since Aristotle claims that thinking and being intelligent would not be easy if 'thought' and the 'common sense' were averse to change.

If we assume, as we no doubt should, that 'thought' and the 'common sense' are parts or aspects of the form (capacities of the soul), rather than parts of the body (organs), the adjective δυσκίνητος, translated here consistently as 'averse to change', must be taken to refer to the state or disposition of being actualized with difficulty, rather than to the state or disposition of being materially changed with difficulty. Surely, whether thought and the common sense are in the state or disposition of being actualized with difficulty or ease depends on the physiological set-up of the body, most notably on the composition of the heart and the pressure exerted on it, which are the two factors that determine the heart's ability to undergo the relevant processes. Thinking and being intelligent, then, are not easy when thought and the common sense are in the state or disposition of being exercised with difficulty due to an unfavourable physiological set-up of the body. And, presumably, the opposite also holds: thinking and being intelligent are easy when thought and the common sense are in the state or disposition of being exercised with ease due to a favourable physiological set-up of the body.

I take it, therefore, that the first pair of conjuncts, 'thinking' (νοεῖν) and 'being intelligent' (φρονεῖν), designate cognitive activities which are closely related to the cognitive capacities designated by the second pair of conjuncts, namely 'thought' (διάνοια) and the 'common sense' (κοινὴ αἴσθησις). In order to see the exact relation between the first and the second pair of conjuncts, we must decide what Aristotle means by 'thinking' and 'being intelligent'.

The terms νοεῖν and φρονεῖν are notoriously ambiguous in Aristotle. They can both refer to the activity of thinking in a broad sense, regardless of the sort of object which is being apprehended in thought, the manner of apprehension, or its liability to error.[26] This broad sense of *νοεῖν* and *φρονεῖν* corresponds to the wide sense of the verb *διανοεῖσθαι*. All these terms are usually correlated with the cognate nouns *νοῦς* and *διάνοια* and the substantives designating the thinking capacity of the soul (*τὸ νοητικόν, τὸ διανοητικόν, τὸ λογιστικόν*).[27] So the formula *νοεῖν καὶ φρονεῖν* can very well refer to the same activity, namely to the activity of thinking, broadly speaking.

The two terms can also refer to two slightly different kinds of thinking. The first conjunct, *νοεῖν*, may be taken in the stricter sense of reasoning specifically about explanatory features of things and the necessary relations between these features, whereby scientific understanding of these things is gained. In the strictest sense, *νοεῖν* may refer to the intuitive apprehension specifically of the first principles of a science, in accordance with the explanation of *νοῦς* spelled out in *EN* VI.6 1140^{b}31–1141^{a}8. The other conjunct, *φρονεῖν*, may be taken in the narrower sense of reasoning about what is good and expedient for one's life, in accordance with the explanation of *φρόνησις* in *EN* VI.5 1140^{a}24–^{b}30. So the formula *νοεῖν καὶ φρονεῖν* can refer to two distinct kinds of thinking, roughly, to theoretical and practical thinking.

Finally, the two terms can stand for two essentially different kinds of cognitive activity. Aristotle says for a considerable number of non-human animals that they are intelligent (*φρόνιμα*).[28] These animals

[26] For the broad sense of the verb *φρονεῖν* see *Phy.* VII.3 247^{b}11; *DA* II.5 417^{b}10–11, III.4 429^{a}10–15; *DS* 1 437^{a}1–3; *DSV* 2 455^{b}23–5; *PA* III.10 672^{b}28–31; *EN* X.7 1177^{b}32; cf. *Rhet.* II.21 1394^{b}24–5. The verbs *νοεῖν* and *φρονεῖν* seem to be used interchangeably in *DA* II.5 417^{b}10–11, III.3 427^{a}18, 19, 26–8, 4 429^{a}10–15; *Prot.* 108.2 (Düring). Cf. Hicks ((ed.)1907: 453), Hamlyn ((ed.)1968: 129).

[27] For *νοῦς* in this sense see *DA* II.3 414^{b}18, III.4 429^{a}22–4; *DM* 1 450^{a}13; *EN* VI.2 1139^{a}18, 33; for *διάνοια* in this sense see *DA* III.3 427^{b}15, 9 432^{a}16, 433^{a}2, 10 433^{a}18, 19; *DM* 2 452^{b}10; *EN* VI.2 1139^{a}1 ff.; *τὸ διανοητικόν*: *DA* II.2 413^{b}12, 3 414^{a}32, ^{b}18, III.7 431^{a}14; *τὸ νοητικόν*: *Phy.* VII.3 247^{b}1; *DA* III.4 429^{a}30, 7 431^{b}2; *DM* 1 450^{a}16; *PA* I.1 641^{b}7; *τὸ λογιστικόν*: *DA* III.9 432^{a}25, ^{b}5, 26; *EN* VI.2 1139^{a}12.

[28] *HA* I.1 488^{b}15, VIII (IX).10 614^{b}18; *PA* II.2 648^{a}5–8; *GA* III.2 753^{a}9–15; *Met.* I.1 980^{b}22; *EN* VI.7 1141^{a}27. Animals expressly said to be intelligent are the deer (*HA* I.1 488^{b}15, VIII (IX).5 611^{a}15–16), the hare (*HA* I.1 488^{b}15), the cuckoo (*HA* VIII (IX).29 618^{a}25–6), and the bee (*PA* II.2 648^{a}5–8). In *HA* VIII (IX).6, Aristotle says that many quadruped animals 'act intelligently for their own benefit' (*ποιεῖ πρὸς βοήθειαν αὑτοῖς φρονίμως*), supporting this with examples of animals which heal themselves, e.g. Cretan wild goats, dogs, the panther, the Egyptian ichneumon, the weasel, etc. The

behave in a way which manifests an ability to discriminate between those things that are beneficial for their lives and those that are not, and they pursue the former and avoid the latter, often with some ingenuity. For instance, the deer gives birth in the vicinity of roads because they are avoided by wild beasts for fear of human beings; dogs eat a particular kind of grass when they are sick because it helps them to vomit; crocodiles let a particular kind of bird fly into their open jaws and feed on the leftovers because that is how they get their teeth cleaned. Such animals obviously show an ability to discriminate what is good and expedient for their life, so there must be a related sense of *φρονεῖν* which applies to non-human animals too.[29] This sense of the verb *φρονεῖν* designates a cognitive activity which cannot be based on the thinking capacity of the soul, because non-rational animals are not endowed with it. Hence, this sort of *φρονεῖν* must be based solely on perception and imagination (including memory, of course). More precisely, this sort of *φρονεῖν* seems to require a joint work of perception and imagination. Take the example of a crocodile opening his jaws and letting a particular kind of bird clean his teeth instead of closing the jaws and devouring the bird.[30] I presume that the crocodile, in order to behave in this way, must not only perceive a certain object in the environment, but also recognize it as a bird of a certain kind, have a memory of birds of this kind having previously flown into his open jaws and feeding on the leftovers (or a memory of seeing other crocodiles' teeth having been cleaned by such birds), must represent that situation as something good, and so on. Be that as it may, it seems that the formula *νοεῖν καὶ φρονεῖν* can very well refer to two essentially different kinds of cognitive activity, the rational kind of cognitive activity accomplished by the thinking capacity of the soul, and the non-rational kind of cognitive activity accomplished by the sensory capacity of the soul.

How should we understand the formula *νοεῖν καὶ φρονεῖν* in our passage of *PA* IV.10, then? I think that the best reading of the passage

weasel is said to handle birds it catches intelligently (*φρονίμως*), for it tears their throats open (*HA* VIII (IX).6 612ᵇ1–2); and there are many evidences of intelligence in cranes (*πολλὰ φρόνιμα*), e.g. they fly very high in order to survey the distance, they land when they spot bad weather approaching, etc. Book VIII (IX) of the *HA* contains a long record of examples of intelligent behaviour of animals. There is a handy table of these examples with references in Coles (1997: 320–3).

[29] This topic is investigated in detail by Labarrière (1990) and Coles (1997). See also G. Freudenthal (1995: 52–6) for a concise discussion of the nature and cognitive basis of animal intelligence, with which I find myself in agreement.

[30] This is Aristotle's example from *HA* VIII (IX).6 612ᵃ20–4.

is achieved if the two conjuncts are taken to refer to two essentially different kinds of cognitive activities. Recall the context of the passage. Aristotle is discussing the erect posture of human beings which is due to their manlike bodily proportion. This makes the human being more intelligent than all other animal species, and more manlike human individuals better at thinking than more dwarflike human individuals, as we learn from the second of the cited passages from *PA* IV.10. It seems, therefore, that Aristotle is talking, on the one hand, of the φρονεῖν of which other animals are also capable, but in which they, all being dwarflike, are far inferior to human beings. And on the other hand, Aristotle is talking of the νοεῖν in which the more manlike human individuals are superior to the more dwarflike human individuals. Both of these cognitive activities depend on the bodily proportion which presupposes a certain composition of the heart and slight pressure exerted on it by the superincumbent parts of the body.

If we decide to understand the formula νοεῖν καὶ φρονεῖν in the way I suggest, as two essentially different kinds of cognitive activity, then the relation between the two pairs of conjuncts, one designating cognitive activities and the other designating cognitive capacities, is pretty clear. 'Thinking' (νοεῖν) is the work of 'thought' (διάνοια), and 'being intelligent' (φρονεῖν) of the 'common sense' (ἡ κοινὴ αἴσθησις), provided that the latter is understood as the sensory capacity of the soul which comprises the perceptual and the imaginative capacity. That the phrase 'common sense' can indeed be thus understood will be verified by the occurrence of the phrase 'common sense' to be discussed in the following chapters.

The interpretation I have outlined in the preceding pages rests on three fundamental assumptions: (1) all kinds of cognitive capacity in one way or another depend on the composition of the heart; (2) 'being intelligent' (φρονεῖν) is accomplished by the common sense; and (3) the common sense is the sensory capacity of the soul as outlined in Part I, Chapter 4. None of these assumptions is unassailable, of course, but I have tried to show that they are true to Aristotle's doctrine, that they enable us to give a cogent reading of the crucial passage in *PA* IV.10, and that they are supported by Aristotle's other texts.

Other interpretations, built on different assumptions, are no doubt possible. For instance, in his gloss on *PA* IV.10 686^{a}31 Michael of Ephesus says: 'And by the "common sense" Aristotle means either touch (for all animals have this sense) or, as I think, all the five senses together.'[31] As for Michael's second suggestion, which he prefers, it would require considerable work to show why Aristotle should choose to refer to the individual senses with the phrase 'common sense' in the singular, and how exactly the individual senses are related to thinking and being intelligent.

Michael's first suggestion, that the phrase 'common sense' refers to the sense of touch, looks more promising.[32] First, we have seen earlier that Aristotle uses the phrase several times to describe the sense of touch. Second, the sense organ of touch is the heart, and the heart figures prominently in this passage.[33] Also, in *DA* II.9 421^{a}19–26 Aristotle expressly associates the sense of touch with intelligence.[34] However, even if one could find an explanation of this association which is both credible and pertinent to the context of *PA* IV.10, it is difficult to see the point of calling the sense of touch the 'common sense' in this particular context. The fact that the sense of touch is shared by all animals, which is presumably what the phrase 'common sense' would be intended to suggest, seems irrelevant for the discussion of erect posture of human beings which enables them to think and be intelligent.

If my interpretation is on the right track, it has a far-reaching consequence for the phrase 'common sense' in Aristotle. The consequence is that the phrase here refers to the sensory capacity of the soul which comprises the perceptual and the imaginative capacity of the soul. Because it is only conceptually divided into these two parts, the sensory capacity of the soul remains a unified thing. And as a unified thing, it can accomplish not only perception or imagination independently of one another, but also their joint work, which is required for being intelligent (*φρονεῖν*), as I have suggested.

[31] *κοινὴν δὲ αἴσθησιν ἢ τὴν ἁφὴν λέγει (ταύτην γὰρ ἔχουσι πάντα τὰ ζῷα) ἢ ὅπερ οἶμαι, ὁμοῦ πάσας τὰς πέντε* (Michael 1904: 84.18–20).

[32] This suggestion seems to be embraced by Van der Eijk (1997: 250; 2000: 71).

[33] Van der Eijk (1997: 250) argues for the view that the phrase 'common sense' in *PA* IV.10 refers to the sense of touch by saying that 'touch is the fundamental sense which is closely concerned with, if not identical to, the "common sense faculty"', followed by a footnote referring to *DSV* 2 455^{a}23. However, all that Aristotle says in the *DSV* 2 passage is that the central sense organ coincides with the proper sense organ of touch. That does not allow us to identify the sense of touch with the common sense, any more than we are allowed to identify, for example, perception with imagination on account of their coinciding in the same system of parts. I shall say more about the *DSV* passage in Part III, Ch. 3.

[34] Discussions of this association can be found in Freeland (1992: 234–42), and Van der Eijk (1997: 249–50; 2000: 71–2).

We may wonder why Aristotle chooses to refer to the sensory capacity of the soul with the phrase 'common sense'. One answer would be that it is simply Aristotle's technical term for the sensory capacity of the soul. However, there are reasons to doubt this answer. First, he uses the same phrase to describe a variety of different things, as I have shown in the preceding two chapters. Second, Aristotle has other names for the sensory capacity of the soul, notably 'primary perceptual capacity of the soul' (*τὸ πρῶτον αἰσθητικόν*). This makes us doubt that in Aristotle the phrase 'common sense' has the status of a technical term.

However that may be, the phrase does seem to be used as a proper name in *PA* IV.10 686^{a}31, rather than as a context-dependent description. I believe Aristotle found the phrase 'common sense' a convenient name for the sensory capacity of the soul in this particular context because the adjective 'common' (*κοινή*) specifies that the type of awareness (*αἴσθησις*) in question is general, encompassing, comprehensive; namely, comprehensive of perception and imagination. I shall argue that this is also how the phrase 'common sense' is used in *DM* 1 450^{a}10, to which I turn next.

4

De Memoria et Reminiscentia 1 450^a10

Aristotle's first concern in the opening chapter of *DM* is to determine the capacity of the soul to which memory belongs.[1] This is a problem because memory is the ability to retrieve past perceptions as well as past thoughts, so it seems to belong to both the perceptual and the thinking capacity of the soul. Contrary to Plato, who seems to have associated memory more closely with thinking when he characterized remembering as something that the soul does by itself,[2] Aristotle finds it crucial to show that memory belongs essentially to the perceptual capacity, and only accidentally to the thinking capacity of the soul. It is not difficult to see why Aristotle should want to make this point. If memory belonged essentially to the thinking capacity of the soul, no non-rational animal would be capable of remembering. However, Aristotle believed, quite rightly, that some non-rational animals are capable of remembering, so it was important for him to show that memory is essentially associated with a non-rational capacity.

Aristotle develops an argument to that effect at 449^b30–450^a14. His argument is complex and difficult to follow, because its parts are not connected as clearly as one would wish. The argument seems to revolve around the idea that there is no memory without the 'perception of time' (*αἴσθησις χρόνου*), as stated at 449^b28–30. At 450^a19–21 Aristotle elucidates what the perception of time amounts to: 'For whenever one is actually remembering, as we have said earlier, one is also aware that one has seen, heard, or learned something before.'[3] So the perception of time in this treatise does not refer to the awareness of the passage of time, but more specifically to the awareness of the temporal relation in which things experienced in the past stand to the subject in the

[1] Cf. *DM* 1 449^b5, 450^a22–5, 451^a14–17, 2 453^b9–11.

[2] *Philebus* 34b6–8; cf. Lang (1980).

[3] I follow Sorabji in reading *πρότερον προσαισθάνεται* at 450^a21; cf. Sorabji ((ed.)1972: 79). The back-reference in the quotation is to 449^b22–3.

present. That is, to perceive time is to be aware that something currently present to the mind has been experienced before.[4] The perception of time is constitutive of memory because we remember something only when we are aware that the thing currently present to our mind has been experienced before. Unless we are aware that something has been experienced before, we are not remembering it but experiencing it anew.

A large part of the argument (450^{a}1–9) is devoted to describing the way we think. Aristotle's strategy is to elicit certain features of thinking on the basis of which he can conclude that memory should *not* be associated, at least not essentially, with the thinking capacity of the soul. Aristotle starts his discussion of the way we think by saying that the thinking capacity requires images (φαντάσματα) for its operation. He claims that when we think, even if we think of things which have no spatial extension, we always put something spatially determined before our mind's eye.[5] For example, when we think of circularity, which itself has no spatial determinations, we imagine a circle, and the circle we imagine is spatially determined in that it has a certain shape and size.

The other feature of thinking is that even when we think of things which are not themselves in time, we cannot think of them without time. Things that are not in time, as we learn from *Physics* IV.12, are entities whose being cannot be measured by time, such as everlasting heavenly bodies or objects of mathematics.[6] To say that we cannot think even of such entities without time seems to imply, among other things, that we can tell whether an object of thought has been thought before. We can tell that, I take it, because our thoughts require manipulation of images, and our images are temporally determined insofar as they occur in time and have a duration; moreover, our images seem to include some sort of time-tags which enable us to say whether the imagined thing has been contemplated before, or even when in the past it was contemplated. For example, the property of having all points on the periphery equidistant

[4] Cf. *DM* 1 449^{b}18–23, 450^{a}19–22. Later on, in 2 452^{b}7–453^{a}4, we learn that the perception of time can be indeterminate or with measure. It is indeterminate when we know that something was experienced in the past but cannot determine when, and it is with measure when we can specify in units of time when in the past the experience took place. Memory does not require perception of time with measure, which is presumably restricted to human beings.

[5] Aristotle in fact speaks of things that have no quantity (ποσόν), but it seems fairly clear from his example that he has spatial extension in mind.

[6] Coope (2005: ch. 9) provides an illuminating discussion of what it means for something to be 'in time', according to Aristotle.

from the centre is not itself temporally determined, yet to think of this property we need to imagine, say, a line and rotate it around one of its end-points. Because this act of imagination is temporally determined and time-tagged, the next time we think of the same property—at least if we think of it by means of the same act of imagination—we shall know that we have thought of that property before. This is what allows us to remember our thoughts. For, unless we are aware that something was thought before, we are not remembering it, but thinking it afresh.

Having shown that images needed for thinking necessarily bring in spatial and temporal determinations, the next step in Aristotle's argument is to demonstrate that the perception of time is the work of the primary perceptual capacity of the soul. And since memory requires a perception of time together with an image of the thing remembered, it follows that memory is the proper work of the primary perceptual capacity, and only accidentally of the thinking capacity of the soul. This step is made in a passage which is immediately relevant to us because it contains the phrase 'common sense'. Here is the translation of the received text of that passage:

(i) But it is necessary to grasp magnitude and change by the same thing as time, and the image is an affection of the common sense; so it is clear that the grasp of these is due to the primary perceptual capacity of the soul; (ii) and memory, including that of objects of thought, is not without an image; (iii) hence memory will belong to the thinking capacity of the soul accidentally, but properly to the primary perceptual capacity of the soul. (*DM* 1 450^{a}9–14; see Appendix (b))

I have divided the passage into three sections. Section (i) presents a short subordinate argument. In its premiss the grasp of magnitude and change is put in a necessary relation with the grasp of time. Skipping for a moment the crucial sentence which mentions the 'common sense', the conclusion of the short subordinate argument establishes that the grasp of all three—magnitude, change, and time—is the work of the primary perceptual capacity of the soul.[7] Section (ii) states that there is

[7] Observe that the logic of the argument requires the common sense to be identical with the primary perceptual capacity of the soul. This passage is probably the basis of Galen's claim, in *On the Doctrines of Hippocrates and Plato* VII.8.2 (De Lacy), that 'it makes no difference whether we call the source (viz. of the single common capacity of all the sense organs) κοινὴ αἴσθησις or πρῶτον αἰσθητικόν'; cf. Michael (1903: 13.3–4). This is true for Aristotle's use of these phrases, but false if the former phrase is used in the later Aristotelian tradition.

no memory, not even of the objects of thought, without images. Finally, section (iii) concludes the argument: memory belongs accidentally to the thinking capacity of the soul, and properly to the primary perceptual capacity of the soul.

The role of the sentence—'and the image is an affection of the common sense'—in the subordinate argument in section (i) is far from obvious. The introduction of an 'image' seems unexpected at this juncture, and its attribution to the 'common sense' is puzzling. Hence, it is a considerable challenge for interpreters of this passage to show how the crucial sentence links the premiss and the conclusion of the subordinate argument in section (i). There are some interpreters who think that this challenge cannot or need not be met, for they propose either to transpose the crucial sentence two lines below, following section (ii),[8] or to excise it from the text altogether.[9]

In this chapter I would like to take up the challenge and offer an interpretation of this passage which allows us to retain the received text. I will start with an analysis of section (i). This will lead us to the standard interpretation of this passage. I will then show that the standard interpretation faces serious difficulties, and I will replace it with a more satisfactory one. Finally, I will consider the advantages and disadvantages of the proposed textual emendations.

Let us take a closer look at section (i). At 450ᵃ9–10 Aristotle submits that it is necessary to grasp magnitude and change with the same thing with which time is grasped, implying that the grasp of all three—magnitude, change, and time—is the work of the 'primary perceptual capacity of the soul' (*πρῶτον αἰσθητσκόν*). I would like to raise three distinct questions in connection with this, and these questions will guide the rest of my discussion. First, why should it be necessary to grasp magnitude and change with the same thing with which time is grasped? Second, granted that it is necessary to grasp magnitude, change, and time by means of the same thing, why should it follow that this thing must be a *perceptual* capacity? Third, what exactly is the 'primary perceptual capacity of the soul' to which the grasp of magnitude, change, and time is explicitly assigned?

In reply to the first question, it will be useful to look at Aristotle's theory of time in *Physics* IV.10–14. What follows is but a simplified

[8] J. Freudenthal (1869: 397–400), W. D. Ross ((ed.)1955: 237–8), Laurenti ((ed.)1971: 47 n. 172).

[9] Kahn (1966: 60 n. 36).

sketch which leaves out many significant details.[10] According to Aristotle, there is an interdependence of time, change, and magnitude. Not only does time ontologically depend on change, and change on magnitude, but the very character of time derives from the character of change, and the character of change in turn derives from the character of magnitude. By 'magnitude' Aristotle probably means spatial magnitude over which a change occurs, and by 'change' he does not mean only spatial movement, but also growth and diminution, and alteration. A thing that moves traverses a certain spatial path, a thing that grows and diminishes also traces out a spatial path, and at least some qualities cover a spatial path in the sense that they gradually spread through the things that undergo alteration.[11]

Aristotle speaks of 'before and after in magnitude', by which he seems to mean that magnitude is an ordered continuum. Something is 'before or after in magnitude' if it is nearer to or further from some place that is the origin either in the absolute sense, determined with reference to that thing's source, or in a relative sense, fixed with reference to any chance spatially located thing.[12] Since every magnitude is a continuum ordered with respect to 'before and after', change is also a continuum ordered with respect to 'before and after' (prior and posterior stages in a process), and since change is such, time is also a continuum ordered with respect to 'before and after' (prior and posterior moments in time).[13]

Moreover, time depends psychologically on change, and change on magnitude. The awareness of change typically depends on the awareness of magnitude. For instance, to see that an object far up in the sky moves, we have to see at least a minimal path that it has traversed; otherwise, it will appear to rest at one place. Similarly, the awareness of time depends on the awareness of change. Aristotle says that if there is no change—or, if there is change, but there is no awareness of it—there can be no awareness of time, either.[14] That is, unless one is aware of at least some change, whether outside or inside the mind, one cannot be aware of two distinct moments and a lapse of time between them. So the awareness

[10] My sketch relies on Coope (2005), esp. chs. 3 and 4. See also Sorabji (1983: chs. 6 and 7).

[11] See Coope (2005: 52–3). [12] Cf. *Met.* V.11 1018^b9–14.

[13] *Phy.* IV.11 219^a10–21.

[14] *Phy.* IV.11 219^a3–10. Of course, we can be aware of something being at rest, and still be aware of time, since time measures not only change, but also the absence of change. This is true, however, as long as there is *some* change going on of which we are aware; cf. *Phy.* IV.11 218^b24–219^a1.

of time implies the awareness of change, and the awareness of change in turn implies the awareness of magnitude. Presumably, this is the background of Aristotle's claim that it is necessary to grasp magnitude, change, and time by the same thing.

Now to the second question: why does Aristotle think that this thing must be a *perceptual* capacity? According to many scholars, this is because magnitude, change, and time are all common perceptibles.[15] They seem to reason in the following way. In *DA* III.1 425^{a}14–27 magnitude and change are said to be the common perceptibles grasped by a 'common sense', which these scholars understand as the higher-order perceptual power which accompanies the individual senses. In *DM* 1 450^{a}9–10 time is said to be grasped by the same capacity by which magnitude and change are grasped. From this they infer, first, that time is perceived by the common sense understood as the higher-order perceptual power which accompanies the individual senses, and second, that time is a common perceptible. I believe this is the essence of the standard interpretation of *DM* 450^{a}9–14.

There are three difficulties with this interpretation. First, time does not seem to be a common perceptible. The common perceptibles are perceived in themselves (*καθ' αὑτὰ αἰσθητά*), and time is not the sort of thing that is perceived in itself. As Kahn writes: 'if a property is to be a common sensible as defined in the *De An.* II 6, it must first be the object of at least two special senses. . . . Time, however, is not directly perceived by any external sense, much less by more than one.'[16]

Perhaps one could suggest a different argument to the effect that time is a common perceptible. Aristotle defines time as the number of change (*Phy.* IV.11 219^{b}1–2); since number and change are both common perceptibles (*DA* III.1 425^{a}16), time too must be a common perceptible.[17] This inference seems too hasty. I take it that time is

[15] Zeller (1921: 542), Kampe (1870: 102–3), Trendelenburg ((ed.)1877: 348), Hicks ((ed.)1907: 362), W. D. Ross (1949: 140; (ed.)1955: 34–5, 185, 208; (ed.)1961: 33), Theiler ((ed.)1959: 119, 131), Siwek ((ed.)1963: 123, 153), Verbeke (1985: 361 n. 23).

[16] Kahn (1966: 53 n. 23). Labarrière (2000: 274 n. 9) and Taormina (2002: 46–9) also argue against the view that time is a common perceptible. Arguments against this view are part and parcel of Taormina's critique of the standard interpretation.

[17] Hicks ((ed.)1907: 362) and King ((ed.)2004: 91) seem to take this line of argument. King does not expressly say that time is a common perceptible, but he does say that 'time can be perceived through different senses', which he relates to the fact that time 'belongs to the things which appertain to several senses in common [viz. magnitude and change]'; cf. King ((ed.)2004: 33).

number in the sense that we can count nows which first have to be marked out in some way. This involves much more than perceiving a number. An eagle-hen, for instance, can perceive threeness of the eggs in her nest, for she will be upset if she finds any other number of eggs in her nest. Yet surely she does not *count* her eggs. So, if something is capable of perceiving number and change, that in itself does not entitle us to conclude that it must be capable of perceiving the number of change, that is time, too.[18]

Second, the result of Part II, Chapter 2 is that the expression 'common sense' in *DA* III.1 425ª14–27 does not in fact refer to the higher-order perceptual power accompanying the individual senses. This result directly undermines the substantive claim of the standard interpretation, namely that magnitude, change, and time are perceived by the higher-order perceptual power accompanying the individual senses. Our result undermines also the standard interpretation's answer to the third question, since the standard interpretation would identify the 'primary perceptual capacity of the soul' and the 'common sense' with the higher-order perceptual power accompanying all the senses.

Third, the standard interpretation cannot explain the introduction of 'image' (φάντασμα) at this juncture of Aristotle's argument. For if magnitude, change, and time are all common perceptibles grasped by the common sense, what is the point of bringing up images and saying that they are affections of the common sense?

Given that the standard interpretation of *DM* 1 450ª9–14 is untenable, I would like to propose a different one, with a different set of answers to the three questions initially raised in connection with the subordinate argument in section (i). To begin with, the earlier answer to the first question has not done justice to the formulation we actually find in the text. Observe that Aristotle does not exactly say that it is necessary to grasp magnitude, change, and time by the same thing, but rather that 'it is necessary to grasp magnitude and change by the same thing as time'. That is, he presupposes that there is a certain capacity by which time is grasped, and then magnitude and change are said to be necessarily grasped by the same capacity. Before we can say more about that capacity, we need to clarify what exactly Aristotle means by the 'grasp of time'. I propose that it is nothing else but the perception of time which was said earlier to be constitutive of memory. That is,

[18] See Sorabji (2004: pp. xxii–xxiv).

to grasp time is to be aware that something was experienced before, or even when in the past it was experienced.[19]

This assumption about the grasp of time provides a link between section (i) and what precedes it. In the preceding lines (450^a8–9) we were told that imagination introduces temporal determinations, which already suggested that the grasp of time is closely connected with imagination. In the premiss of the subordinate argument in section (i) we are told that the grasp of magnitude and change is closely connected with the grasp of time. Now the crucial sentence at 450^a10 picks up the suggestion that the grasp of time is closely connected with imagination. Namely, the image which is said to be an affection of the 'common sense', I take it, is the image by means of which we grasp time. Let me elaborate on this a bit more.

The idea that the grasp of time is closely connected with imagination is confirmed by *DM* 2 452^b23–9.[20] There Aristotle says that we remember when the image of a thing occurs together with the image of time, presumably the time of experiencing that thing.[21] Images of time have a certain degree of autonomy, since they can occur without images of things and vice versa, which explains various memory failures. Aristotle does not specify these memory failures, but we can easily do that on his behalf. First, if an image of a thing does not occur together with an image of time, one will mistakenly think that something is merely imagined, rather than something experienced in the past. Second, if an image of time does not occur together with an image of a thing, one will feel that there is something one has experienced in the past, but cannot remember what. The autonomy of images of time admittedly allows for a third type of memory failure: if an image of a thing occurs together with a wrong image of time, one will remember this thing as happening at a wrong point in the past. The facility with which Aristotle's theory explains familiar memory failures speaks strongly in its favour. Indeed, Aristotle's theory seems to anticipate the contemporary

[19] Observe that Aristotle's much-debated diagrammatic explanation of the way we apprehend temporal relations in *DM* 2 452^b7 ff. is introduced by saying that 'the most important thing [viz. for memory] is that one must grasp the time (*γνωρίζειν τὸν χρόνον*), with measure or indeterminately'.

[20] The same idea seems to underlie the interpretations of *DM* 1 offered by Wiesner (1985), Labarrière (2000), Taormina (2002), and King ((ed.)2004: 30–6, 91).

[21] Aristotle speaks of *κίνησις τοῦ πράγματος* and *τοῦ χρόνου*. It is fairly uncontroversial that *κινήσεις* here, as in the rest of the chapter, refer to images; cf. Sorabji ((ed.)1972: 110), Cooper (1975: 66–7), Sisko (1997: 167–8), King ((ed.)2004: 139–41).

theories of 'time-tags', which are taken to be automatically stored with representations of events at the time when these events take place.[22]

Although imagination clearly plays a crucial role in our ability to grasp time, Aristotle does not identify the thing by which we grasp time simply with the imaginative capacity of the soul, but with the 'common sense'. That is quite surprising. Why does Aristotle not say that we grasp time simply with the imaginative capacity?

As we have seen from our earlier sketch of Aristotle's theory of time, our awareness of the passage of time depends on our awareness of change. We experience change not only when we perceive the relevant type of common perceptible (change), but also when we perceive a succession of objects, be they changing or not. And even when we perceive nothing with our senses, we experience change when we manipulate images. It is these processes of perception and imagination that our awareness of the passage of time follows upon. More to the point, it is these processes of perception and imagination that our grasp of time follows upon. We can be aware that we have experienced something before when the thing is given to us by perception as well as when it is given to us by imagination. For example, I can see a person on the street and realize that I've met that person before; or I can imagine a certain person and know that I've met that person before. This is, I have argued, what it means to grasp (or to perceive) time, and what Aristotle considers to be essential for memory. The point I wish to make is this: had Aristotle assigned the grasp of time specifically to the imaginative capacity of the soul, he would be suggesting that time is grasped solely in relation to things imagined, whereas in fact time is grasped also in relation to things perceived.

It is true that we need a certain sort of images to grasp time, but these images do not accompany only things experienced through imagination, but also things experienced through perception. That is why Aristotle needs to assign the grasp of time to something more general than the imaginative capacity of the soul, to something capable of combining perception and imagination. We have seen in the preceding chapter that the phrase 'common sense' in *PA* IV.10 686ᵃ31 refers to the sensory capacity of the soul which comprises the perceptual and the imaginative capacity and combines their activities. I submit that it refers to the same thing in *DM* 1 450ᵃ10, too.

[22] See Yntema and Trask (1963), Hasher and Zacks (1979), Friedman (1993); cf. Friedman (1990: ch. 3).

When Aristotle says that 'the image is an affection of the common sense', I take him to be saying that the image by means of which we grasp time is an affection of the sensory capacity of the soul operating as the imaginative capacity; however, the image by means of which we grasp time accompanies not only images of things but also perceptions of things. When the latter happens, that is, when the image by means of which we grasp time accompanies a perception of something, the sensory capacity of the soul operates at the same time both as the imaginative and as the perceptual capacity, combining their activities. Without the joint work of perception and imagination, then, we would not be able to grasp time with respect to things perceived, that is, we would not be able to tell that something we currently perceive has been experienced before.

We are now in a position to give answers to all three questions initially raised in connection with section (i). First, it is necessary to grasp magnitude and change with the same thing with which time is grasped, because the grasp of time accompanies things imagined as well as things perceived. Had the grasp of time accompanied only things imagined, Aristotle would be entitled to ascribe the grasp of time specifically to the imaginative capacity of the soul; however, since the grasp of time accompanies also things perceived, Aristotle must ascribe the grasp of time to a more general capacity which comprises both the perceptual and the imaginative capacity, and that is what Aristotle calls the 'common sense' at 450^{a}10 and the 'primary perceptual capacity' at ^{a}11 and 14. This foreshadows our answer to the third question. The primary perceptual capacity of the soul to which the grasp of magnitude, change, and time is attributed is what I have called the 'sensory capacity of the soul'. The sensory capacity of the soul is a unity which comprises the perceptual and the imaginative capacity as its conceptually distinct parts, and in effect it constitutes the non-rational cognitive capacity of the soul.

Our passage shows quite clearly that the primary perceptual capacity of the soul comprises the imaginative capacity as well as the perceptual capacity strictly speaking. That it comprises the imaginative capacity is clear from the fact that the grasp of time and memory, both of which rely on imagination, are assigned to it. Furthermore, images are explicitly said to be affections of the common sense, and the common sense is identical with the primary perceptual capacity of the soul. On the other hand, that the primary perceptual capacity of the soul comprises the perceptual capacity strictly speaking is clear from the fact that the grasp of magnitude and change is assigned to it, and one way, if not the fundamental way, in which we grasp magnitude and change is by perception. In addition, Aristotle's choice of words is highly indicative, for he speaks of the primary *αἰσθητικόν* and of the common *αἴσθησις*.

This leads us back to the second question: why does Aristotle assign the grasp of magnitude, change, and time to a *perceptual* capacity? My interpretation requires us to take the adjective 'perceptual' (*αἰσθητικόν*) in its wider sense. To be sure, we can grasp magnitude and change by perception in the narrow sense, but I have argued that we cannot grasp time in the same way. To grasp time with reference to something perceived, i.e. to realize that a perceived thing has been experienced before, joint work of perception and imagination is required. For Aristotle, such joint work goes beyond perception in the narrow sense, but it remains within the boundaries of perception in a wider sense.

If we look at the whole of Aristotle's argument, we see that only two alternatives are in play: either the grasp of magnitude, change, and time belongs to the primary perceptual capacity of the soul, or it belongs to the thinking capacity of the soul. We might rephrase this by saying that the grasp of magnitude, change, and time is the work either of the non-rational or of the rational cognitive capacity of the soul. Of course, it is important for Aristotle to establish the former, because otherwise he would be unable to attribute memory, for which the grasp of time is essential, to non-rational animals. I have suggested that imagination, which provides the images by means of which time is grasped, plays a crucial role in establishing that the grasp of magnitude, change, and time belongs to the non-rational cognitive capacity of the soul. My suggestion was motivated by an attempt to explain the role of the sentence 'and the image is an affection of the common sense' within the subordinate argument in section (i). But even if we disregard this complication in Aristotle's argument, it is easy to see why he should find it easy to decide which one of the two cognitive capacities furnishes the grasp of magnitude, change, and time. The objects of the thinking capacity of the soul are, at least paradigmatically, entities which have no magnitude, which are unchangeable, and which are not in time; hence, the grasp of magnitude, change, and time must belong to the other, non-rational cognitive capacity.

My interpretation of *DM* 1 450^{a}9–14 rests on four assumptions. The first is that the perception of time, which is said to be constitutive of memory at 449^{a}28–30 and 450^{a}19–22, is not the awareness of the passage of time, but the awareness of the temporal relation in which things experienced in the past stand to the subject in the present. The second is the assumption that the 'grasp of time' at 450^{a}9–10 (implied also by τούτων ἡ γνῶσις at ^{a}12) is the same as the perception of time. The third is the assumption that the grasp of time is closely connected with imagination. The fourth is the assumption that the phrase 'common sense' (ἡ κοινὴ αἴσθησις) refers to the sensory capacity of the soul which comprises both the perceptual capacity and the imaginative capacity of the soul. I hope that the preceding discussion has convinced the reader that these four assumptions are reasonable and well founded. They allow us to construe a sufficiently cogent interpretation of *DM* 1 which is not subject to the difficulties that undermine the standard interpretation.

I have mentioned that one of the difficulties with the standard interpretation of *DM* 1 450^{a}9–14 is that it cannot explain the introduction of 'image' (φάντασμα) between the premiss and the conclusion of the subordinate argument in section (i). This particular difficulty can be circumvented by transposing the sentence 'and the image is an affection of the common sense' two lines below, following the statement in section (ii) that there is no memory without images. The transposition was first proposed by Freudenthal, and it was followed by Ross and Laurenti.[23]

The advantage of this transposition is that the sentence becomes grammatically well connected with the preceding clause. Having said that there is no memory without images, the sentence 'and the image is an affection of the common sense' follows quite neatly. With the transposition we get the following line of reasoning. Memory, including that of the objects of thought, requires images, and since images are affections of the common sense (and the common sense is the same thing as the primary perceptual capacity of the soul), it follows that memory belongs only accidentally to the thinking capacity of the soul, and essentially to the primary perceptual capacity of the soul.

In itself, this is quite sensible. Memory operates by means of images, and since images are affections of the primary perceptual capacity, memory belongs to that capacity essentially. Of course, there is memory also of the objects of thought, but since memory even of such objects crucially depends on images, memory belongs only accidentally to the thinking capacity of the soul.

Although sound in isolation from the preceding lines, this reading fails to appreciate the complexity of Aristotle's argument. In fact, it severs lines 450^{a}12–14 from the preceding discussion, and renders

[23] See n. 8 above.

the whole passage from 449^{b}31 all the way down to 450^{a}12 one long and unnecessary digression. For if the lines 450^{a}12–14 do all the work of proving that memory belongs properly to the primary perceptual capacity of the soul, and only accidentally to the thinking capacity, as they seem to do if we transpose the sentence, how does that connect with the previously established fact that memory requires the perception of time? And what could possibly be the point of arguing (1) that imagination brings in spatial and temporal determinations in the process of thinking, (2) that magnitude and change are necessarily grasped by the same thing by which time is grasped, and (3) that this thing is the primary perceptual capacity of the soul?

So, with the transposition the sentence becomes grammatically well connected, but it makes Aristotle's argument at 450^{a}12–14 disconnected from the preceding passages. A more radical suggestion is to excise the sentence at 450^{a}10 altogether. Kahn writes that '[i]t may well represent a marginal gloss which has become incorporated into the text'.[24] Although not impossible, I find this suggestion dubious. The interpretation I have offered, however, can stand even without the crucial sentence in the text, although the connection between the grasp of time and imagination would then be left hanging in the air. The real disadvantage of excising the sentence, however, would be the loss of one of the very few occurrences of the phrase 'common sense' in Aristotle. Fortunately, there is no need to tamper with the received text of *DM* 1 450^{a}10.

In *DM* 1 450^{a}10, then, the common sense is identified with the primary perceptual capacity of the soul. My interpretation of Aristotle's argument shows that this is best understood as the sensory capacity of the soul sketched in Part I, Chapter 4. Assuming that this is correct, the phrase 'common sense' in *DM* 1 450^{a}10 is used in the same way as in *PA* IV.10 686^{a}31, that is, as a proper name for the sensory capacity of the soul which comprises the perceptual capacity and the imaginative capacity as its conceptually distinct parts or aspects. Indeed, we shall see in the next chapter that the phrase 'common sense', in all probability, has the same reference once more in Aristotle's works.

[24] Kahn (1966: 60 n. 36).

5

De Anima III.7 431^b5

I have noted earlier that modern commentators speak of three or four occurrences of the phrase 'common sense', depending on their views of a passage in *DA* III.7. In line 431^b5 the words *τῇ κοινῇ* occur in the context mentioning an act of perception, which makes some commentators think that these words ought to be supplemented with the noun *αἰσθήσει*. In other words, these commentators suggest that at 431^b5 the phrase 'common sense' occurs in an elliptical form.[1] However, there are many textual and interpretative difficulties with this passage, so that other commentators prefer not to take these words to constitute an incomplete occurrence of the phrase 'common sense'.[2] They interpret the words *τῇ κοινῇ* in some other way, or propose an emendation of the received text by way of altering these words or omitting them altogether.

It is our task in this chapter to see whether we indeed have an elliptical occurrence of the phrase 'common sense' at 431^b5, and if we do, to try to establish the reference of that phrase. This is very difficult, because our passage occurs within a chapter which poses serious problems to the editors of *De Anima* and commentators alike. The text of the whole chapter is poorly preserved, and it is hard to see a coherent line of thought which connects different parts of the chapter. That is why the chapter yields an impression of an assemblage of disconnected parts. In addition, most of these parts are in themselves hard to follow, which makes the whole endeavour rather tentative.

DA III.7 can be analysed into seven sections: (i) 431^a1–4; (ii) 431^a4–7; (iii) 431^a8–17; (iv) 431^a17–20; (v) 431^a20–$^b1$; (vi) 431^b2–12; and

[1] Trendelenburg ((ed.)1877: 432–3), Wallace ((ed.)1882: 169), Rodier ((ed.)1900: I.195, II.511), Smith ((ed.)1918: ad loc.), De Corte (1932: 212–13), Siwek ((ed.)1933: 267), Theiler ((ed.)1959: 62), Jannone and Barbotin ((eds.)1966: 84), Thillet ((ed.)2005: 172).

[2] Torstrik ((ed.)1862: 211), Bywater (1888: 61), Hicks ((ed.)1907: 143, 539), Ross ((ed.)1961: 307), Hamlyn ((ed.)1968: 64, 148), Lawson-Tancred ((ed.)1986: 209). Individual solutions will be considered later.

(vii) 431^{b}12–19.[3] The line containing the words τῇ κοινῇ occurs in section (vi), which appears to be connected primarily with section (iii). In that section Aristotle links perception with action by showing that pleasure and pain are a matter of perception. Namely, some things are perceived as pleasant and some as painful. Since perceiving something as pleasant or painful is a form of recognizing it as good or bad, the pleasant things are desired and hence pursued, whereas the painful things are disliked and hence avoided. This explains how beings endowed with perception are moved to act by their perceptions. At the end of (iii), at 431^{a}14–17, Aristotle seems to extend the same line of reasoning to thinking. The thinking capacity of the soul recognizes certain things as good or bad, and those things that are recognized as good are desired and pursued, whereas those things that are recognized as bad are disliked and avoided. However, this explanation of how rational beings are moved to act by their thoughts is complicated by the fact that the thinking capacity requires images (φαντάσματα). That is, things which are recognized as good or bad by the thinking capacity of the soul are present to rational beings by means of images. This is not pursued further in (iii), but seems to be picked up again in (vi).

Here is my translation of the relevant passage of (vi) which contains the words τῇ κοινῇ:

> The thinking capacity of the soul, therefore, thinks the forms in images, and just as in those [cases which involve perception] it determines what is to be pursued and avoided, also [in the cases] excluding perception, when it attends to images, it is moved; for instance, perceiving a beacon because it is fire, by the common [sense?] grasps, seeing it move, that it is the alarm signal; and sometimes [one] calculates by means of images or thoughts in the soul, as if seeing, and deliberates what is going to happen with reference to what is happening; and when [the thinking capacity of the soul] pronounces [what is to be pursued and avoided], just as there [viz. in the cases when the perceptual capacity of the soul pronounces] the pleasant or unpleasant, also here [in the cases when the thinking capacity determines what is to be pursued and avoided, it] avoids or pursues, and so in action generally. (*DA* III.7 431^{b}2–10; see Appendix (c))

On account of its vagueness, this passage is susceptible to a variety of different interpretations, and my translation incorporates the one that I

[3] This division of the chapter is proposed by Ross, marked by en-dashes inserted in the text. For a slightly different division, with a helpful summary of each part, see Osborne (1998: 433).

find most plausible. As a starting point, I assume that the main purpose of the passage is to show that the thinking capacity of the soul is able to determine what is to be pursued and avoided both in the presence and in the absence of perception. In the presence of perception, I take it, the thinking capacity determines what is to be pursued and avoided with respect to things that are given to us by perception. Things that are given to us by perception are properties and objects available to our senses, present here and now.[4] In the absence of perception, on the other hand, the thinking capacity determines what is to be pursued and avoided with respect to things that are given to us by imagination (φαντασία). Such things are properties and objects which we contemplate by means of images (φαντάσματα). Things we imagine are not themselves present here and now, at least not typically, although we can very well think of them as having been present at some point in the past, as being present here and now, or as becoming present at some point in the future. In short, things we imagine can belong to the past, present, and future, whereas things we perceive invariably belong to the present. The main point of the passage is to ascertain that the thinking capacity of the soul can determine what is to be pursued or avoided both in things we perceive and in things we imagine.

In section (iii), 431^{a}8 ff., we learn that, in addition to perceiving this or that, we might also perceive it as pleasant or unpleasant. This is the difference, I take it, between 'merely saying' and 'affirming and denying' something, which is here ascribed to perception. Perception of something as pleasant ('affirming') is a form of recognizing it as good, whereas perception of something as painful ('denying') is a form of recognizing it as bad. So when an animal perceives something as pleasant, the animal recognizes it as good. Having recognized it as good, the animal desires it, which in turn explains why the animal moves in such a way as to get it. When an animal perceives something as painful, the animal recognizes it as bad. Having recognized it as bad, the animal dislikes it, which in turn explains why the animal moves in such a way as to avoid it. So the perceptual capacity of the soul moves an animal by determining what is to be pursued and avoided in terms of what is pleasant and painful.

The thinking capacity of the soul similarly 'affirms' and 'denies' things as good or bad, and thus brings about pursuit or avoidance. That is, when the thinking capacity recognizes something as good, it brings

[4] Cf. *DM* 1 449^{b}13–15, 27.

about desire for that thing, which makes one act in such a way as to obtain it. When the thinking capacity recognizes something as bad, it brings about dislike for that thing, which makes one act in such a way as to avoid it. However, as we learn from *DA* III.10, the standard of good and bad for perception is the pleasant and painful, whereas for thought the standard is the true good and bad. Now the true good and bad necessarily involve temporal perspective, because what is truly good or bad for someone is not good or bad for the moment only, but in the long run.[5] What is good or bad in the long run is something that cannot be perceived because it is not present here and now. It is something that may become present at some point in the future, and hence it can be only imagined. This is why Aristotle insists that the thinking capacity requires images for its operation.

Let us now connect this point from section (iii) with the passage we are looking at. I assume that 'to determine what is to be pursued and avoided' (*ὥρισθαι τὸ διωκτὸν καὶ φευκτόν*) mentioned at 431^{b}3 amounts to recognizing something as good or bad. And the main point of the passage, as I understand it, is that the thinking capacity can recognize as truly good or bad both (a) things that we perceive and (b) things that we imagine, and thus initiate the appropriate kind of action with respect to either. It is easy to see why Aristotle should wish to make this point. If the thinking capacity was confined to things we perceive, it would not be able to deal with anything that is not present here and now. Since the true good and bad are rarely present here and now (they are usually in store for us in the future), the thinking capacity confined to things that we perceive would be unable to determine what is truly good and bad, and this would clearly amount to the abolishment of the practical intellect and a happy life for human beings.

The interpretation I outlined largely corresponds to the way a majority of ancient and contemporary commentators understand the general intention of this passage. However, the details are much more difficult to grasp, and that is where disagreements among the commentators begin. Since it would be too laborious, and ultimately unnecessary, to account for all unclear aspects of this passage, I shall restrict my discussion only to those details which are relevant to our immediate task.

Let us take a closer look at the sentence in lines ^{b}5 and 6 in which the words *τῇ κοινῇ* occur. I understand the sentence to be saying that one

[5] *DA* III.10 433^{a}25–30, ^{b}5–13; cf. III.11 434^{a}11–15; *MA* 6 700^{b}28–35, 7 701^{a}16–20, 27–36.

perceives a beacon because it is fire, and that, seeing it move, one grasps by something common that it is the alarm signal. I would like to make several preliminary points to justify this understanding of the sentence.

First, I agree with the commentators who claim that the subject of this sentence is an individual human being. The subject of the verb γνωρίζει is qualified as αἰσθανόμενος and ὁρῶν, and these can refer only to an individual human being. Thus the sentence must be saying that when a human being perceives a beacon and sees that it moves, he or she grasps by something 'common' that it is the alarm signal.

Second, the commentators understand the words ὅτι πῦρ as introducing the content of perception, so they argue for some construction such as 'one perceives that a beacon is fire'.[6] There is certainly something odd about this way of construing the sentence. We would expect that, if anything, one perceives that a fire is a beacon, rather than vice versa. According to the prevalent interpretation, however, what one perceives seems to be a fire, and this fire happens to be a beacon. In this case, that of which one is certainly aware is indicated by the word 'fire', whereas the word 'beacon' gives a description of the fire of which the perceiver may or may not be aware. In other words, the perceiver may or may not be aware that the fire he or she perceives is a beacon. I am emphasizing this point because I will argue that it is actually necessary for the perceiver to be aware that the fire he or she perceives is a beacon, and this is guaranteed by the alternative interpretation of the words ὅτι πῦρ that I shall presently offer.

In any case, according to the prevalent interpretation, one perceives a fire and then, seeing that it moves, one realizes that it is πολέμιος. The adjective πολέμιος is interpreted as saying that 'it signals the approach of the enemy' (e.g. Wallace, Rodier, Hicks) or that it 'signifies an enemy' (e.g. Smith, Hett). But the adjective by itself can hardly mean what these interpreters say it means. Ross and Hamlyn are more cautious. They translate the adjective as 'belonging to the enemy'.[7] With the adjective πολέμιος thus interpreted, the sentence is saying that one perceives a fire and then, seeing that it moves, one realizes that it belongs to the enemy.

[6] So Wallace ((ed.)1882: 169), Hicks ((ed.)1907: 143), Smith ((ed.)1918: ad loc.), Siwek ((ed.)1933: 267), Hett ((ed.)1957: 179), Ross ((ed.)1961: 302), Jannone and Barbotin ((eds.)1966: 84), Lawson-Tancred ((ed.)1986: 209), Thillet ((ed.)2005: 172). The two commentators who take it the way I shall propose are Rodier ((ed.)1900: I.195) and Theiler ((ed.)1959: 62); cf. n. 9 below.

[7] Ross ((ed.)1961: 302), Hamlyn ((ed.)1968: 64); similarly Seidl's ((ed.)1995: 183) revised translation of Theiler ((ed.)1959).

However, it is clear that the adjective *πολέμιος* goes with *φρυκτός*, rather than with *πῦρ* because the adjective is in the masculine, as the noun *φρυκτός*, whereas the noun *πῦρ* is in the neuter. Therefore, it must be the beacon, not the fire, which one realizes to be *πολέμιος*.

The reason why the interpreters tend to misconstrue this sentence is that they fail to see, or to take fully on board, that *φρυκτός πολέμιος* is an idiom referring to the alarm signal. When an ancient city expected a siege, torches were placed on visible spots around the city. They would remain steady for as long as there was no threat, but as soon as a threat was spotted, the sentry would swing the torches and thus warn the city of the threat.[8] This would be called 'the beacon of danger' (*ὁ φρυκτὸς πολέμιος*), that is the alarm signal. If this fact is fully appreciated, it is clear that what the perceiver is said to realize is that something is the alarm signal, not that something belongs to the enemy. Since the adjective *πολέμιος* picks up the preceding *τὸν φρυκτόν*, what the perceiver grasps is that the beacon seen to be moving is the alarm signal.

To grasp that the beacon seen to be moving is the alarm signal, a person must be aware of at least four things: first, of a fire; second, of the motion of the fire; third, of the fact that the fire is not just a random fire, but that it is actually a beacon; and fourth, of the fact that motion of the beacon-fire is the alarm signal. Therefore, if one is to realize that a fire seen to be moving is the alarm signal, one must be aware not only of the fire and its motion, but also of the fact that the fire is a beacon. For instance, a person familiar with the described convention of signalling the alarm can perceive a fire and see that it moves, but unless he believes that this particular fire is a beacon, rather than a random torch someone is carrying, he is not going to take it as the alarm signal. Hence, what the sentence should say is that it is a beacon that one perceives. And the sentence can very well be construed so as to say exactly that.

How should we interpret the clause *ὅτι πῦρ*, then? Instead of interpreting the conjunction *ὅτι* as the one used with verbs of perceiving ('*that* it is a fire'), it can be interpreted causally ('*because* it is a fire').[9] The advantage of this interpretation is that it makes the sentence say that one perceives a beacon, and the clause *ὅτι πῦρ* serves as a brief

[8] Cf. Thucydides II.94, III.22 and the scholiast ad loc.; Ps-Aristotle, *De Mundo* 6 398^{a}32–5; Aeneas Tacticus, *Poliorcetica* 7.4; Torstrik ((ed.)1862: 209).

[9] So Rodier ((ed.)1900: II.511) and Theiler ((ed.)1959: 62).

explanation of why the beacon is perceived, namely because it is fire, that is, the sort of thing which is clearly visible in the day and at night, as Aristotle points out in *DA* II.7 419^{a}23–4.

So much for justifying my interpretation of the sentence. Let us take a fresh look at the sentence and make a general observation about its purpose. With a majority of commentators I assume that the purpose of this sentence is to introduce an example of a case in which the thinking capacity of the soul determines what is to be pursued and avoided in the presence of perception. The following sentence (431^{b}6), which opens with the contrasting ὅτε δέ, provides an example of a case in which the thinking capacity determines what is to be pursued and avoided in the absence of perception.

However, both of these examples are incomplete, and they are incomplete in the same way. The first example specifies a complex perceptual act, but does not proceed to mention how the thinking capacity of the soul determines what is to be pursued and avoided with reference to things perceived. The second example states a complex intellectual cognitive activity of calculating by means of images and deliberating about a set of possible situations with reference to a present situation. However, such a calculation and deliberation does not itself amount to determining which one of these situations is good or bad, and hence which one of them is to be pursued or avoided. It is only when a particular situation is envisaged and recognized as good or bad that it determines what is to be pursued and avoided, thus initiating the appropriate kind of action. But again, that is not spelled out in the example.

Whichever way the examples are supposed to work, the sentence introducing the first one could work just as well without the phrases ὅτι πῦρ and τῇ κοινῇ. We would thus get the sentence, 'Perceiving a beacon, [one] grasps, seeing it move, that it is the alarm signal', which would essentially amount to the same thing that we actually have in the received text. What, then, is the function of these two phrases which do not really contribute much to the example? As I have pointed out earlier, Aristotle added the clause ὅτι πῦρ most probably as a brief explanation of why the beacon is perceived. The words τῇ κοινῇ, on the other hand, are meant to specify the means of grasping the alarm signal. However, 'the means of grasping the alarm signal' can refer to at least two different sorts of thing: to the cognitive capacity by which one grasps the alarm signal, or to some particular feature in the world by means of which the alarm signal is grasped.

There are interpreters who take the words τῇ κοινῇ in the latter way. Philoponus reports that some people claim that it is by motion (τῇ κινήσει) of the fire that the alarm signal is grasped.[10] With some support from a marginal note in the *editio Basileensis*, which is most probably inspired by this comment of Philoponus, Torstrik proposed to emend the text by replacing τῇ κοινῇ with τῇ κινήσει. However, with Torstrik's conjecture the sentence is unduly repetitive: τῇ κινήσει γνωρίζει, ὁρῶν κινούμενον κτλ.

Following the Latin translation of William of Moerbeke, which is unreliable in this chapter due to the obtuseness of the Greek original, Thomas Aquinas mentions the possibility that it is 'according to what commonly happens' that one knows that a conflict is raging.[11] To translate Aquinas's suggestion into terms that I have used, a person grasps the alarm signal by means of what commonly happens when the alarm is signalled, for example sudden commotion among people. Although this suggestion is not logically impossible, it is hard to see how the Greek τῇ κοινῇ could possibly be interpreted as 'what commonly happens'.

There is another suggestion for reading the words τῇ κοινῇ as some feature by means of which the alarm sign is grasped. Given that it is a matter of convention that the motion of a beacon signifies alarm, it can be argued that Aristotle intended to say that a person grasps the alarm sign by some such thing as 'common agreement' (τῇ κοινῇ συνθήκῃ). This suggestion is appealing, but συνθήκη is hardly a term that can be casually omitted and presumed as a matter of course.

It is more promising, then, to interpret the words τῇ κοινῇ with reference to a cognitive capacity by means of which the alarm signal is grasped. The most plausible assumption is that these words have to be supplemented with the noun αἰσθήσει, so that we have an elliptical occurrence of the phrase 'common sense'. This is what the majority of ancient and modern commentators think, and I am inclined to follow them. However, they also think that the alarm signal can be grasped only by a rational, not by a perceptual, capacity of the soul.[12] Of course, this creates a problem: if the alarm signal can be grasped only rationally, what should we do with the text which effectively says that one grasps the alarm signal with the common sense?

10 Philoponus (1887: 561.32–3). 11 Thomas Aquinas (1951: 449).

12 This seems to be the view of Simplicius (1882: 274.10–17), Philoponus (1887: 561.27–30), Beare (1906: 286), and Kahn (1966: 46).

Some commentators are prepared to change the text. Simplicius ingeniously proposes to transpose *γνωρίζει* after *ὁρῶν κινοῦμενον*, with the effect that the words *τῇ κοινῇ* are now joined with *ὁρῶν κινοῦμενον*, not with *γνωρίζει*.[13] Thus, *ἡ κοινή* is that by means of which one sees a beacon-fire move, not that by means of which one grasps that it is the alarm signal. Simplicius' proposal is attractive if one assumes that the phrase 'common sense' invariably refers to the higher-order perceptual power that emerges from the unity of the perceptual capacity of the soul, and if one additionally assumes, relying on the standard but nonetheless problematic reading of *DA* III.1 425^{a}27, that the common perceptibles are perceived by means of that higher-order perceptual power.[14] If one does not make these two assumptions—as I think one should not—the attractiveness of Simplicius' proposal evaporates.

More radically, Bywater suggested excising the phrase *τῇ κοινῇ* altogether, claiming that it is a superfluity which obscures the contrast between things that one sees (*ὁρῶν*), and things that one *as it were* sees (*ὥσπερ ὁρῶν*), that is, between things that one perceives and things that one imagines. Bywater maintains that the words *τῇ κοινῇ* are 'due to some annotator who was aware that *κίνησις* was one of the *κοινὰ αἰσθητά*, but did not understand the Aristotelian theory as to how we know them'.[15] Assuming that the common perceptibles are perceived by something called 'common sense', then, an early annotator was prompted by the word *κινούμενον* in line ^{b}6 to add the words *τῇ κοινῇ* in the margin, or between the lines, and these words at some point became integrated in the text. So, according to Bywater, these words do not belong in the text and should be excised. To some editors and commentators this appears to be the most satisfactory solution.[16]

However, it is possible to preserve the received text and take the words *τῇ κοινῇ* as an elliptical occurrence of the phrase 'common sense', provided we give up the idea that the alarm signal can be grasped only rationally. This move certainly goes against our intuitions about

13 Simplicius (1882: 274.14–17).

14 These assumptions were made by Ross, who seems to have been so impressed by Simplicius' conjecture that he printed it in his *editio maior* of 1961. The conjecture is not even mentioned in the critical apparatus in the more conservative *editio minor* of 1956.

15 Bywater (1888: 61–2).

16 Bywater's conjecture has been adopted by Susemihl (1892: 110), Hicks ((ed.) 1907: 143, 539) and Hamlyn ((ed.)1968: 64, 148; 1968: 195). Ross ((ed.)1961: 307) commends the proposal, but prefers Simplicius' conjecture. Hett ((ed.)1957: 179) prints *τῇ κοινῇ* in the text, but does not translate it.

reason, language, and thought, but it is not necessary to assume that Aristotle shared these intuitions. For Aristotle, grasping the alarm signal was, I think, a matter of perception, not of thought. To defend this suggestion, I would like to make the following two points.

First, one should not be tempted to assume that the verb *γνωρίζειν* ('grasping', 'realizing') is loaded with epistemological connotations which necessarily confine it to the activity of thinking. This verb covers activities of both fundamental cognitive capacities, perception and thought, so it can often be found applied to perception too.[17] Therefore, nothing in the expression 'to grasp that it is the alarm signal' bars it from referring to an act of perception.

Second, there can be no doubt that only rational beings are capable of grasping the motion of a beacon-fire as the alarm signal. This cognitive act presupposes, for instance, an understanding of the convention according to which a fire planted at a particular place functions as a beacon, and its motion as the alarm signal; this in turn presupposes an understanding of the concepts of beacon and alarm signal, as well as a more general understanding of language and human practice by which one comes to know this convention. These requirements certainly cannot be satisfied by perception only, since they involve a good deal of memory, experience, and the sort of rationality which enables us to acquire, manipulate, and express concepts. However, when these requirements are satisfied, that is, when one has an understanding of the convention according to which the motion of a beacon signifies the alarm, grasping the alarm signal upon seeing a beacon move can very well be a matter of perception. The idea, very briefly, is that our rationality informs our perception in the sense that it expands the scope of things in the world that we perceive.[18]

Assuming that grasping the alarm signal is indeed a perceptual act, it is no doubt an instance of perceiving an accidental perceptible, since the alarm signal is not the sort of thing which is perceived in itself. If the alarm signal is an accidental perceptible, and if the words *τῇ κοινῇ* specify the cognitive capacity by which one grasps the alarm signal, it is reasonable to suppose that in *DA* III.7 $431^{b}5$ we have an elliptical

[17] e.g. *APo.* II.19, $99^{b}34$ ff.; *Top.* II.7 $113^{a}30$–2, V.3 $131^{b}23$–7; *DA* I.2 $404^{b}28$, 5 $409^{b}26$–32; *DM* 1 $449^{b}14$; *DI* 1 $458^{b}3$; *Met.* I.1 $980^{a}26$, VII.10 $1036^{a}6$; cf. *GA* I.23 $731^{a}31$–4; *Met.* I.1 $981^{b}10$.

[18] This idea is pursued further in Gregoric and Grgic (2006).

occurrence of the phrase 'common sense', and that the perception of the accidental perceptibles is the work of the 'common sense'. This is what a number of interpreters who keep the words τῇ κοινῇ in the text actually claim.[19] However, they tend to be unaware of the ambiguity in the phrase 'common sense' in Aristotle. We have seen that the phrase 'common sense' can refer to different things, so our next task is to determine the exact reference of the phrase at this particular place. There are several possibilities.

One is that it refers to some individual sense, in this case sight. This is not very likely, because it is hard to see what could possibly motivate Aristotle to describe sight in this passage as 'common'. Another possibility is that the phrase refers to the ability of the individual senses to grasp certain features in the world, namely accidental perceptibles such as alarm signals, in analogy with the *DA* III.1 passage in which Aristotle refers to the ability of the individual senses to grasp the common perceptibles. However, the phrase used in *DA* III.1 425ᵃ27 is αἴσθησις κοινὴ, not ἡ κοινὴ αἴσθησις, and I have argued in Chapter 2 of this Part that the omitted article and the reversed word order are rather significant. So the second possibility also has to be rejected.

The third possibility is that the phrase refers to the higher-order perceptual power emerging from the unity of the perceptual capacity of the soul. I do not find this possibility appealing, for two reasons. One reason is that this passage in *DA* III.7, where the phrase occurs in truncated form, would be the only place in the whole body of Aristotle's works where the phrase 'common sense' is actually used with reference to the higher-order perceptual power. Second, it is reasonable to assume that the perception of the accidental perceptible is a complex cognitive act which requires, if not rational capacities, than at least joint work of perception and imagination.[20] However, the higher-order perceptual power does not involve imagination, and hence it is not up to the task.

The only other thing to which the phrase 'common sense' in *DA* III.7 431ᵇ5 can refer, given our assumptions, is the sensory capacity of the soul which comprises both the perceptual and the imaginative capacity. This is exactly how the phrase was used twice before, in *PA* IV.10 and *DM* 1, both times in the context of complex cognitive activities (being

[19] e.g. Ross (1949: 140–50; (ed.)1955: 35; (ed.)1961: 34–5), Siwek ((ed.)1933: 198), Cashdollar (1973).

[20] See Ross ((ed.)1961: 34), Block (1960: 94), Graeser (1978: 90), and Everson (1997: 187–228).

intelligent, perceiving time). Moreover, if the phrase 'common sense' indeed refers to the sensory capacity of the soul as I suspect, we find that the passage in *DA* III.7 in effect brings out the contrast between the non-rational cognitive capacity of the soul and the rational cognitive capacity of the soul. The same contrast, we remember, was found in *PA* IV.10 686^{a}31 and *DM* 1 450^{a}10.

Due to the opacity of our passage in *DA* III.7, then, it is hard to tell with certainty what to do with the words *τῇ κοινῇ* at 431^{b}5. A strong case has been made for deleting them from the received text. If these words are nevertheless preserved, it is best to take them as an elliptical occurrence of the phrase 'common sense'. In that case, there are reasons to take the phrase 'common sense' with reference to a non-rational cognitive ability by which accidental perceptibles, such as alarm signals, are grasped, and I have suggested that this should be identified with the sensory capacity of the soul.

6

Conclusions on the Terminology

Our discussions of the passages in Aristotle's extant works in which the phrase 'common sense' occurs yield several interesting results. We have seen that the phrase has different uses in Aristotle. In the previously unnoticed occurrences, it is used (i) as a context-dependent description for a specific individual sense, namely touch (*HA* I.3 489^a17; cf. *EN* III.10 1118^b1), or for all individual senses indiscriminately (*Met.* I.1 981^b14).

Once (*DA* III.1 425^a27) it describes (ii) sensitivity of the individual senses to a certain type of feature in the world. In a significant degree this sensitivity is due to the fact that the individual senses are integrated in the perceptual capacity of the soul, but I have insisted that the passage in *DA* III.1 does not *say* that the perception of the common perceptibles is the work of any perceptual power distinct from the individual senses.

Finally, there are three passages in the received text (*PA* IV.10 686^a31, *DM* 1 450^a10, and *DA* III.7 431^b5) where the phrase is best interpreted (iii) as the proper name for the sensory capacity of the soul which comprises the perceptual and the imaginative capacity of the soul. The sensory capacity of the soul amounts to the unified non-rational cognitive capacity of the soul, and in all three passages it stands in a more or less prominent opposition to the thinking capacity of the soul.

If my interpretation of the latter three passages is accepted, we find consistency in Aristotle's use of the phrase 'common sense' there. On its own, this would commit us to the view that the phrase is a technical term for Aristotle, functioning as a proper name for the sensory capacity of the soul. However, the other uses we surveyed manifest variation which leads us to suspect that the phrase really did not have the status of a technical term for Aristotle. We have seen that, depending on the context, the terms which make up the phrase—the noun *αἴσθησις* and the adjective *κοινή*—can take different nuances in meaning within their respective semantic horizons and assume different word order to express different ideas. Aristotle takes advantage of this variability in different contexts. I suppose he would not be inclined to do so had the phrase been fixed in his mind as a technical term.

There is one more reason to doubt the idea that the phrase 'common sense' was a technical term for Aristotle. Aristotle's successors, notably Theophrastus and Alexander of Aphrodisias, do not follow their master in using the phrase with reference to the sensory capacity of the soul. The evidence we have of Theophrastus' views on the matter, preserved in Priscian of Lydia's *Metaphrasis in Theophrastum*, suggests that he used the phrase with reference to the higher-order perceptual power emerging from the unity of the perceptual capacity of the soul. Or, to put it more cautiously, there is nothing in the available evidence of Theophrastus' views to suggest otherwise.[1] On the other hand, we have positive evidence that Alexander used the phrase with reference to the unified perceptual capacity which he keeps safely apart from the imaginative capacity of the soul.[2]

Although these reasons are not conclusive, I am inclined to think that the phrase 'common sense' has not yet crystallized into a technical term with Aristotle. Nevertheless, there can be little doubt that, owing to Aristotle, it became a technical term at some point between Theophrastus and Alexander. This is part of my excuse for diverging from Aristotle's use of the phrase 'common sense' in this book and for concentrating on the higher-order perceptual power emerging from the unity of the perceptual capacity of the soul, to which I turn in the next Part.

[1] See Priscian (1886: 21.16–22.23) and Gregoric (2003: ch. 4, sec. 2A).

[2] See Alexander (1887a: 62.16–22; cf. 63.6–8, 13–15, 65.2–10) and Gregoric (2003: ch. 4, sec. 2B).

PART III

FUNCTIONS OF THE COMMON SENSE

Mine eyes he closed, but open left the cell
Of fancy, my internal sight, by which,
Abstract as in a trance, methought I saw,
Though sleeping, where I lay, and saw the shape
Still glorious before whom awake I stood.

John Milton, *Paradise Lost*

1

Simultaneous Perception and Cross-modal Binding

Despite the curious lack of interest in Aristotle's discussion of simultaneous perception in the scholarly literature, I think that it merits a separate discussion for at least three reasons. First, Aristotle conceives of simultaneous perception as a distinct perceptual function of the common sense. Second, this function has a parallel in contemporary psychology and neuroscience. Third, Aristotle's discussion of simultaneous perception is directly relevant for his consideration of perceptual discrimination, an important function to be discussed in the following chapter. Certain things Aristotle says about simultaneous perception in *De Sensu* 7 will have to be squared with what he says about perceptual discrimination in *De Anima* III.2 and 7.

Simultaneous perception is the special topic of the last, longest, and structurally most complex chapter of *DS*. No individual aporia receives as much attention in this treatise as 'whether it is possible to perceive simultaneously two things in the same and indivisible time, or not' (*DS* 7 447^{a}13–14). From 447^{a}12 to 448^{a}19 Aristotle works towards the conclusion that there can be no simultaneous perception of two distinct special perceptibles, be they the same or different in kind. From 448^{a}19 to 449^{a}2 he briefly outlines and rejects a solution which was current at the time, thus sharpening the aporia before resolving it with his own solution at 449^{a}5–20.

Simultaneous perception, as it is discussed by Aristotle, is the perception of two special perceptibles at one time. Let me explain the restrictions implied in this perfunctory characterization. First, Aristotle's treatment of simultaneous perception in *DS* 7 is confined to special perceptibles, presumably because they are the most fundamental kind of object on which perception of all other kinds of object depends. Besides, there is nothing problematic about the simultaneous perception of a special perceptible and a common or accidental perceptible, simply because common and accidental perceptibles are by definition perceived together with special perceptibles.

Second, Aristotle restricts the number of special perceptibles which are simultaneously perceived to two, and I believe he does so only for the sake of brevity. The idea is that if it is shown that two special perceptibles cannot be perceived at the same time, neither can three or more; and if it is shown that two special perceptibles can be perceived at the same time, it must be possible, by extension, to perceive three or more.

Finally, throughout his discussion of simultaneous perception Aristotle speaks of 'time which is one and indivisible'. Of course, 'time which is one and indivisible' cannot be meant here in the absolute sense, because time is a continuum, that is, something that by definition does not have indivisible parts.[1] Moreover, in his discussion of simultaneous perception Aristotle does not rely on the strict notion of simultaneity. To perceive simultaneously is not to perceive two things in 'one and the same now', the 'now' being an indivisible temporal point of no duration by which time is limited (*Phy.* IV.10 218^{a}25–7). Rather, it is perceiving 'in time which is one and indivisible *relative to things perceived*'.[2] That is to say, two things are perceived simultaneously if the time of perceiving one cannot be distinguished from the time of perceiving the other. Thus we can perceive two things for a shorter or longer period of time, but as long as we cannot identify distinct intervals in which one thing was perceived without the other, we have a case of simultaneous perception. This is a flexible notion of simultaneity which is suitable for discussing the sort of experience Aristotle wants to explain.

It can be argued, however, that we do not really perceive two things simultaneously, because it is unlikely that we perceive one thing at *exactly* the same time as another thing. Rather, there is always some interval between perceiving one and perceiving the other thing, and as long as this interval is below the threshold of perception, it *appears* to us that we perceive both things at the same time. This view has in fact been espoused by certain unnamed theorists of musical harmonies in Aristotle's time, and it meets Aristotle's resolute disapproval at 448^{a}19–449^{a}2.[3]

[1] Cf. *Phy.* VI.9 238^{b}8–9, VIII.8 263^{b}27–8.

[2] τὸ δ᾽ ἅμα λέγω ἐν ἑνὶ καὶ ἀτόμῳ χρόνῳ πρὸς ἄλληλα (*DS* 7 448^{b}19).

[3] The same view is endorsed in Ps.-Aristotle's *De Audibilibus* 803^{b}26–804^{a}8.

In effect, this view reduces simultaneous perception to consecutive perceptions with imperceptible intervals in between. Aristotle, by contrast, believes that perception can be genuinely simultaneous. Moreover, the view of the unnamed theorists introduces a strict notion of simultaneity and the notion of an imperceptibly short interval of time. We have seen that Aristotle avoids the strict notion of simultaneity in his discussion of simultaneous perception and adheres to a more flexible one which is more suitable for describing the sort of experience he wants to explain. What Aristotle finds most objectionable, however, is the notion of an imperceptibly short interval. All three arguments that he offers in rebuttal of the aforementioned view are directed against this notion.[4] Very briefly, Aristotle maintains that any given period of time is divisible into ever shorter intervals. These intervals exist only potentially, as parts of some period taken as a whole. To exist actually, they would have to be separated from the whole period. To separate an interval it is necessary to isolate some change occurring in that interval. So the shortest separable interval is the time in which the smallest change can be registered. In a world without sophisticated instruments, the smallest change that can be registered is the smallest change detectable by the unaided sense. Consequently, the shortest actual interval of time is for Aristotle the shortest interval perceptible by the unaided sense.

In a world of advanced electronic instruments, by contrast, the smallest change that can be registered is the motion of elementary particles. Hence, the shortest actual interval is the shortest interval detectable by instruments, and that interval is certainly much too short to be perceived by the unaided sense. So we may concede to Aristotle that there are no intervals of time so short that no change could be registered in their duration, but we cannot deny the existence of intervals too short to be registered by the unaided senses, that is, too short to be perceived. This is why we find nothing embarrassing about the view Aristotle criticizes. One has only to think of the principle on which cinematography works to see that the impression of continuity can be created by a succession of things with intervals of time which are imperceptible to our senses. And if an impression of continuity can be thus created, so can an impression of simultaneity.

However, I doubt that we would be inclined to explain simultaneous perception with reference to imperceptibly short periods of time.

[4] The first argument is expounded at 448^a26–30, the second at 448^a30–$^b10$, and the third, which is structurally closely connected with the second, at 448^b10–12.

Instead, we would probably argue that the perceptual apparatus—from the receptors in the peripheral sense organs through the neural network to the specialized centres in the brain—is sufficiently complex to allow parallel input, transmission, and processing, which is what makes simultaneous processing of information possible. In essence, Aristotle follows the same explanatory strategy, although he does not look for the required complexity in the material, but in the formal cause of perception. In other words, what enables Aristotle to explain simultaneous perception in *DS* 7 is not the complexity of the sensory apparatus, but the complexity of the perceptual capacity of the soul.

Let me briefly state the background of the problem of simultaneous perception and sketch Aristotle's solution in order to facilitate understanding of the remainder of this chapter. According to Aristotle, the sense is a capacity to perceive objects of a certain kind. When actualized by an object of the right kind, that is, in an act of perception, the sense and its object are one. There are three corollaries which can be drawn from this principle, and Aristotle adheres to all of them. First, of an object which is one in number there is one act of perception. This is the objective restriction: a single object of perception produces a single act of perception. Second, in one act of perception the perceived object is pronounced to be one in number. This is the subjective restriction: in a single act of perception the object of perception is grasped as a single thing. Third, one act of perception occurs at one time, that is, at a time which is indivisible. This implies that two acts of perception necessarily occur at two moments, that is, at a time which is divisible with reference to each act of perception.[5]

It is the stated principle with its three corollaries that generates the problem of simultaneous perception. The problem can be formulated in the following manner. If we assume, quite naturally, that simultaneous perception consists of *two* acts of perception occurring at one time, we are in difficulty. What makes two acts of perception two is precisely that they are of two objects. And because they are of two objects, they necessarily occur in a time which is divisible into the moment of perceiving one object and the moment of perceiving the other. In other words, as soon as we have two acts of perception, we have

[5] For the three corollaries, see *DS* 7 447^{b}12–21. Charles (2000: 113) puts it succinctly: 'what makes a perception one perception is that it is of one object at one time. This is how (according to Aristotle) we individuate perceptions: by their objects and their times.'

two perceived objects, and as soon as we have two perceived objects, the time of perceiving is divided into two: the moment in which the first object is perceived and the moment in which the second object is perceived. Therefore, two acts of perception cannot occur at *one* time. Consequently, there can be no simultaneous perception under the assumption that it consists of two acts of perception occurring at one time. If, on the other hand, we assume that simultaneous perception consists of *one* act of perception occurring at one time, we find ourselves in difficulty again. In one act of perception only one object is perceived. And if only one object is perceived, there is no simultaneous perception, since simultaneous perception implies that *two* objects are perceived at one time. Hence, there can be no simultaneous perception under the assumption that it consists of one act of perception occurring at one time, either.

How does Aristotle solve this problem? Essentially, he argues that simultaneous perception is indeed one single act of perception occurring at one time, but this one act of perception is nevertheless such that two objects are grasped in it. This solution must satisfy several requirements. First, recall the subjective restriction mentioned above: in one act of perception the perceived object is pronounced to be one in number. Aristotle shows that there is a sense in which two objects grasped in a single act of simultaneous perception are pronounced to be one, while remaining two distinct objects. Second, that which performs simultaneous perception must be, on the one hand complex enough to grasp both objects, and on the other hand sufficiently unified to produce a single act of simultaneous perception. We shall see in the following pages how Aristotle meets these requirements.

Now that we understand the framework of the problem of simultaneous perception, let us look at its presentation. The discussion can be divided into four sections, the first two developing the aporia and the latter two developing a solution. (i) Aristotle offers arguments to show that two homogeneous perceptibles cannot be perceived ($447^{a}29$–$^{b}21$). (ii) He offers an argument to show that simultaneous perception of two heterogeneous perceptibles is even more problematic ($447^{b}21$–$448^{a}19$). Of course, all of this clearly runs against our intuitions, and Aristotle's solution is supposed to save them. (iii) His solution tackles the tougher problem of simultaneous perception of heterogeneous perceptibles ($449^{a}5$–18). (iv) Having settled that problem, Aristotle extends the same solution to the problem of simultaneous perception of homogeneous perceptibles ($449^{a}18$–20). Let us discuss each section in turn.

(i) Two homogeneous perceptibles are perceived by the same individual sense, and the question is whether an individual sense can be actualized by two of its perceptibles in such a way that there is one single act of perception in which both perceptibles are grasped, each remaining distinct from the other. Aristotle proceeds by saying that two homogeneous special perceptibles either form a mixture or remain discrete. If they form a mixture, there is really *one* single special perceptible which is composed of, and analysable into, two special perceptibles. So the individual sense, strictly speaking, is not actualized by two special perceptibles, but by one single special perceptible, namely the mixture of the two constitutive special perceptibles.

Two discrete homogeneous perceptibles, on the other hand, actualize the same individual sense at two different times. 'With respect to one capacity and at one time,' Aristotle writes at 447^b17–19, 'the activity is necessarily one.' Of two discrete homogeneous perceptibles, then, there are two acts of perception occurring at two different times, which means that there is no simultaneous perception of them. And even if two discrete homogeneous perceptibles could produce a single act of perception, in that act they would be conflated into one single special perceptible, rather than remaining two distinct special perceptibles. That is to say, two homogeneous perceptibles would be perceived as a mixture due to the subjective restriction. It follows that there can be no simultaneous perception of two homogeneous perceptibles, except in the diluted sense in which they objectively or subjectively form a mixture.

(ii) As for simultaneous perception of two heterogeneous perceptibles, Aristotle says that it is even less possible than simultaneous perception of two homogeneous perceptibles. The argument he offers to that effect introduces the notion of co-specific perceptibles (εἴδει ἕν, σύστοιχα).[6] Co-specific perceptibles are two heterogeneous perceptibles which occupy the same spot on their respective qualitative spectrums. I have explained in Part I, Chapter 2, that each kind of special perceptible constitutes a qualitative spectrum between a positive and a negative extreme, that is, the state and its privation. Thus white and sweet are co-specific perceptibles, since white is among colours what sweet is among flavours, namely the positive extreme.

Co-specific perceptibles seem to be introduced as a pair of perceptibles which, in terms of their similarity, follows right after a pair of

[6] The first part of this argument runs from 447^b24 to 448^a1, the second from 448^a13 to 19.

homogeneous perceptibles. Here is what I have in mind. Two homogeneous perceptibles are similar in that they share the same kind (i.e. genus). Two heterogeneous perceptibles, by contrast, do not share the same genus, and in that respect they are dissimilar. However, two co-specific heterogeneous perceptibles are similar insofar as they belong to the same side of their respective qualitative ranges. Thus a pair of co-specific heterogeneous perceptibles (e.g. white and sweet) is closer to a pair of homogeneous perceptibles than a pair of heterogeneous perceptibles which are not co-specific (e.g. black and sweet) and which have nothing in common.[7] That is, I take it, why in this argument Aristotle introduces co-specific perceptibles rather than heterogeneous perceptibles *simpliciter*.

Now although two co-specific perceptibles do have something in common, they differ from one another more than two homogeneous perceptibles. Hence, Aristotle concludes at 448ª13–19 that it is even more difficult for two co-specific perceptibles to be perceived simultaneously than for two homogeneous perceptibles. And since two heterogeneous perceptibles which are not co-specific have nothing in common, we may add, they are even more different from one another, and hence they are even less likely to be perceived simultaneously. In short, if two homogeneous perceptibles cannot be perceived simultaneously, much less can two heterogeneous perceptibles.

Why should Aristotle think that two heterogeneous perceptibles are more difficult to be perceived simultaneously on account of their being more different from one another than two homogeneous perceptibles? The answer, I think, can be found at 449ª5–8. Two homogeneous perceptibles are said to be simultaneously perceived only insofar as they form a mixture. Since two heterogeneous perceptibles are so different from one another that they cannot mix (only things of the same kind mix), two heterogeneous perceptibles cannot be simultaneously perceived.

Although logically valid, this whole argument is not very convincing. However, Aristotle needs it to round off the aporia before offering his solution.

(iii) The solution to the problem of simultaneous perception is delivered in the following passage:

If, then, the soul perceives sweet with one part and white with another part, then what is made up of these parts is either some one thing, or not. But it must

[7] Of course, they have in common the same higher genus of 'special perceptible', but that is irrelevant here.

be one; for the perceptual part is one thing. (Of what one object is it then? For no one thing is made up of these [sc. of heterogeneous special perceptibles].) Therefore, there must be some one thing of the soul with which everything is perceived, as has been said before, each kind [of special perceptible] through one [part, i.e. individual sense]. In that case, (i) is that which is perceptive of sweet and white some one thing as undivided in actuality, but different [things] when it becomes divided in actuality? Or (ii) just as it is possible with things themselves, so it is with the soul too? Namely, numerically one and the same thing is white and sweet and many other things; for even if such properties are not separable from one another, each one of them is different in being. The same should then be supposed to be the case with the soul, that which is perceptive of everything is numerically one and the same thing, but its being is different—of some things [viz. heterogeneous perceptibles] different in genus, and of others [viz. homogeneous perceptibles] different in species. So there can be simultaneous perception with that which is one and the same, but not the same in account. (*DS* 7 449^{a}5–20; Appendix (d))

In this passage Aristotle argues that the individual senses are distinct parts or aspects of one and the same thing: the perceptual part of the soul.[8] However, Aristotle suggests that this can be understood in two different ways. First (i), the perceptual part of the soul can be construed as something which is in some cases one and undivided in actuality, and in other cases many and divided in actuality.[9] What Aristotle has in mind, I take it, is the idea that the perceptual part of the soul is actually undivided in some cases, as when it perceives white and sweet simultaneously, and actually divided in other cases, as when it perceives white and sweet consecutively, for then it is two different things, first sight and then taste. I suppose this idea is unattractive because it implies

[8] This is one of the many passages in which Aristotle talks of parts of the soul. No doubt these are 'parts' only in the weak sense of conceptual or logical parts, as I have explained in Part I, Ch. 1. It makes no difference whether we speak of the 'perceptual part of the soul' or 'perceptual capacity of the soul'.

[9] Alexander (1901: 164.19–165.20) has a different interpretation of the first conception of the perceptual part of the soul, which is followed by some modern commentators, e.g. G. R. T. Ross ((ed.)1906: 242) and Charlton (1981: 107–8). According to that interpretation, the first conception in our passage is the one developed in analogy with a geometrical point in *DA* III.2 427^{a}9–14. There is one obvious problem with this interpretation. In *DA* III.2 Aristotle endorses the conception in analogy with a geometrical point, whereas here he seems to reject the first conception in favour of the second. So, if Alexander's interpretation of the first conception were correct, this would mean that *DA* III.2 and *DS* 7 espouse two different views. I do not think we need to force this inconsistency on Aristotle. See Ch. 2 below, p. 149.

that the perceptual part of the soul cannot be both divided and undivided in actuality, and that is what Aristotle needs, as will be clear presently.

Second (ii)—and this is the conception Aristotle endorses—the perceptual part of the soul can be construed as something which is numerically one and indivisible, but different 'in account'. This is illustrated by analogy with physical objects. Physical objects, while remaining one in number, have many different properties. For instance, one and the same sugar cube is white and sweet and dry and rough, and so on. Note that it is not the case that one and the same sugar cube is white in one part, sweet in another; rather, it is white and sweet throughout. So the sugar cube is something one in number but different in being; namely, it is one thing for the sugar cube to be white and another to be sweet. Likewise with the perceptual part of the soul. It is one and the same thing capable of perceiving all five kinds of special perceptible. Insofar as it perceives colours it is sight, insofar as it perceives sounds it is hearing, and so on. Because it is one thing for the perceptual part of the soul to perceive colours, another to perceive sounds, and so on, it is said to be different in being, while remaining one and the same thing in number.

It follows that the individual senses are not self-subsistent capacities, as the usual manner of speaking misleadingly suggests, but distinct capacities of the perceptual part of the soul, each a capacity to perceive one kind of special perceptible. Hence, instead of saying that it is sight that perceives colour, it would be more accurate to say that it is the perceptual part of the soul *qua* sight that perceives colour. Since the capacity of the perceptual part of the soul to perceive colours is different from its capacity to perceive sounds, it is perfectly feasible for one and the same perceptual part of the soul to perceive a colour and a sound at the same time. Indeed, there is nothing problematic about *two* senses perceiving two different special perceptibles at the same time. Each sense is actualized by one object, and in each act of perception the object is pronounced to be one, and these two acts of perception can very well occur at the same time.

While this is no doubt true, it does not capture the essence of Aristotle's solution to the problem of simultaneous perception. Unless these two acts of perception are somehow unified in a single act, that is, unless there is really *one* single act of perception in which both special perceptibles are grasped, this will not happen in time which is one and indivisible, and hence there will be no simultaneous perception. For such a single act of perception to be possible, there must be a single capacity to perceive both heterogeneous perceptibles at the same time. Such a capacity emerges from the unity of the perceptual part of the soul.

The perceptual part of the soul is a single thing, indivisible in number but different in being. As I have explained earlier, by saying that the perceptual part of the soul is different in being, Aristotle means that it comprises different individual senses as its conceptually distinct parts or aspects. Hence, the perceptual part of the soul grasps two heterogeneous perceptibles insofar as it is different in being. However, it perceives them simultaneously insofar as it is one in number. That is, the perceptual part of the soul perceives two heterogeneous perceptibles through the activity of the corresponding individual senses, but it does so in *one* single act of perception which is discharged insofar as the perceptual part of the soul is a single thing. When the perceptual part of the soul operates as a single thing, I have argued, we are talking about the higher-order perceptual power that goes by the name 'common sense'.

In an act of simultaneous perception, then, the relevant individual senses are no doubt active, but it is really a single act of the common sense. We can say that the act of simultaneous perception is one in number but different in being: its unity is due to the common sense and its difference in being to the individual senses, each apprehending its own special perceptible. This allows us to conclude that Aristotle solves the problem of simultaneous perception with his concept of the perceptual capacity of the soul which is sufficiently complex to access both heterogeneous perceptibles, and yet at the same time sufficiently unified to do so in a single act of perception. As Catherine Osborne writes: 'the sense corresponds in a fundamental way to the objects to which it is attuned, and while the individual senses are specially adapted to their own class of the proper sense-objects, the sense-faculty as a whole is like the total object to which it is attuned, and it recognizes that object as a unity, in virtue of itself being such a unity with sensitivity to all the various classes of sensible qualities that the object possesses.'[10]

Let us now explore how Aristotle's solution to the problem of simultaneous perception meets the subjective restriction. Aristotle believes that in one act of perception the perceived object is pronounced to be one in number.[11] We have seen what this is supposed to mean in the case of homogeneous perceptibles: in a single act of an individual

[10] Osborne (1998: 444); cf. Lories (1991: 418–19).

[11] *DS* 7 447^{b}12–21 and 447^{b}24–5.

sense two discrete homogeneous perceptibles are conflated into one special perceptible, that is, they are perceived as a mixture. What about heterogeneous perceptibles? In a single act of the common sense two heterogeneous perceptibles surely cannot be perceived as a mixture, for things which are different in kind do not mix. Is there a sense, then, in which two heterogeneous perceptibles—say, white and sweet—can be pronounced to be one in number? Aristotle believes that there is. They are pronounced to be one in number in the sense that they are bound together, forming a single bundle of perceptible qualities. In *Met.* V.6 1015^b21–2 Aristotle says that the just and the musical are one because they accidentally belong to the same substance, and the accidental unity of different properties that coincide in the same substance is a case of oneness in number.[12] So, in an act of simultaneous perception white and sweet can be pronounced to be one in number in the sense that they are perceived as forming an accidental unity. In an act of simultaneous perception, then, white and sweet are integrated in some way.

Integration of various perceived properties of objects into coherent wholes, or 'binding', is a multifaceted and intensely studied subject in contemporary psychology and neuroscience. We can distinguish different kinds of perceptual binding, depending on the sort of properties being integrated in perception. Here we are interested in the kind of binding in which two or more heterogeneous perceptibles are integrated. This is called 'cross-modal binding'.[13]

What we have just seen is that cross-modal binding is achieved, according to Aristotle, by simultaneous perception, and simultaneous perception is the work of the common sense. Although simultaneous perception and cross-modal binding can be regarded as two distinct functions of the common sense, it is important to keep in mind that they occur in the same perceptual event. In other words, one and the same perceptual event can be described with reference to the time of perceiving two perceptibles, or with reference to the way they are apprehended.

Our discussion of cross-modal binding brings us very close to perception of accidental perceptibles. It seems that very little is needed to get us from the grasping of the accidental unity of two heterogeneous perceptibles to the grasping of something to which both perceptibles

[12] Cf. *Top.* I.7 103^a25–32.

[13] Bayne and Chalmers (2003: 25) speak of 'objectual unity across different sensory domains'.

belong, that is, of a physical object.[14] In fact, I would be prepared to argue that the ability to perceive objects is initially developed from simultaneous perception. It seems that human infants come to apprehend physical objects by noticing first that certain perceptible features regularly go together. This is confirmed by experiments in developmental psychology which show that human infants realize that certain sensible qualities belong together within the first three months of their life, and by the fifth month they realize that these qualities come together in objects which can be manipulated.[15] Of course, there is no evidence that Aristotle himself argued for this position, but I think this is a reasonable position to take and one that naturally follows from his arguments.

I would like to add one remark before I proceed to consider how Aristotle's solution addresses the problem of simultaneous perception of homogeneous perceptibles. Cross-modal binding of two heterogeneous perceptibles, I have argued, depends on nothing other than their being perceived simultaneously. As Aristotle says, 'it seems that the soul affirms numerical unity by nothing other than simultaneity' (*DS* 7 447^b24–5).[16] I presume this could lead, at least theoretically, to two kinds of error. On the one hand, an act of simultaneous perception could fail to occur where it should. Suppose there is an object which is white and sweet, say a sugar cube. It is seen and tasted at the same time, but for some reason its white colour and sweet flavour are not perceived in a single act of simultaneous perception. In that case, the white colour and sweet flavour would be perceived separately, in two consecutive acts of perception. They would not be perceived as bound together, although they do in fact coincide in the same object and form an accidental unity. That is to say, the mistaken omission of simultaneous perception would amount to a failure to perceive that the two heterogeneous perceptibles go together, and hence that the same thing is *both* sweet and white.

On the other hand, an act of simultaneous perception could perhaps occur where it should not occur. Suppose there is a box containing brown sugar cubes. Someone decides to play a practical joke by planting a few white salt cubes of the same size in the box. Without paying much attention, an unsuspecting person picks two cubes, the sugar cube on

[14] I assume that physical objects are paradigmatic accidental perceptibles.

[15] According to Vernon (1962: 18), who reports the findings of Gesell and Piaget.

[16] William James (1983: 462) seems to be in agreement with Aristotle: 'any number of sensory sources, falling simultaneously on a mind which has not experienced them separately, will fuse into a single undivided object for that mind.'

top of the salt cube. So he sees the brown sugar cube, but does not see the white salt cube which he licks. If the salty flavour of the tasted salt cube and the brown colour of the seen sugar cube are mistakenly grasped in one act of simultaneous perception, I presume that they would be perceived as forming an accidental unity when in fact they belong to two different objects. That is, the two heterogeneous perceptibles would be mistakenly perceived as going together, and hence *one* object, the seen sugar cube, would be perceived as salty and brown.

(iv) Simultaneous perception of two heterogeneous perceptibles is clearly possible, and we have seen how Aristotle conceives of the capacity which performs it. What about simultaneous perception of two homogeneous perceptibles? So far we have seen Aristotle arguing that two homogeneous perceptibles can be perceived simultaneously only insofar as they form a mixture. Perhaps this could settle the question of simultaneous perception of sounds, smells, and flavours; for I suppose it would not be particularly strange to claim that two sounds or two smells or two flavours can be perceived simultaneously only as a mixture. But surely it would be odd to make this claim for two tangible qualities or two colours. When I touch a chessboard, I feel its coldness and its smoothness at the same time and distinctly from one another. To be sure, this may be due to the complexities of the sense of touch, which apprehends different kinds of tangible properties, so perhaps it is better to focus on the sense of sight. If I look at that same chessboard from an arm's length, I cannot distinguish the time of perceiving white squares from the time of perceiving black squares; I seem to perceive simultaneously white and black—not as a mixture, but as discrete colours.

Aristotle considers the suggestion that an individual sense is itself divisible in the same way as the perceptual part of the soul, which would render it sufficiently complex to be able to perceive two of its perceptibles simultaneously. For instance, if sight was divided into two parts or aspects, say one for positive and one for negative colours, it might perceive positive colours with one part and negative colours with another.[17] The suggestion that the senses are themselves divisible is decisively rejected at $448^b22–449^a2$.[18] If sight were divided in two parts

[17] Again, this would not explain how two colours which belong to the same side of the qualitative spectrum are simultaneously perceived, e.g. dark grey and black or white and yellow.

[18] This is, by the way, why it is especially fitting to speak of the five 'individual' senses in Aristotle.

as described, effectively there would be two senses of sight in one and the same soul. Such proliferation of capacities is repugnant to Aristotle. He defines each capacity with reference to one genus of objects (e.g. sight with reference to colours), not with reference to one species of objects of the same genus (e.g. positive and negative colours), much less with reference to particular objects of one genus (e.g. this shade of white here or that shade of red there). What marks off one capacity from another is that one capacity can be actualized by any particular object of one genus, whereas the other capacity can be actualized by any particular object of another genus. So, for instance, just as there is one science of geometry for all geometrical figures, rather than many geometries, one for triangles and one for quadrangles, there must be one sense of sight for all colours.

Sight is thus a capacity which is one and indivisible, and it is defined with reference to perceptibles of one kind, namely colours.[19] As such, sight is capable of perceiving any particular colour; as Aristotle would put it, sight is an indivisible capacity which potentially perceives white and black and all colours in between. However, when it *actually* perceives white and black (or any other colour), it is divided in actuality, because there are two acts of perception, one in which white is grasped and one in which black (or any other colour) is grasped. Sight cannot actually perceive two colours and remain undivided in actuality. It follows that we cannot see two distinct colours in a single act of perception.

Nevertheless, Aristotle seems to think, quite rightly, that it *is* possible to perceive two distinct colours simultaneously.[20] Having solved the more problematic case of simultaneous perception of heterogeneous perceptibles, he believes that he has *a fortiori* solved the less problematic case of simultaneous perception of homogeneous perceptibles. Although his solution is no doubt focusing on the purportedly tougher case of heterogeneous perceptibles, Aristotle clearly extends it to the case of

[19] This is considerably simplified, since luminescent things constitute another kind of special perceptible of sight; cf. *DA* II.7 419^{a}1–7.

[20] Here I agree with Sorabji (1972: 301) and disagree with Barker (1981: 266 n. 9) who sees 'no reason to dissent from Ross's brief account [viz. Ross ((ed.)1955: 228)] of the structure of *De Sensu* 7, including his contention that on Aristotle's view no one sense can have more than a single object at a time, while 449a5 ff. explains how objects of several *different* senses may be perceived simultaneously'. I see a good reason to dissent from Ross and Barker in Aristotle's statement at 449^{a}16–19 that the perceptual part of the soul is different in being not only generically but also specifically.

homogeneous perceptibles. At 449^{a}16–19 he concludes that 'that which is perceptive of everything is numerically one and the same thing, but its being is different—of some things different in genus, and of others different in species'.[21] What Aristotle must mean here is that the perceptual part of the soul accesses two heterogeneous perceptibles at the same time insofar as it is different in genus (ἕτερον γένει), and it accesses two homogeneous perceptibles at the same time insofar as it is different in species (ἕτερον εἴδει).

This should make us pause. It turns out that the perceptual part of the soul is not different in being *simpliciter*, but different in being in two distinct ways, or at two different levels—generically and specifically. It is easy to see what it means for it to be different in being generically: the perceptual part of the soul is conceptually differentiated into the individual senses, each one of which is geared to one genus of special perceptible. But what does it mean for it to be different in being specifically? Surely the perceptual part of the soul cannot be conceptually differentiated into items each one of which is geared to one species of special perceptible, for such items would be incompatible with Aristotle's notion of the individual sense.

It is difficult to see what Aristotle has in mind here solely on the basis of *DS* 7, since he leaves us with very few clues. His discussion of perceptual discrimination in *DA* III.2 is potentially more informative, so I propose to postpone an answer to those questions for the next chapter. Here I would like to reiterate that the quoted conclusion of *DS* 7, as well as the relevant passages in *DA* III.2 and 7, clearly indicate Aristotle's commitment to the view that simultaneous perception of two homogeneous perceptibles is indeed possible, even when they do not form a mixture. Moreover, all these passages show that Aristotle was determined to explain simultaneous perception of homogeneous perceptibles in the same fashion in which he explained simultaneous perception of heterogeneous perceptibles. That is to say, two homogeneous perceptibles are perceived simultaneously because the perceptual capacity of the soul is sufficiently complex to access both homogeneous perceptibles—even though none of the individual senses is able to do

[21] I take the words τῶν μέν and τῶν δέ at ^{a}18–19 to go with αἰσθητικόν from the previous clause. Osborne (1998: 444) takes these words to go with ἕτερον, so she translates '. . . different from some in genus and others in species'. I am not sure I understand this interpretation. What would be the point of saying that the perceptual part of the soul is different from some things generically and from others specifically?

so—and at the same time it is sufficiently unified to achieve that in one single act.

It is fairly clear, then, that Aristotle took the view that simultaneous perception of homogeneous perceptibles, as well as of heterogeneous perceptibles, is accomplished by the common sense. It is the higher-order perceptual power which performs that one single act in which both perceptibles, homogeneous or heterogeneous, are apprehended simultaneously and in which they are bound together. What is far from clear is how exactly Aristotle thought this is accomplished in the case of homogeneous perceptibles.

2

Perceptual Discrimination

The last part of *DA* III.2 (426^b8–427^a16) opens with Aristotle's statement that each individual sense is concerned with one kind of perceptible object, and that it discriminates (κρίνει) the differences found in the relevant kind of perceptible object.[1] What he has in mind, I take it, is the fundamental ability of each individual sense to pick out various qualities in the spectrum which constitutes one kind of special perceptible, for example, sight can pick out white from non-white, taste can pick out sweet from non-sweet. After this relatively uncontroversial opening, Aristotle goes on to say that we can also discriminate between white and sweet, and indeed between any two special perceptibles. Contrary to Plato, who thinks that this is achieved by some sort of thinking, as we have seen, Aristotle insists that we discriminate between white and sweet perceptually, since these are proper objects of perception. In the rest of *DA* III.2 we find out that there is a problem with this, and in the end we learn the solution to this problem.

I would like to start with some introductory remarks. In the passages we shall be looking at, Aristotle's discussion of perceptual discrimination is restricted to the cases which involve two special perceptibles. Not less than two, because here Aristotle is not interested in the more fundamental ability of a sense to pick out, say, red from non-red. Rather, he is interested in the more specific ability to differentiate between red and green, or between red and bitter. Hence, when we talk of perceptual discrimination, we shall always think of two special perceptibles being differentiated from each other. On the other hand, I presume that Aristotle does not discuss perceptual discrimination in the cases which involve three or more special perceptibles for the same reason that his discussion of simultaneous perception was restricted to two special perceptibles. The idea is that if there can be no perceptual

[1] For the verb κρίνειν in Aristotle, and for the reasons why it is better to translate it as 'to discriminate' rather than as 'to judge', see Ebert (1983).

discrimination between two special perceptibles, neither can there be among three or more. And if perceptual discrimination between two special perceptibles is permitted, perceptual discrimination among three or more should be possible too. Furthermore, Aristotle's discussion of perceptual discrimination is sensitive to the difference between the cases involving two heterogeneous perceptibles and the cases involving two homogeneous perceptibles, in particular those involving two opposite perceptibles, such as white and black. I shall presently explain why Aristotle is especially concerned with opposites.

In the relevant places Aristotle speaks of 'that which discriminates' or 'the discriminating thing' (*τὸ κρῖνον*). Which cognitive capacity of the soul is the discriminating thing in a particular case depends on what is being discriminated. If objects of perception are discriminated, the discriminating thing is a perceptual capacity, and if objects of thought are discriminated, the discriminating thing is an intellectual capacity. In these passages Aristotle discusses discrimination of objects of perception, but his frequently added references to thinking (426^b22, 427^a1, 9) clearly indicate that his explanation of the discriminating thing in the case of objects of perception is intended to hold for the discriminating thing in the case of objects of thought too.

Finally, it is worth stressing that Aristotle's discussion of perceptual discrimination, much like his discussion of simultaneous perception, is aporetic in character. The aporia is generated by putting certain constraints on perceptual discrimination, and then by evoking a principle which seems to undermine the possibility of perceptual discrimination in the case of two opposite perceptibles. However, our everyday experience shows that perceptual discrimination between two opposite perceptibles is perfectly possible. Aristotle solves the problem by giving an explanation of the discriminating thing according to which it is capable of discriminating between two opposite perceptibles without violating the stated principle. In that way, the constraints put on perceptual discrimination are preserved, the principle is respected, and our experience accommodated.

At 426^b17–29 Aristotle posits two constraints on discrimination: one on the discriminating thing, and one on the time of discrimination. First, the discriminating thing must be a single thing to which both special perceptibles are present. Unless that which discriminates between two special perceptibles is a single thing, the discrimination cannot be intuitive, but inferential. What Aristotle has in mind is the following. Suppose that one soldier hiding in the Trojan horse is assigned to look through the holes drilled in the place of the horse's eyes, and another to listen through the holes drilled in the place of the horse's ears. The difference between the visual information reported by the first soldier and the auditory information reported by the second soldier could perhaps be *inferred* from the fact that what is perceived by one is not perceived by the other, but surely it would not be *perceived* by either one of them, or by anyone else inside the horse.

Second, Aristotle's constraint on the time of discrimination is formulated in a fairly complicated way, but it can be simplified as follows. The time in which the two perceptibles are present to the discriminating thing and differentiated from one another must be indivisible. In other words, perceptual discrimination does not take time which is divisible into two moments, one moment in which one perceptible is perceived and differentiated from another, and another moment in which the other perceptible is perceived and differentiated from the former. Rather, both special perceptibles are present to the discriminating thing and differentiated from one another at a time which is one and indivisible.[2]

Given that the discriminating thing is some numerically one thing to which both special perceptibles are present, and given that they are discriminated at a time which is one and indivisible, we must suppose that the two special perceptibles are discriminated in one single act of the discriminating thing. And it is precisely because they are discriminated in one single act that the time of their discrimination is indivisible. The problem with this is the following: the perceptual capacity of the soul is sufficiently complex to allow perceptual discrimination between two *heterogeneous* perceptibles, for we have seen that two heterogeneous perceptibles can very well be simultaneously perceived—and, by the same token, discriminated from each other—in one single act occurring at one time. However, when it comes to discriminating between two *homogeneous* perceptibles, none of the individual senses seems to be complex enough to simultaneously perceive two of its perceptibles and thus to discriminate between them in a single act and at a time which

[2] The second constraint on discrimination seems to be mistaken. Succession of qualities is more conducive to their discrimination than their simultaneity: 'the differing objects should not come to us simultaneously but fall in immediate *succession* upon the same organ. It is easier to compare successive than simultaneous sounds, easier two compare two weights or two temperatures by testing one after the other with the same hand, than by using both hands and comparing both at once. . . . The reason why successive impression so much favours the result seems to be that there is a real *sensation of difference*, aroused by the shock of transition from one perception to another which is unlike the first.' (James 1983: 468–9).

is one and indivisible. It would appear that perceptual discrimination between two homogeneous perceptibles is not possible.

Aristotle comes to the heart of the problem in *DA* III.2 426^{b}29–427^{a}1: 'It is impossible for the same thing to be changed simultaneously by opposite changes, insofar as it is indivisible and in an indivisible time. For if something is sweet, it changes the sense or thought in one way, whereas the bitter changes it in the opposite way, and the white changes it in yet another way.'[3] The problem is formulated in terms of 'change' (κίνησις), rather than in terms of 'activity' (ἐνέργεια), which is not unusual for Aristotle. This formulation makes a straightforward point in non-technical language. Also, it seems to contain an allusion to the principle which underlies Plato's tripartite division of the soul, and which was no doubt familiar to Aristotle's audience.[4] Aristotle's formulation of the problem puts an emphasis on opposites because the case of opposites appears to be particularly difficult. As such, it is a test case for an adequate explanation of perceptual discrimination. That is to say, if perceptual discrimination between two *opposite* perceptibles is adequately explained, other cases present no worry, whereas an adequate explanation of perceptual discrimination between other combinations of special perceptibles does not remove the worry concerning the hardest case, that of two opposite perceptibles.

Aristotle seeks a solution to this problem in an adequate explanation of the discriminating thing. Two explanations are offered. In the first one (427^{a}2–5), the discriminating thing is said to be one in number but different in being. The idea is familiar: insofar as the discriminating thing is different in being, it has both special perceptibles present to it, and insofar as it is one in number, it discriminates them in a single act at a time which is one and indivisible. This clearly works for heterogeneous perceptibles: the perceptual part of the soul has both heterogeneous perceptibles present insofar as it is different in being (i.e. two heterogeneous perceptibles are accessed by the individual senses), and it discriminates them insofar as it is a single thing (i.e. the two heterogeneous perceptibles are differentiated from each other by the common sense).

[3] Cf. *DS* 7 448^{a}1–5; *Cael.* II.13 295^{b}14–15.

[4] Plato says that it is impossible 'for the same thing at the same time in the same respect and in the same relation to suffer, be, or do opposites' (*Republic* IV 436e9–437a2). Hence, if the same thing is changed at the same time and in the same respect with two opposite changes, it cannot be indivisible. Rather, it is divided into parts such that one part changes in one way and the other part changes in another way.

However, this explanation does not suffice for homogeneous perceptibles. Two homogeneous perceptibles, notably two opposite perceptibles, are perceived by an individual sense, and we have seen that the individual senses are not themselves conceptually differentiated so that they can be affected by both opposites at the same time. An individual sense can be affected by both opposites only at two different times—it is 'divided in actuality', as Aristotle puts it at 427^{a}7. Hence, a different explanation of the discriminating thing is needed.

But before the second explanation is spelled out, I should like to make a brief digression. Some modern interpreters seem to follow Alexander of Aphrodisias in identifying the first explanation of the discriminating thing in *DA* III.2 (427^{a}2–5) with the second conception of the perceptual part of the soul in *DS* 7 (449^{a}13–20), there offered as Aristotle's final solution to the problem of simultaneous perception.[5] I do not think that this identification is correct. In *DA* III.2 427^{a}2–5 the discriminating thing is said to be one in number but different in being *simpliciter*, whereas in *DS* 7 449^{a}16–19 the perceptual part of the soul is said to be one in number but different in being *in two distinct ways*—generically (in the case of heterogeneous perceptibles) and specifically (in the case of homogeneous perceptibles). We shall see that this second conception of the perceptual part of the soul in *DS* 7 is in fact parallel with the second explanation of the discriminating thing in *DA* III.2, which will render the two passages mutually consistent.

Aristotle's second explanation of the discriminating thing comes in a passage which is extremely compressed and textually problematic. Here is a translation of the Greek text which seems to me to give tolerable sense:

> Rather, it [sc. the discriminating thing] is like what some call a point, which is divisible insofar as it is one or two. Insofar as it is indivisible, then, the discriminating thing is one and [it discriminates] at one time, whereas insofar as it is divisible, it uses the same dot twice at one time. Insofar as it uses the boundary as two, it discriminates two separate [things], [since what is used] is in a way separated; whereas insofar as [it uses the boundary as] one, [it discriminates] one [thing] and at one time. (*DA* III.2 427^{a}9–14; see Appendix (e))

There are many acute difficulties with this passage. For instance, Aristotle uses three different words: point (στιγμή), dot (σημεῖον), and boundary

[5] Cf. Alexander (1901: 165.21–166.4), Rodier ((ed.)1900: II.390–1), G. R. T. Ross ((ed.)1906: 230), Siwek ((ed.)1963: 125–6); cf. Part III, Ch. 1, p. 136 n. 9.

(πέρας). One would think that these three different words are used in order to mark certain distinctions in the subject-matter, but it is difficult to say with certainty what these distinctions are.[6] Moreover, in the first sentence the discriminating thing is compared to what some people, presumably mathematicians, call a point. Two lines below, however, it seems to be the discriminating thing that is said to *use* a dot and a boundary. Should we attach significance to this shift, or disregard it as a 'confusion between the illustration and the fact it is intended to illustrate'?[7] Furthermore, what does it mean 'to use the same dot twice', or 'to use the boundary as two' and 'as one'? These difficulties can be solved only within a broader interpretation of the passage, so let us attempt one.

Aristotle compares the discriminating thing to a geometrical point. A geometrical point is defined as that which is quantitatively entirely indivisible and has a position.[8] Its function is to limit and divide lines.[9] Every line is limited by two points, each at one end of the line. Also, every line is divisible at any point lying between the two ends. When a line becomes actually divided at some point, this point performs two roles at the same time: that of a beginning and that of an end. In line AC divided at point B, point B is both the end of section AB and the beginning of section BC. Insofar as point B is a single point, it is one in number. On the other hand, insofar as it has two roles, it is different in being.[10] It is different in being because it is one thing for point B to be the end of section AB and quite another to be the beginning of section BC.

Since 'beginning' and 'end' are opposites, one might be tempted to think that point B can be said to have two opposite qualifications at the same time. This would allow one to conclude that, if the discriminating thing is indeed like a geometrical point, it should be able to have two opposite perceptibles present to it at the same time. However, this cannot

[6] As far as I know, the majority of ancient and modern commentators think that these words, plus the word ὅρος in the parallel passage in *DA* III.7 431^{a}22, stand for the same thing, namely the discriminating thing; e.g. Neuhaeuser (1878: 46), Wallace ((ed.)1882: 259), Rodier ((ed.)1900: II.395, 500), G. R. T. Ross ((ed.)1906: 231), Hicks ((ed.)1907: 450), Hamlyn ((ed.)1968: 128), Modrak (1981*b*: 417 n. 29), Osborne (1998: 440).

[7] Hicks ((ed.)1907: 451).

[8] *Met.* V.6 1016^{b}24–6; cf. *Met.* III.5 1002^{b}4, V.6 1016^{b}31, XIII.8 1084^{b}26; *Phy.* V.1 231^{a}25; *Cael.* III.1 299^{b}6.

[9] *DA* III.6 430^{b}20; *Met.* III.5 1002^{b}10, V.17 1022^{a}4–6, XI.2 1060^{b}15, 18, XIV.3 1090^{b}6.

[10] *Phy.* VIII.8 263^{b}12–14 and *DA* III.7 431^{a}29.

be the gist of Aristotle's analogy with a geometrical point. 'Beginning' and 'end' are opposites in the relevant sense only if they limit the same thing. For instance, the beginning of line AB and the end of line AB are opposites in the sense that makes the principle of non-contradiction applicable; indeed no point can be both the beginning of AB and the end of AB. This is precisely the sense in which white and black are opposites. What we find in Aristotle's example, however, is the beginning of *one* section (AB) and the end of *another* section (BC). Here the principle of non-contradiction does not apply. One single point can very well be both the beginning of one section and the end of another section, just as Socrates can be both small and large at the same time, namely small in relation to Theodorus and large in relation to Theaetetus. The force of the analogy with a geometrical point, therefore, must lie elsewhere.[11]

Before we can appreciate the force of Aristotle's analogy, it is important to observe that a point is not only one in number and different in being when it *divides* one line, but also when it *connects* two or more lines. If two lines, say AB and CB, meet at point B, point B is again one in number and different in being. It is different in being insofar as it is the end of line AB and the end of line CB (or the beginning of line AB and the beginning of line CB). Still, point B is one in number, so that the ends of the two lines coincide in one single point.

This is how the point analogy has been understood in the tradition. The point with which Aristotle compares the discriminating thing is taken to be the centre of a circle in which different radii meet.[12] This is a neat illustration not only of the perceptual capacity of the soul, but possibly also of the sensory apparatus, as it reminds us of the sense organs on the periphery which are connected with the heart at the centre. Thus interpreted, however, the point analogy seems to boil down to the idea that the perceptual capacity of the soul is a single thing conceptually

[11] I thank David Sedley for insisting on this point against my earlier interpretation in Gregoric (2003).

[12] The earliest evidence of this interpretation is found in Alexander of Aphrodisias (1887*a*: 63.6–28; 1887*b*: 96.14–34; 1901: 165.12–20). It is reiterated by all ancient commentators: Themistius (1899: 86.18–28), Simplicius (1882: 196.31–2, 200.21–6, 270.25–8), Philoponus (1887: 169.21–9, 481.7–11, 560.20–2, 25–33), Michael (1903: 47.30–48.2), Sophonias (1883: 114.24–8). Some contemporary scholars also endorse this interpretation, e.g. De Corte (1932: 200), Kahn (1966: 57), Modrak (1981*b*: 418; 1987: 66). The geometrical point appears to be the standard analogy for incorporeal substances in later antiquity, and I suspect that this may be due to the *DA* III.2 passage under discussion; cf. Plotinus IV.7.6, 11–19, IV.2.1, 24–9; Proclus, *In Platonis Rem Publicam* II.46.21–8 (Kroll).

differentiated into the individual senses, that is, one thing in number but different in being *simpliciter*. This idea can account only for perceptual discrimination of two or more heterogeneous perceptibles, whereas the analogy with a geometrical point seems to be introduced precisely in order to account for the hard case of perceptual discrimination of two *opposite* perceptibles. This problem has been spotted by those scholars who insist that the point in Aristotle's analogy must be a point dividing a single line.[13] However, it is not necessary to insist that the geometrical point in Aristotle's analogy is *either* a point connecting two or more lines, *or* a point dividing one single line. It can very well be both, depending on whether it describes the discriminating thing in the case of two heterogeneous perceptibles or in the case of two homogeneous perceptibles.

Let me elaborate on this suggestion. We have seen that one and the same point can perform two functions: the function of dividing a single line and the function of connecting several lines. In each of these two functions the point is one in number but different in being insofar as it plays multiple roles. When it divides a single line, the same point has two roles, that of the beginning of one section and that of the end of another section. When it connects two or more lines, as in the case of the centre in which radii of a circle meet, the same point again has two or more roles, being the limit of each line.

This is crucial because it shows that the point is not different in being *simpliciter*, but in two different ways: when performing the second function, point B is different in being insofar as it is, say, the end of line AB, the end of line CB, and the end of line DB; when performing the first function, say of dividing line AC, point B is different in being insofar as it is the end of section AB and the beginning of section BC. These two ways in which point B is different in being, I submit, correspond to Aristotle's statement in *DS* 7 449^a16–19 that the part of the soul which is perceptive of everything is different in being—'of some things different *in genus*, and of others *in species*'.

It will be helpful to unpack this correspondence more fully. The perceptual part, as we have seen, is conceptually differentiated at two levels, such that its differentiation at one level (different in being generically) can account for simultaneously accessing heterogeneous perceptibles,

13 Neuhaeuser (1878: 45), Wallace ((ed.)1882: 259), Rodier ((ed.)1900: II.394), G. R. T. Ross ((ed.)1906: 230), Hicks ((ed.)1907: 450), W. D. Ross ((ed.)1961: 36), Hamlyn ((ed.)1968: 128), Charlton (1981: 106).

whereas its differentiation at another level (different in being specifically) can account for simultaneously accessing homogeneous perceptibles. Insofar as it is a single thing, on the other hand, the perceptual part achieves simultaneous apprehension and discrimination of both heterogeneous and homogeneous perceptibles. In all of this the perceptual part is analogous to a geometrical point. A geometrical point can likewise be conceptually differentiated at two levels, such that its differentiation at one level (the function of connecting several lines) can account for its being the end of several lines, and its differentiation at another level (the function of dividing a single line) can account for its being the beginning of one section and the end of another section of a single line. Insofar as it is one in number, on the other hand, the point achieves its functions of connecting and dividing the lines.

This should suffice to establish that the second explanation of the discriminating thing in *DA* III.2 (427^a9–14) overlaps with the second conception of the perceptual part of the soul in *DS* 7 (449^a13–20). What we have just seen is how Aristotle's formulation of the perceptual part of the soul in *DS* 7 can be applied to the explanation of the discriminating thing in analogy with a geometrical point. However, what really interests us is whether the point analogy in *DA* III.2 explains something that Aristotle's discussion of the perceptual part of the soul in *DS* 7 left unspecified, namely *how* the perceptual part simultaneously perceives two homogeneous perceptibles.

Of course, there is little in our passage from *DA* III.2 that amounts to an explanation, strictly speaking. Nevertheless, I think that it does offer us a clue as to how the discriminating thing simultaneously accesses and discriminates two perceptibles. This clue is available, however, only if we read the text for what it says and if we attach significance to the shift from describing the discriminating thing as a point (στιγμή) at 427^a10, to saying that it uses a dot (σημεῖον) or a boundary (πέρας) in lines 12 and 13. That is, we have to assume that what is compared to a 'point' is not the same as what is called a 'dot' or 'boundary'. What is compared to a point is, no doubt, the discriminating thing, and that is the perceptual part of the soul.[14] On the other hand, I suggest that 'dot' and 'boundary' stand for the juncture of two or more perceptibles.[15]

[14] I shall explain shortly why the discriminating thing cannot be an individual sense, even in the case of homogeneous perceptibles.

[15] We shall see that this 'juncture' is rather different in the case of heterogeneous and in the case of homogeneous perceptibles.

If we accept this suggestion, we can make some progress. When Aristotle says that the perceptual part of the soul uses the same dot twice, or that it uses the same boundary as two, I take him to mean the following. The perceptual part apprehends the boundary of a white square on the chessboard, on the one hand as that which divides white from black, and on the other hand as that which divides black from white. In thus apprehending the boundary, the perceptual part of the soul gains access to two opposite perceptibles at the same time. That is, I take it, what is communicated in lines ^{a}13–14: 'Insofar as it [viz. the discriminating thing] uses the boundary as two, it discriminates two separate [things].'[16] However, the boundary needs to be apprehended as a single thing too, if the discrimination is to take place at one time.[17] That is what the next sentence says: 'And insofar as [the discriminating thing uses the boundary as] one, [it apprehends] one [thing] and at one time.'

Before I proceed, let me sum up our discussion so far. The quoted passage in *DA* III.2 can be divided into two parts. In the first part (427^{a}10–12) we find a description of the discriminating thing. The discriminating thing is compared to a geometrical point which is a single thing playing multiple roles. If we accept the suggestion that a point can have two distinct functions—the function of connecting different lines and the function of dividing a single line, each function involving multiple roles for the point to play—then we can establish a parallel between *DA* III.2 and *DS* 7. This is desirable not only because it renders Aristotle's thought on these matters consistent across two different texts, but also because it explains why he says nothing in *DS* 7 about how the perceptual part of the soul simultaneously perceives homogeneous perceptibles; namely, he assumes that he has already dealt with the issue in *DA* III.2.

In the second part (427^{a}13–14) we find an explanation of how the discriminating thing performs discrimination of two perceptibles at one time. So far I have suggested an interpretation of that explanation only

[16] I am not sure what to make of the following clause, ἔστιν ὡς κεχωρισμένῳ, which comes in many textual variants. In this variant, favoured by the majority of editors and translators, I take it with Trendelenburg ((ed.)1877: 366) to clarify that two separate things are discriminated when the boundary is used as two. It is possible to interpret the same textual variant differently (e.g. Hicks (ed.)1907: 451), or to advocate different variants (e.g. Ross (ed.)1961: 281).

[17] Remember the second corollary from the principle that the sense and its object are one in an act of perception (the subjective restriction): in one act of perception the perceived object is pronounced to be one in number; cf. Part III, Ch. 1, p. 132.

as far as it concerns discrimination of two opposite perceptibles, and this should also work for any other two or more homogeneous perceptibles. I have argued that the boundary of a special perceptible is a single thing which functions as an interface, so to speak, through which two or more perceptibles of the same kind are accessed simultaneously. The boundary of a white square is also the boundary of the neighbouring black square, so the boundary seems to be both white and black.[18] Because the perceptual part of the soul is able to regard the boundary as a single thing and as something which is both white and black, the perceptual part can simultaneously access and discriminate white and black. Before I extend my interpretation of Aristotle's explanation to the case of heterogeneous perceptibles, I should like to make a few more remarks about the case of homogeneous perceptibles.

If my interpretation of Aristotle's explanation is on the right track, it is legitimate to raise some questions concerning the role of the individual senses in discriminating homogeneous perceptibles. When we discriminate white and black, what do we actually perceive by sight? Hicks thinks that '[s]ight, as a special sense, apprehends white and black successively: *sensus communis*, employing sight as its instrument, apprehends white and black simultaneously.'[19] This cannot be right. If the perceptual part of the soul employs sight to discriminate two colours, as it surely does, discrimination will not be simultaneous if the colours are apprehended successively—the time of perceiving one colour preceding the time of perceiving the other colour. What happens when we discriminate two colours, rather, is that sight perceives one colour, whereas the common sense uses its boundary to discriminate it from the neighbouring colours.

To be sure, my account is not unproblematic. When we look at a chessboard, for instance, we seem to perceive simultaneously and discriminate not only one white and one black square, but an elaborate pattern of white and black squares. This appears to involve more than a single boundary. Furthermore, when we look at a chessboard we seem to perceive simultaneously and discriminate a host of other colours in our field of vision,[20] and we tend to bind them together in

[18] I suppose that having two opposite qualifications in this weak sense is not ruled out by the principle of non-contradiction.

[19] Hicks ((ed.)1907: 536–7).

[20] Hamlyn ((ed.)1968: 128) correctly observes that Aristotle did not 'pay any attention to the fact that the objects of perception may occupy a field'.

our perception of objects. It is difficult to see how Aristotle's account relying on the notion of boundary could accommodate what may be called 'unimodal binding', that is, binding of various homogeneous perceptibles into coherent wholes. I hasten to add, however, that it is not my interpretation that makes Aristotle's account problematic, but Aristotle's fundamental assumption that only one special perceptible can actualize the corresponding individual sense at one time.

This is precisely why Aristotle is committed to the view that the discriminating thing in the case of homogeneous perceptibles is the perceptual part of the soul, rather than the relevant individual sense.[21] He does not think it is *sight* that uses the boundary between white and black, because using the boundary as two implies a sort of simultaneous presence of both white and black, and this in turn implies a sort of division for the sense of sight. As we have seen in the preceding chapter, Aristotle is unwilling to admit any sort of division in the individual senses. Hence, he has to relegate this sort of division to the perceptual part of the soul. Given that the perceptual part of the soul is already divided at one level into the individual senses, we should not find its division at another level particularly vexing. Thus we end up with the perceptual part of the soul which is different in being generically and specifically.

Let us now consider whether our interpretation of Aristotle's explanation can accommodate discrimination of heterogeneous perceptibles. There is one major obstacle to this effort. Saying that the perceptual part of the soul uses the same boundary as two and as one is perhaps applicable to the case of homogeneous perceptibles, but not to the case of heterogeneous perceptibles, since there is no boundary between white and sweet. The problem is nicely formulated by William Charlton: 'If we see a pale object, we will see its boundary, and to see its boundary is to differentiate it from the dark background. In the case of pale and sweet we can point out that the same thing can be both, but we cannot so easily speak of boundaries. There is no boundary between the colour and the flavour of a lump of sugar.'[22]

[21] A number of ancient and modern interpreters agree that the discriminating thing even in the case of homogeneous perceptibles is not to be found among the individual senses, but in the unified perceptual capacity of the soul. These interpreters include Alexander of Aphrodisias (1887*a*: 62.20–65.2, esp. 64.4–22), Thomas Aquinas (1951: 373–4, 449), Rodier ((ed.)1900: II.396, 498–509), G. R. T. Ross ((ed.)1906: 232–4), Hicks ((ed.)1907: 536–7), Siwek ((ed.)1933: 333), and Hamlyn ((ed.)1968: 128).

[22] Charlton (1981: 107).

The only way to surmount this obstacle is to assume that words 'dot' and 'boundary' at 427ª12 and 13 can, after all, refer to physical objects in which two or more heterogeneous perceptibles coincide. Although by no means straightforward, this assumption is not entirely unfounded. If a dot or a boundary can be something in which two or more things (lines and surfaces) meet, and a physical object is something in which two or more properties (heterogeneous perceptibles) coincide, then perhaps calling a physical object 'dot' or 'boundary' is not an entirely inappropriate choice of metaphor.

With this assumption, our interpretation of Aristotle's explanation works in the case of heterogeneous perceptibles too. When Aristotle says that the perceptual part of the soul uses the boundary as two, he means that it simultaneously apprehends, for instance, a sugar cube's whiteness and sweetness. The perceptual part can do this because it is conceptually differentiated into the individual senses, in analogy with a geometrical point which plays different roles when it connects several lines. On the other hand, when Aristotle says that the perceptual part of the soul uses the boundary as one, he means that it apprehends the sugar cube as a single thing which is both white and sweet, and this ensures the unity of the act of discrimination. The perceptual part can do this because it is numerically one, in analogy with the geometrical point which, despite its different roles, is numerically one.

The flexible notion of a boundary—in some cases taken literally as the limit between two or more homogeneous perceptibles, in other cases taken metaphorically as the physical object in which two or more heterogeneous perceptibles coincide—allows us to credit Aristotle with a single explanation of discrimination of both homogeneous and heterogeneous perceptibles. If anything is clear from the notoriously difficult passage in *DA* III.7 431ª20–ᵇ1, it is that Aristotle indeed intended to provide a single explanation for both cases of perceptual discrimination.

This passage is even more obscure and textually problematic than the one in III.2 427ª9–14. It seems to refer to a diagram, but it does not explain all the symbols used in it. Moreover, it is hard to see what exactly are the relations that hold among the things symbolized. Instead of reviewing all the available interpretations of this difficult passage—and there is quite a number of them[23]—I shall offer one

[23] A review of the pre-1900 interpretations can be found in Rodier ((ed.)1900: II.500–9). Apart from the interpretations offered in various editions and commentaries

which is in line with the proposed interpretation of the point analogy in *DA* III.2. Also, I shall refrain from discussing many textual variants and their possible significance, because that would require a separate chapter.

Although it has already been said what it is by which [the soul] discriminates what the difference is between sweet and hot, the following needs to be said as well: it is one thing, and that as a limit. These things too, being analogously and numerically one, stand to one another as those other things stand to each other. For what is the difference whether we puzzle over how it discriminates [perceptibles that are] not homogeneous or [how it discriminates] opposites, such as white and black? Let A (white) stand to B (black) as C stands to D. So that the converse will be true as well [viz. A is to C as B is to D]. Now if C and D are to belong to one thing, they will be just like A and B—one and the same thing, but not the same in being—and likewise with those others. The same account would hold if A were sweet and B white. (*DA* III.7 $431^{a}20–^{b}1$; see Appendix (f))

Any interpreter of this passage faces three main difficulties, namely how to understand (i) 'these things' (ταῦτα) at $^{a}22$; (ii) 'those other things' (ἐκεῖνα) at $^{a}23$; and (iii) symbols 'C' and 'D' (Γ and Δ) at $^{a}26$. With a majority of interpreters, I take (i) 'these things' to be 'sweet and hot', mentioned in the previous sentence.[24] With a minority of interpreters, I take (ii) 'those other things' to be the corresponding perceptions, in this particular case the perceptions of sweet and hot.[25]

At $^{a}22–3$, then, Aristotle says that the items of the first pair (sweet and hot), being one in analogy and one in number, are related to each other in the same way as the items in the second pair (the perception of sweet and the perception of hot). It is not entirely clear whether it is necessary to infer from this that the perception of sweet and the perception of hot are also one in analogy and one in number, not least because there are significant textual variations in the relevant clause, but I believe that we can make sense of the text even if the inference is made.

on the *De Anima*, different interpretations can be found in De Corte (1932), Charlton (1981), and Osborne (1998).

24 So Simplicius (1882: 271.13–14), Torstrik ((ed.)1862: 200–1), Ross ((ed.)1961: 305), Hamlyn ((ed.)1968: 147), Charlton (1981: 107), Lawson-Tancred ((ed.)1986: 208, 248), Osborne (1998: 441–4).

25 So Hamlyn ((ed.)1968: 147), and Charlton (1981: 107); see n. 29 below. Brentano (1867: 94 n. 49), Baeumker (1877: 73), Neuhaeuser (1878: 53–60), and Wallace ((ed.)1882: 167) take 'these things' (ταῦτα) to be the perceptions of sweet and hot, and 'those things' (ἐκεῖνα) to be sweet and hot.

Numerical unity is not a problem. Sweet and hot are one in number in the sense that they belong to the same object. Likewise, the perception of sweet and the perception of hot are one in number in the sense that they belong to the same act of the perceptual part of the soul.[26] However, it is more difficult to say in what sense sweet and hot are one in analogy. This depends on whether we take sweet and hot to be random examples, or whether it matters that they occupy the same spot on their respective spectrums. I am inclined to believe that it does matter that sweet and hot are co-specific perceptibles.

At 431^{a}19, immediately preceding our passage, Aristotle claims that the perceptual part of the soul is 'a single mean, but its being is multiple'. If the perceptual part of the soul is a single mean, someone might object, it will have no way of distinguishing between two heterogeneous perceptibles that occupy the same spot on their respective spectrums. As Osborne puts it: 'Surely, someone might say, it will be capable of registering "something at the hot/white/sweet end", but not *which* of those qualities, severally, might be in play.'[27] Of course, the answer is that the perceptual part of the soul is a single mean but *different in being*, which is what enables it to register which of these qualities are in play. That is to say, because it comprises taste and touch as its conceptually distinct parts, the perceptual capacity of the soul will be perfectly able to distinguish between any flavour and any tangible quality, including those that occupy the same spot on their respective spectrums, such as sweet and hot. Because it is a single mean, on the other hand, the perceptual capacity of the soul will be able to detect that they occupy the same spot within their spectrums, that is, that they are co-specific or 'one in analogy'.[28]

Let us assume, then, that sweet and hot are one in analogy in the sense that they are co-specific perceptibles. What about the second pair—the perceptions of sweet and hot; in which sense are they one in analogy? I can only speculate and suggest that they are one in analogy in the sense that they are acts of the same intensity. For, in an act of simultaneous perception, the perceptual part of the soul registers that sweet and hot are co-specific perceptibles because they actualize the corresponding senses

[26] It has been established in the preceding chapter (p. 138) that one and the same act of simultaneous perception comprises as its conceptually distinct aspects the perceptions of two heterogeneous perceptibles.

[27] Osborne (1998: 441).

[28] This is clearly expressed by Aristotle in *DS* 7 447^{b}24–448^{a}1, where he speaks of two heterogeneous perceptibles being 'one in species' (τῷ εἴδει ἕν, 447^{b}25).

with equal intensity. Should we fear, then, that the perceptual part will fail to discriminate sweet and hot because it will register only one thing, namely the spot that both perceptibles occupy within their respective spectrums? Not at all. Discrimination of two co-specific perceptibles is no more problematic than discrimination of two opposite perceptibles which occupy as different spots on a spectrum as they possibly can (one is a form, the other its privation).

This seems to be demonstrated by means of a diagram which was probably drawn on Aristotle's blackboard. Two symbols are known: 'A' stands for white, 'B' for black. I take (iii) symbols 'C' and 'D' to stand for the corresponding perceptions, the perception of white and the perception of black.[29] As we have seen, the relation between A and B holds between C and D. The *alternando* relation also holds: A (white) is to C (the perception of white) as B (black) is to D (the perception of black).

Now if C and D are to belong to one thing, Aristotle says, they will be related just like A and B. In other words, if the perception of white and the perception of black are going to belong to one thing[30]—as they must, if they are to be discriminated perceptually—they will be related to each other in the same way in which white and black themselves are related to each other. Well, how are white and black related? Assuming that the idea of a boundary comes into play here, white and black are related as two distinct aspects of one and the same thing. The boundary is one thing which is in a way both white and black, for it belongs to both colours and marks off each one from the other. That is what its 'difference in being' amounts to. Similarly, the perception of white and the perception of black are two conceptually distinct aspects of a single act of discrimination performed by the perceptual part of the soul. Indeed, we have seen that the perceptual part of the soul, in perceiving the boundary, simultaneously accesses two or more homogeneous perceptibles that meet in that boundary. It does so because it is different in being (specifically), whereas it discriminates them in one act and one time because it is one in number.

[29] So Brentano (1867: 94 n. 49), Kampe (1870: 109 n. 3), Baeumker (1877: 73–4), Neuhaeuser (1878: 59–60), Hamlyn ((ed.)1968: 147), and Charlton (1981: 107). Similarly, Wallace ((ed.)1882: 169) has 'the idea of white and the idea of black'.

[30] I agree with Rodier ((ed.)1900: I.193, II.503), Siwek ((ed.)1933: 265, 332–3), and Hamlyn ((ed.)1968: 147) that the one thing to which C and D belong is the discriminating thing, i.e. the perceptual part of the soul or the common sense. Similarly, Wallace ((ed.)1882: 169) has 'some one act of mind'.

The crucial move comes in the last sentence. The same account, Aristotle says, can be given if A were sweet and B white. Let us spell out this account. If the perception of sweet and the perception of white are going to belong to one thing, they will be related to each other in the same way in which sweet and white are related to each other. Sweet and white are two conceptually distinct aspects of one and the same thing, say a sugar cube. The sugar cube is a single thing which is both sweet and white. Since its being sweet is not the same as its being white, it is 'different in being'. Similarly, the perception of sweet and the perception of white are two conceptually distinct aspects of a single act of discrimination performed by the perceptual part of the soul. We have seen that the perceptual part simultaneously accesses two or more heterogeneous perceptibles that coincide in the same object. The perceptual part can do that because it is different in being (generically), whereas it discriminates them in one act and one time because it is one in number.

Before I conclude, I wish to stress that the interpretation of the *DA* III.7 passage I have offered is neither foolproof nor the only one possible. However, it seems to me to be at least as cogent and charitable to Aristotle as the other ones on the market. Its main advantage (or shortcoming) is that it relies on my interpretation of the *DA* III.2 passage. My interpretation of the latter passage in turn rests on a few acceptable assumptions. It may be helpful to list these assumptions here. First, I have argued that a geometrical point can have two distinct functions, that of connecting several lines and that of dividing a single line. Accordingly, the point in Aristotle's analogy should not be interpreted exclusively, as either the centre in which radii meet or the point in which a line is divided, but inclusively, as both the centre in which radii meet and the point in which a line is divided. Second, I have maintained that there is a shift from talking about the discriminating thing as a point, to talking of its using a dot or boundary. Thus, in *DA* III.2 427^{a}9–14 we have not only a description of the discriminating thing in analogy with the point, but also a (woefully condensed) explanation of how the discriminating thing does the work. Third, I have argued for a flexible notion of boundary which covers the cases of adjacent homogeneous perceptibles as well as of heterogeneous perceptibles coinciding in physical objects. With these three assumptions, I provide not only a tolerable interpretation of the *DA* III.2 passage, but one which sits well with what Aristotle says in *DS* 7 and which can be projected into the *DA* III.7 passage, thus rendering Aristotle's thoughts on the matter of simultaneous perception and discrimination consistent.

The main result of that interpretation can be summarized as follows. The perceptual part of the soul is sufficiently complex to simultaneously access and discriminate two or more heterogeneous perceptibles as well as two or more homogeneous perceptibles, including the opposites. This complexity is formulated in terms of 'difference in being' which is operative at two different levels, at one level for heterogeneous and at another level for homogeneous perceptibles.

The view that two or more homogeneous perceptibles are discriminated, properly speaking, not by their corresponding individual sense but by the unified perceptual capacity of the soul—that is, by the common sense—is no less counterintuitive than Aristotle's explanation as to how that takes place. I have suggested that Aristotle was stuck with that view because he was committed to the idea that only one special perceptible can actualize an individual sense at one time. Supposing that two or more homogeneous perceptibles must be discriminated by the unified perceptual capacity of the soul, Aristotle's explanation as to how that happens was bound to be rather complicated and, ultimately, disappointing.

3

Waking, Sleep, and Control of the Senses

Some of the most important features of animals come in four pairs of contraries. The first pair mentioned by Aristotle is sleep and waking (*DS* 1 436^{a}11–15), and it is the subject of the *De Somno et Vigilia*, the first in the series of three short treatises dealing with the phenomena of sleeping and dreaming in the collection *Parva Naturalia*.

The first question Aristotle addresses concerns the part of the animal to which sleep and waking appertain. He observes that sleep and waking, being two contrary states, must affect the same part of the animal. This must be the part with which the animal perceives, since to be awake is to have the senses either active or capable of becoming active, whereas to be asleep is to have the senses incapacitated, that is, incapable of becoming active. Because sleep and waking are states of the part with which the animal perceives, no plant can be either asleep or awake.

In the next step, Aristotle wants to show that it is necessary that sleep and waking periodically alternate in an animal, so that no animal can always be awake or always be asleep. This is established by an a priori argument which goes as follows. No natural activity can go on forever (at least not in the sublunary sphere). An extended period of activity is naturally followed by an incapacitation which is called rest. Since perceiving is a natural activity of the perceptual part of an animal, after an extended period of perceiving, the part with which the animal perceives necessarily becomes incapacitated and has to rest. Hence, it is necessary that waking, after a period of time, be replaced by sleep. Also, it is necessary that sleep, after a period of time, be replaced by waking. Rest is a deprivation of the natural activity which essentially preserves the ability to act. In other words, rest exists for the sake of activity. And as soon as the activity can be resumed, rest is naturally replaced by the activity. Thus, when the perceptual part has had enough of rest and can resume its activity, the animal wakes up and stays awake until the perceptual part becomes naturally incapacitated again. It is necessary, therefore, that waking and sleep alternate in an animal.

Aristotle's initial characterization of sleep as an incapacitation of perception after an extended period of waking is later qualified by specifying its material cause.[1] Such a qualification is necessary in order to distinguish sleep from other forms of incapacitation of the perceptual part, such as short faints and extended periods of unconsciousness. Sleep is the incapacitation of perception caused by the physiological processes following the intake of food. These processes can be summarized as follows. Ingested food is concocted in the stomach, and this process creates exhalations. The exhalations pass into the blood-vessels and ascend towards the brain, carrying chunks of food upwards. Upon reaching the brain, these chunks agglomerate, cool down, and then start to descend, pressing the blood and the heat therein downwards. This is supposed to explain a whole range of facts related to sleep: why we feel drowsy after meals, why our head and eyelids become heavy, why we have to lie down, why our limbs cool down in sleep, and so forth.

Most pertinent for our endeavour is Aristotle's discussion of the question he raises at the beginning of chapter 2. The question is this: due to which sense—or which senses, if there be more than one—does an animal sleep or wake? This question appears to ask which one, or several, of the individual senses is responsible for an animal's being asleep or awake. A satisfactory answer to this question must accommodate two facts. First, not all animals have all the five senses, and yet all animals sleep and wake. Second, sleep affects simultaneously all the senses that an animal has. Aristotle points out that when an animal sleeps none of its senses can perceive in an unqualified way.[2] Had sleep not affected all the senses that an animal happens to have, the sleeping animal would be perceiving in an unqualified way with the sense that is not affected by sleep, and that, Aristotle claims, is impossible. Hence, sleep must at once affect all the senses that an animal has.

Aristotle's answer occurs in a passage which may be quoted in full. I will divide it into five sections to facilitate its analysis.

(i) Since each particular sense has something special and something common—for instance, seeing is special to the sense of sight and hearing to the

[1] *DSV* 2 455^{b}2–13, 3 456^{b}9–12.

[2] The point of the reservation 'in an unqualified way' (ἁπλῶς, 455^{a}9) is to leave room for dreams, which are often treated as objects of perception in the *De Insomniis*, and possibly also for the faint sort of perceiving which may sometimes occur during sleep (*DI* 3 462^{a}19–27; cf. *DDS* 1 463^{a}12–17).

sense of hearing and likewise for each one of the senses—there is also some common power which accompanies all of them by which one also perceives that one is seeing and hearing; (ii) for certainly it is not by sight that one sees that one sees, and certainly one does not discriminate and is not capable of discriminating that sweet things are different from white things either by taste or by sight or by both, but by some common part of all the sense organs; (iii) for there is a single perceptual capacity, and the controlling sense organ is one, but the being of the perceptual capacity is different for each genus [of special perceptible], e.g. for sound and colour; (iv) and this is present most of all together with the sense organ of touch, for the latter can exist separately from the other sense organs, but the others are inseparable from it (these things have been treated in the studies on the soul); (v) hence it is clear that waking and sleep are affections of that sense organ. (*DSV* 2 455^{a}12–26)

In section (i) Aristotle says that the individual senses have special and common functions. Special functions, exemplified by sight seeing, are presumably functions peculiar to each sense. Common functions are due to 'some common power which accompanies all the senses'. Having introduced a common power which accompanies all the senses, Aristotle adds in the same breath that it is in charge of one common function, and that is 'perceiving that one sees and hears'. What this common function amounts to will be discussed shortly.

Section (ii) adduces some evidence for ascribing this particular function to a common power. The evidence is twofold: (a) it is not by sight that we see that we see, and (b) it is neither by sight nor by taste nor by both of them together that we discriminate white from sweet. We are familiar enough with (b). Neither sight nor taste alone can discriminate sweet from white because neither sense has access to the special perceptibles of the other sense. It is also clear from the preceding chapter that sight and taste together cannot discriminate white from sweet—unless accompanied by the common sense—because discrimination requires one single thing to which both special perceptibles are present at the same time. So (b) evidently mentions a common function, that is, a function only a common power which accompanies the senses can perform.

It is unclear whether (a) is also a common function that only a common power can achieve, because in *DA* III.2 425^{b}12–25 Aristotle seems to leave room for the possibility that it is by sight that we perceive that we see, indeed even that we *see* that we see. Nevertheless, it is evident from the grammar of the sentence (γὰρ δή, 455^{a}17) and its context that (a) is introduced to corroborate the preceding claim that it is by a common power that we perceive that we see and hear. The idea is usually taken to be this: when Aristotle says that it is not by sight that we see that we see, he means only that it is not by sight as a special sense, that is, in virtue of its 'special function' (*τι ἴδιον*), that we perceive that we see; hence, it must be in virtue of its 'common function' (*τι κοινόν*) that we do so, that is, by 'some common power which accompanies all the senses'.[3] Although I have no objections to the substance of this interpretation, I have some doubts about the text on which it is based.

The received text does not seem to be entirely sound at 455ª17, for *καὶ κρίνει δὴ καὶ δύναται κρίνειν* ('. . . and certainly one does not discriminate and is not capable of discriminating . . .') seems rather pointless, if not redundant. It was suggested to me by David Sedley that *κρίνει* conceals a corrupted *ἀκούει*.[4] If that is correct, (a) says that it is not by sight that we see that we see *and hear*. This makes perfect sense: sight has no access to hearing and its objects, so it cannot be by sight that we perceive that we see and hear. The emended text has three advantages. First, it ceases to be pointless or redundant. Second, it removes even the slightest appearance of contradiction between *DSV* 2 and *DA* III.2. Third, (a) now offers a straightforward piece of evidence for the preceding claim that it is by a common power that we perceive that we see and hear.

Whether or not we accept the emendation, it is clear that in section (ii) we find denials of two common functions to the individual senses, the first function being no other than the one explicitly ascribed to the common power ('perceiving that we see and hear'). The two denials in (a) and (b) are thus supposed to strengthen Aristotle's preceding claim that it is by some common power that we perceive that we see and hear.

Having denied these two common functions to the individual senses, in lines ª19–20 Aristotle assigns them to 'some common part of all the sense organs'. The phrase 'common part of all the sense organs' can be taken in various ways, but a reference to the controlling sense organ at ª21 makes it perfectly clear that Aristotle has in mind the central sense organ, the heart or its analogue in bloodless animals. The switch from talk of 'some common power' to talk of 'some common part of all sense organs' is somewhat unexpected, but it is not particularly problematic.

[3] Cf. Ross ((ed.)1961: 35), Kosman (1975: 517–18), Caston (2002: 779), Johansen (2006: 271–2).

[4] I suppose that Sedley's emendation requires excision of δή following the corrected *κρίνει*. A less intrusive alternative is to excise *κρίνει* altogether, leaving us with the adverbial *καὶ δὴ καί* ('and especially', 'and in particular').

Aristotle seems to suppose that if a function is ascribed to a capacity, it can also be ascribed to the bodily part in which this capacity is located, and vice versa. This is why he switches freely between talk of senses and talk of sense organs throughout this whole passage in *DSV* 2.[5]

The described situation in which we have the individual senses and the common power which accompanies them is briefly explained in a digression which marks section (iii). Aristotle reminds us that the perceptual capacity is one, but its being is different for each kind of special perceptible. It is also appended that the 'controlling sense organ is one'. This controlling sense organ should no doubt be equated with the 'common part of all the sense organs' from ^{a}19–20 and identified with the heart or its analogue in bloodless animals. I have explained in Part I, Chapter 3 why the unified perceptual capacity of the soul requires a central sense organ, so we can see where the appended sentence comes from.

Having established that the evoked common function, 'perceiving that we see and hear', belongs to the central sense organ, in section (iv) Aristotle says that this organ 'is present most of all together with the sense organ of touch'.[6] Although this means only that the central sense organ is present in an animal whenever the sense organ of touch is present, we know that the same organ, the heart or its analogue in bloodless animals, is both the central sense organ and the sense organ of touch.[7] The statement that the central sense organ coincides with the sense organ of touch is followed by an excursus at ^{a}23–5, incorporating a back-reference to the *DA*,[8] in which Aristotle says that the sense organ of touch is separable from the other sense organs, whereas the other sense organs are inseparable from it. That is to say, the sense organ of touch can be found in animals that have no other sense organ, whereas

[5] At 455^{a}4–19 Aristotle talks about the senses, at ^{a}19–26 about the sense organs, at ^{a}26–33 about the senses, and at ^{a}33–^{b}2 about the sense organs again.

[6] The construction *ἅμα τῷ ἁπτικῷ μάλιστα ὑπάρχει* is ambiguous. First, the phrase *τὸ ἁπτκόν*, 'that which is capable of touch', can refer to the sense of touch and to the organ of touch. Following Ross ((ed.)1955: 257), and contrary to the majority of interpreters, e.g. Beare ((ed.)1908: ad loc.), Hett ((ed.)1935: 327), Siwek ((ed.)1963: 179), Gallop ((ed.)1990: 65), I take it to refer to the *organ* of touch, because in the next sentence it is contrasted with 'the other sense organs' (*τῶν ἄλλων αἰσθητηρίων*). Second, *τῷ ἁπτικῷ* can be taken as the object of *ὑπάρχει* ('belongs to the *ἁπτικόν*'), as Gallop takes it, in which case *ἅμα* is somewhat difficult. Alternatively, *τῷ ἁπτικῷ* can be taken with *ἅμα*, leaving *ὑπάρχει* without an object, as I have done following the Latin translations and Beare. Ross, Hett, and Siwek translate the clause more descriptively.

[7] Cf. *DS* 2 438^{b}30–439^{a}2; *DJS* 3 469^{a}10–23; *PA* II.10 656^{a}27–31.

[8] Cf. *DA* II.2 413^{b}5–7, 414^{a}2–3, 3 415^{a}3–5, III.13 435^{a}12–14.

no other sense organ can be found without that of touch. As we shall see shortly, the move in section (iv) is relevant for the ensuing application of Aristotle's answer to one of the facts that it has to accommodate.

From all that has been said it should be obvious (φανερὸν τοίνυν, 455ª25), (v) that sleep and waking are affections of the sense organ of touch, which is also the central sense organ and the seat of the common power. This is essentially Aristotle's answer to the initial question. Let me extrapolate the premisses of the argument by which Aristotle arrived at his answer: (1) there is some common power which accompanies all the senses by which we perceive that we see and hear; (2) this function belongs to the central sense organ; (3) the central sense organ coincides with the sense organ of touch; (4) it follows that sleep and waking are affections of that organ.

The argument works if and only if there is a sufficiently close connection between perceiving that one sees and hears on the one hand, and sleep or waking on the other hand. That is, Aristotle ascribes sleep and waking to an organ on the basis of having ascribed perceiving that one sees and hears to that organ;[9] hence we must assume that perceiving that one sees and hears stands in a tight relationship with sleep and waking. This relationship with sleep and waking is a precious piece of information that can help us clarify what Aristotle means by 'perceiving that one sees and hears'. I think it is safe to assume that perceiving that one sees and hears is something characteristic of waking, and its lack something characteristic of sleep. This sort of relationship suffices to make Aristotle's argument work.

Now what is characteristic of waking that can be plausibly described as 'perceiving that one sees and hears', the lack whereof is characteristic of sleep? I suppose the first thing that comes to mind is—consciousness. When we are awake we are conscious, and when we are asleep we are unconscious. True enough, but being conscious involves all sorts of mental states, whereas 'perceiving that one sees and hears' seems to involve only perceptual states. Is Aristotle talking about perceptual consciousness, then? But perceptual consciousness is primarily concerned with mental states that represent the world through the senses, or, if we are perceptual realists like Aristotle, with things such as colours and sounds out there. For Aristotle, it is sight and hearing that are concerned with such things, and he is not talking about seeing and hearing, but

[9] More precisely, Aristotle ascribes sleep and waking to an organ on the basis of having ascribed perceiving that we see and hear to the *capacity* located in that organ.

about perceiving that we see and hear. Aristotle's use of a 'that' clause may suggest to the modern reader that he is talking about something rather conceptual, but Aristotle does not seem to make a difference between verbs of perception construed with direct object and with 'that' clauses. To Aristotle's mind, the perception *that* we see and hear does not differ significantly from the perception *of* seeing and hearing.[10]

David Armstrong speaks of introspective consciousness, 'a perception-like awareness of current states and activities in our own mind'.[11] He distinguishes two kinds of introspective consciousness. One is introspection proper, when we deliberately attend to our mental states and activities. This is a complex, fairly sophisticated, and relatively seldom used ability that cannot be taken for granted in all perceivers, and hence it is an unlikely candidate for Aristotle's 'perceiving that we see and hear'. The other kind of introspective consciousness is simpler, effortless, and usually present while we are awake. Armstrong calls it 'reflex' introspective consciousness, by analogy with mere reflex seeing which is always going on when we are awake, as opposed to careful scrutinizing of our visual environment. This 'reflex' introspective consciousness is what the truck-driver lacks before he 'comes to' and realizes that he has been driving for some time without being aware of what he has been doing. He has been seeing the road all along and responding appropriately by turning the steering-wheel, braking, and accelerating, but he has not been aware of doing so. Could it be that Aristotle's 'perceiving that we see and hear' is this sort of introspective consciousness that we normally have and only occasionally lose? I shall postpone a final answer to this question until the end of the next chapter. However, I think that Armstrong's notion of introspective consciousness—which he expressly links with Locke's notion of reflection and Kant's notion of 'inner sense'—gives the reader a rough idea of what Aristotle has in mind when he speaks about perceiving that we see and hear.

Let us return to the text of *DSV* 2 and proceed on the minimalist assumption that 'perceiving that we see and hear' amounts to the awareness of the activity of our senses. When we are awake, we are aware that our senses are active. For instance, when we attend someone's lecture, we are aware that our senses of sight and hearing are exercised.

10 Cf. Graeser (1978: 92 n. 2), Caston (2002: 770 n. 41), and Johansen (2006: 257, 262 n. 54).

11 Armstrong (1997: 724). See also Armstrong (1968: 92–115, 323–38).

If we happen to catch a whiff of the lecturer's perfume, we are also aware that our sense of smell is exercised. In short, when we are awake, we are aware of the activity of any number of our senses that happen to be actualized by their respective special perceptibles. When we are asleep, by contrast, we are not aware that we are not seeing and not hearing. Indeed, we are oblivious to the fact that none of our senses, not just sight and hearing, is active.

If this awareness of the activity of one's senses is at least part of what Aristotle means by 'perceiving that we see and hear', we can readily understand why he can conclude that the organ by which we sleep and wake is the organ by which we perceive that we see and hear. Awareness of the activity of one's senses is characteristic of waking, just as the lack of that awareness is characteristic of sleeping; hence, the organ to which that sort of awareness belongs is the organ to which waking and sleep belong. I suppose this allows us to infer that Aristotle's answer to the initial question posed at 455^a4–5 is the following: the sense (or, more appropriately, the perceptual capacity, *αἴσθησις*) due to which an animal sleeps and wakes is not any of the individual senses, but the common power which accompanies them all, that is, the common sense.

It is perfectly reasonable to ascribe the awareness of the activity of our senses to the common sense. Perhaps an individual sense might have access to its own activity, as *DA* III.2 suggests, but it certainly cannot have access to other individual senses and their activities. The common sense, by contrast, is the sort of thing that can have access to all the individual senses, and hence it is just the sort of thing to provide us with awareness of the activity of any number of senses that happen to be actualized by their respective special perceptibles. Note that this implies that the awareness in question is unified, for it is a single awareness attending to the activity of any number of senses.

It is equally reasonable to ascribe sleep and waking to the common sense. Sleep and waking require some sort of control of the individual senses, such that they are all turned on when the animal is waking, and all shut off when the animal is sleeping. None of the individual senses can have that sort of control over the other senses, but the common sense is precisely the sort of thing that can. The state of the common sense dictates the state of the individual senses: when the common sense is on, all the individual senses are on; when the common sense is off, all the individual senses are off. On the other hand, it is not the case that when an individual sense is off, the common sense is off too. Otherwise the permanent loss or temporary incapacitation of an individual sense would incapacitate the common sense too. As Aristotle says at 455ª33–ᵇ2 (and reiterates at ᵇ10–13): 'When the sense organ which controls all the others, and in which all others converge, has undergone some affection, all others must also be affected with it, whereas if any of them is incapacitated, it need not be incapacitated as well.'

Before I proceed to explain how Aristotle's answer accommodates the two facts it ought to accommodate, I would like to make a brief digression. The interpretation I have offered in this chapter clearly demands a sharp distinction between the common power which accompanies all the senses, that is, the common sense, and the imaginative capacity of the soul.[12] Since dreams are images experienced in sleep, it is necessary that the imaginative capacity of the soul be active in sleep, whereas the common sense is necessarily inactive in sleep. This is important for two reasons. First, it demonstrates that the 'common sense' to which images are ascribed in *DM* 1 450ª10 cannot be the same thing as 'some common power which accompanies all the senses' to which perceiving that we see and hear is ascribed in *DSV* 2 455ª16. Second, in *DI* 2–3 Aristotle explains that we are taken in by dream-images because there is something in us that 'affirms' them. If the common sense is necessarily inactive in sleep, it cannot be the thing that 'affirms' dream-images.[13]

The first fact Aristotle's answer has to accommodate is that not all animals have all the senses, and yet all animals sleep and wake. In section (ii) of his argument Aristotle assigned common functions of the senses, including the awareness of the activity of one's senses, to the controlling sense organ. The crucial move came in section (iv), where he established that the central sense organ coincides with the sense organ of touch. Since there is no animal without the sense organ of touch, it follows that there is no animal without the controlling sense organ either. Hence, all animals, including those very modest ones with the sense of touch

[12] Cf. *DI* 1 459ª8–22.

[13] Cf. *DI* 3 461ᵇ4–7. A few interpreters—Zeller (1921: 544)), Block (1960: 98–9), Van der Eijk ((ed.)1994: 50, 76)—think that a function of the common sense is to 'affirm' the changes coming from the peripheral sense organs, be they caused by external objects or by earlier perceptions, which is how we take their content to have objective reference. This is a difficult topic, brimming with textual and interpretative problems, and it requires a separate study. My hunch, however, is that 'objectification' is not a distinct activity of any particular cognitive capacity of the soul, but an integral part of every cognitive activity. Unless opposed by a higher cognitive capacity, we go along with reports of a lower one.

only, or touch and taste,[14] are aware of the activity of their senses, which implies that all animals without exception wake and sleep.

The second fact that has to be accommodated is that sleep simultaneously affects all the senses that an animal has. Aristotle sees a problem with the suggestion that 'the capacities which need not, and in a way cannot, be active simultaneously, should necessarily be inactive and immobilized simultaneously'.[15] The problem of simultaneous inactivity of several senses is to some extent parallel to the problem of simultaneous perception. We have seen in Part III, Chapter 1 that Aristotle adhered to the principle that only one act of perception can occur at one time. Consequently, two senses produce two acts of perception, and two acts of perception necessarily occur at two different times. Hence, there can be no simultaneous perception. This is, I take it, what Aristotle has in mind when he says that the senses 'in a way (τρόπον τινά) cannot be active simultaneously'. Namely, the senses cannot be active simultaneously if they operate independently from one another.

We know, however, that the senses need not operate independently from one another. Being distinct parts or aspects of one and the same thing, namely the perceptual capacity of the soul, they can operate jointly. That is, we perceive two things simultaneously, say red and sweet, not in two independent acts of sight and taste, but in a single act of the common sense. Of course, the relevant individual senses, sight and taste, are both active in that act of perception, but they are involved, strictly speaking, as two distinct parts or aspects of one and the same thing—the perceptual capacity of the soul—rather than as two mutually independent capacities.

The perceptual capacity of the soul, as we have seen earlier, can perform certain acts as a unity, in which case we can speak of a higher-order perceptual power in addition to the individual senses; that is what Aristotle calls the 'common power which accompanies all the senses' in *DSV* 2, and what we have been calling the 'common sense' throughout this book. Simultaneous perception of red and sweet, therefore, is in fact one single act of the common sense which unifies two distinct acts of the individual senses, seeing a colour and tasting a flavour.

[14] At 455^{a}27 Aristotle says that touch is the only sense that all animals have. Earlier on, at 455^{a}7, he said that all animals have touch *and taste*. We must remember that for Aristotle the sense of taste is a form of the sense of touch, both because it operates through direct contact and because its special perceptibles are tangible qualities. This topic is discussed at length by Johansen (1998: 178–225).

[15] *DSV* 2 455^{a}29–31.

This solution to the problem of simultaneous perception is neatly applied to the problem of simultaneous inactivity of the senses during sleep. Just as the individual senses can be simultaneously active because they are integrated in the perceptual capacity of the soul, they can be simultaneously inactive for the very same reason. That is to say, just as simultaneous perception is made possible by the activity of the common sense which unifies the activities of the individual senses, simultaneous inactivity of the individual senses is made possible by the inactivity of the common sense which affects all the individual senses. The individual senses can thus all be simultaneously inactive during sleep due to the inactivity of the common sense.[16] As we have put it earlier, when the common sense is on, all the individual senses are on; when the common sense is off, all the individual senses are off. This can be further elucidated by saying that the perceptual capacity of the soul must be off as a unity for its conceptually distinct parts, namely the individual senses, to be all off at the same time. Similarly for waking: the perceptual capacity of the soul must be on as a unity in order for its conceptually distinct parts to be all on at the same time.

To conclude. The analysed passage in *DSV* 2 tells us that the common sense is in charge of perceiving that we see and hear, and hence also of waking and sleep. We have seen that sleep and waking entail control of the senses which consists in keeping them all on in periods of waking, as well as in keeping them all off in periods of sleep. The importance of the controlling function is evident enough. Without it an animal would be placed in a situation similar to Plato's wooden horse. Neither awake nor asleep, the animal would be in some strange state in which the senses are turned on or shut off independently of one another, each taking a break for some time and reactivating itself after a while, without any co-ordination with the other senses. No doubt that would render life very difficult, and probably quite short.

As for perceiving that we see and hear, we have interpreted it provisionally as the awareness of the activity of our senses which characterizes the waking state. We have seen that it is the work of the common sense and that none of the individual senses can achieve it. Building on the results of this chapter, let us turn to another passage which deals with 'perceiving that we see and hear'.

[16] Of course, sleep does not entail just any type of inactivity of the individual senses. It is not merely that the senses do not happen to be exercised in sleep, but rather that they are temporarily incapacitated, unable to become exercised.

4

Perceiving That We See and Hear, and Monitoring of the Senses

The theme of perceiving that we see and hear crops up again in a well-known passage at the beginning of *DA* III.2. The passage has received a lot of scholarly attention in the past, largely because it can be fruitfully related to our notions of consciousness.[1] In this chapter, I do not wish to discuss the merits of individual interpretations. What I want to do instead is to provide an account of that passage with an eye on the results from the preceding chapter.[2] That will enable us to probe more deeply into the phenomenon of 'perceiving that we see and hear'.

Since we perceive that we see and hear, it must be either by sight that one perceives that one sees, or by another [sense]. But then the same [sense] will be of sight and of colour as its object. Hence, either there will be two [senses] of the same thing or one [sense will be] of itself. Moreover, if the sense which is of sight were indeed another [sense], either they will go *ad infinitum* or some will be of itself. So that should be admitted of the first [sense]. But there is a difficulty. If to perceive by sight is to see, and what is seen is colour or that which has colour, then if one is to see the seeing thing, the primary seeing thing will also have colour. Well now, it is clear that to perceive by sight is not one thing; for even when we do not see, we discriminate darkness and light by sight, although not in the same way. Moreover, the seeing thing is also in a way coloured; for each sense organ is receptive of the perceptible without its matter; that is why

[1] Notable discussions of the passage are Kahn (1966), Hardie (1976), Modrak (1981*a*), Kosman (1975), Osborne (1983), Brunschwig (1991: 465–70), Caston (2002), and Johansen (2006).

[2] Discussions of the problem of 'perceiving that we see and hear' in the literature usually start with an interpretation of the *DA* III.2 passage, and then proceed to explore how the proposed interpretation fits the *DSV* 2 passage. My strategy is reverse. I opt for it because Aristotle's statement in *DSV* 2 as to how we perceive that we see and hear is forthright, whereas in *DA* III.2 his discussion is aporetic. Hence, it seems more promising to approach *DA* III.2 with an interpretation of *DSV* 2 at hand, rather than to proceed the other way round.

perceptions and representations are present in the sense organs even when the perceptibles are gone. (*DA* III.2 425^b12–25)

I assume that 'perceiving that we see and hear' in the opening line refers to the same phenomenon mentioned in *DSV* 2, namely the awareness of the activity of our senses. Aristotle takes this phenomenon for granted, I take it, because it is characteristic of the waking state, and hence obvious to everyone. The idea is that if you are awake, it can be assumed that you are aware of the activity of your senses. Observe, however, that Aristotle does not introduce this phenomenon in order to ask by which perceptual capacity we achieve awareness of the activity of our senses of sight *and hearing*. That would be a non-starter as far as the argument in this passage goes. Neither sight nor hearing nor any other individual sense could provide that sort of awareness, as we have seen in the preceding chapter. What he asks, rather, is by which perceptual capacity we achieve the awareness of the activity of some one sense, namely sight. This awareness of the activity of a single sense is what he needs to get his argument going, and it is something logically implied by the awareness of the activity of two, three, or any number of senses that happen to be actualized: perceiving that we see is part and parcel of perceiving that we see and hear.

The first sentence formulates two alternatives as to how we perceive that we see, and I assume, moreover, that the second alternative is restricted not only to perceptual capacities, as opposed to rational capacities, but more narrowly to the level of the individual senses, excluding the common sense. Although the pronoun *ἑτέρα* at ^{b}13 could in principle stand for any cognitive capacity, and the noun *αἴσθησις* with its cognates could perhaps be taken very widely to include types of awareness afforded by rational capacities, there is no indication whatsoever that this is how the text was intended to be read, given its place and role in *DA* III.[3] Moreover, the pronoun *ἑτέρα* could in

[3] I suppose that later Platonists would attempt to read the passage with reference to rational capacities. Plutarch of Athens is reported to have thought that the capacity by which we perceive that we perceive is belief (δόξα), and belief belongs to the rational part of the soul; cf. Philoponus (1897: 464.23–7). Damascius, Simplicius, and Philoponus agree that we perceive that we perceive by means of a rational capacity, although they disagree in detail. Damascius thinks that it is the so-called 'attending part of the rational soul' (*τὸ προσεκτικὸν τῆς λογικῆς ψυχῆς*) that monitors all actions of the soul, and hence also perceptions; cf. Damascius (1977: I.269.4–6, 271.2–3, II.19.2–5, 21.1–3). Simplicius and Philoponus seem to be true to the Neoplatonic teaching according to which reason permeates other parts of the soul, and hence also the senses. And it is in virtue of being permeated by reason that the senses are capable of perceiving themselves;

principle stand for any perceptual capacity, including the perceptual power which emerges from the unity of the perceptual capacity of the soul. I submit, however, that in this argument that is not an option. My reason for excluding the common sense from the range of possible referents of the pronoun ἑτέρα at ᵇ13 is twofold. First, in this passage Aristotle is taking issue with Plato, who does not operate with a notion of a perceptual capacity over and above the individual senses, and I shall argue below that Aristotle wants to refute Plato fairly, relying only on those terms recognized by Plato. Second, the inclusion of the common sense would render Aristotle's argument invalid on more than one step. Look at the first step. The whole argument proceeds on the assumption that the alternatives specified in the first premiss are exhaustive and mutually exclusive ('it is *either* by sight . . . *or* by another [sense]'). Now if the common sense were a possible referent of the pronoun ἑτέρα at ᵇ13, the alternatives would cease to be mutually exclusive. Presumably, perceiving that we see requires our perceptual capacity of the soul to be active both as sight and as a unity, so the right thing to say would be that we perceive that we see by sight *and* by the common sense.

To say that the common sense is not a possible referent of the pronoun ἑτέρα at ᵇ13, however, does not imply that the notion of the common sense is incompatible with what Aristotle says in the argument. For instance, one could argue that when Aristotle speaks of sight (ὄψις) in this passage, he does not take it narrowly, with reference to its special function only, but more widely, to include its common function. An indication that he might speak of sight more widely is found at ᵇ20–2, where Aristotle suggests that to perceive by sight is not a simple thing. I shall say more about this below.

Now the question that naturally comes up is this: why does Aristotle refrain from making the common sense explicit in this passage? Why is this passage centred on the individual senses? Many commentators have observed the connection between this passage and Plato's *Charmides*. I am inclined to think that our passage is in fact written in response to the problems raised in that dialogue.

In the *Charmides*, Critias suggests that temperance is knowledge which is not knowledge of some object, but only of itself (167d11–c2). To show that such a notion is implausible, Socrates takes a series of relatives and puts each one of them in relation to itself instead of its

cf. Simplicius (1882: 187.35–188.3), Philoponus (1897: 464.30–467.12). Discussions of this topic can be found in Bernard (1987) and Lautner (1994).

co-relative. He starts with examples of perception and shows that there could be no such thing as a sight that sees no colour but sees itself, or hearing that hears no sounds but hears itself. 'Take, then,' Socrates says to Critias, 'all the senses together and consider whether there is any one of them that seems to you to be a sense of the other senses and of itself, but which perceives none of the things which the other senses perceive', to which Critias gives a negative answer (167d7–10). Socrates proceeds with examples of emotions, a desire that is a desire for no pleasure but for itself and for other desires, similarly with wish, love, fear, and culminating with the example of an opinion that opines nothing other than itself. All such cases are regarded as unsound, which calls into question the existence of a knowledge which is not knowledge of anything other than itself.

Socrates carries on with his investigation by taking another series of relatives and ascribing to each one of them the character of its respective co-relative. The larger is normally larger than something smaller. Hence, if there is something that is larger than itself, it would at the same time be smaller than itself. Similarly with the double, the heavier, the lighter, the older, and the younger. All such cases are pronounced to be 'absolutely impossible', whereas another set of relatives is said to be 'very doubtful', though not impossible. This other set of relatives includes perception. 'Take the example of hearing,' Socrates says to Critias; 'don't we say that hearing is of nothing other than sound? . . . Then if it hears itself, it will hear itself by having sound, for otherwise it would not be able to hear. . . . And sight, I take it, my good man, if it sees itself, it is necessary for it to have some colour; for sight could certainly never see anything that has no colour' (168d3–e1). Socrates says that such cases 'also produce disbelief in some people, though perhaps there are some in whom it does not'. To this Socrates significantly adds: 'What we need, my friend, is some great man to give an adequate interpretation of this point in every detail' (168e9–169a3).

What I want to suggest, then, is that Aristotle accepts Plato's challenge, and that the opening passage of *DA* III.2 is a reply to the difficulties raised by Plato. Since Plato does not have a conception of a perceptual capacity other than the individual senses, to meet Plato's challenge in a fair manner, using only those terms that were accepted by him, Aristotle must leave out the common sense and talk of the individual senses.

This serves the purpose of *DA* III.2 quite well. We have seen earlier that the overall aim of *DA* III.1 is to show that there can be no sense in addition to the five senses discussed in *DA* II.7–11. In the first part of *DA*

III.1 (424^b22–425^a13) Aristotle argued that there can be no additional sense for the special perceptibles, and in the second part (425^a14–29) that there can be no special sense for the common perceptibles. In *DA* III.2 Aristotle wants to show that no additional individual sense needs to be postulated to account for further, more complex perceptual operations. Provided that the five senses are integrated in the perceptual capacity of the soul, even the complex perceptual operations, such as perceiving that we see or perceptual discrimination, can receive a satisfactory explanation. So there is no need to postulate any additional individual sense to explain such operations, much less to explain them with reference to higher cognitive capacities, as Plato and his heirs have been inclined to do. To put it differently, if one refuses to explain complex perceptual operations by appealing to higher cognitive capacities—and we have seen why Aristotle should like to refuse that line of explanation—one does not need to postulate additional individual senses; it will suffice to show that the five familiar senses are appropriately integrated in the perceptual capacity of the soul, which is precisely what Aristotle does at the end of *DA* III.2.

Let us now return to our passage and discuss some details. Whether one perceives that one sees by sight or by another sense, it follows that there will be a sense both of sight and of colour. But why does Aristotle think that should follow? An explanation can be found a little later, at 425^b26–426^a26, where Aristotle tells us that the activity of a sense and the activity of the respective object of perception is one and the same activity only different in being. Because the activity of sight is inseparable from the activity of colour, the sense by which we perceive that we see could not perceive sight without perceiving colour too.

Now given that there will be a sense both of sight and of colour, it follows either (a) that there will be two senses of colour, or (b) that one sense will be of itself.[4] Both options are prima facie problematic. (a) is usually taken to be problematic on account of Aristotle's definition of colour as a special perceptible (τὸ ἴδιον) of sight, which means that no other sense can perceive it.[5] Note, however, that there would be

[4] To say that a sense is 'of itself' means that it perceives its own activity. Caston (2002) argues that the whole passage is not concerned with the capacity by which we perceive that we see, as it is traditionally thought, but only with the activity by which we do so. For criticisms of Caston's activity reading, see Johansen (2006).

[5] Osborne (1983: 401–2) and Caston (2002: 765–6) challenge this analysis. The other sense, they think, may be a second sense of sight, and there is nothing problematic about two senses of sight having colour as their object. However, we have seen in Ch. 1

nothing problematic about this alternative if the common sense were a candidate for the 'other sense', since the common sense does not apprehend colour as its special perceptible, but supposedly through apprehending the activity of sight. (b) is problematic because Plato's *Charmides* has been shown to doubt the idea of a sense related to itself. It may also be problematic because Aristotle claimed earlier that there was no perception of the sense itself.[6]

Apart from these, there are further problems for (b). If we perceive that we see by a sense other than sight, then either an infinite regress will ensue, or else there will be a sense which is of itself. It is not entirely clear what makes Aristotle assume that the infinite regress is necessary. I suppose the underlying assumption is that the activity of every sense is perceived. Note that this is true of every individual sense, since we perceive that we see, that we hear, that we smell, and so on. Now if the activity of every sense is perceived, and if it is perceived by another sense, then this other sense's activity also has to be perceived, and so on ad infinitum.[7] The way to break the regress is to assume that some sense perceives its own activity. Aristotle then prudently suggests that we should assume this of the first sense in the series: it is better to suppose that we perceive that we see by sight, rather than by a series of senses which must end with some sense that is of itself. Again, I do not think we would have this problem if the common sense were a candidate for the 'other sense'. The underlying assumption that the activity of every sense is perceived does not seem to be true if the common sense is counted in. The activity of an individual sense and the activity of the common sense have different explanations, as we shall see, so there is no reason to suppose that if the activity of every individual sense is perceived, the activity of the common sense must be perceived too.

So there are two problems for the alternative that we perceive that we see by a sense other than sight: duplication of the senses concerned with the same type of special perceptible, and the infinite regress. The other alternative, namely that we perceive that we see by sight, is not devoid of problems either. If to perceive by sight is to see, and what is seen

of this Part that the idea of two individual senses of the same object within the same soul is unacceptable to Aristotle.

[6] This claim was made in *DA* II.5 417^{a}2–9, in the context of Aristotle's explanation of why the senses do not perceive themselves *prior to* being actualized by their respective objects. In *DA* III.2 Aristotle suggests that the senses perceive themselves *while* being actualized by their respective objects.

[7] For a different interpretation of the infinite regress, see Caston (2002: 773–5).

is a colour or something coloured, then it follows that if one is to see the seeing thing, the first-order seeing thing would have to be coloured. Observe that this paraphrases Plato's objection in the *Charmides*: 'If sight sees itself, it is necessary for it to have some colour; for sight could certainly never see anything that has no colour' (168d3–e1).

Aristotle offers two different solutions to this problem. The first solution consists in contesting the objection: perceiving by sight is not a simple thing. Aristotle gives an example: even when we do not see, it is by sight that we discriminate darkness and light. It is not entirely clear what is implied in this example, and what is the contrast intended by 'although not in the same way'.[8] Aristotle might have in mind that even when we have our eyes shut ('when we do not see'), it is by sight that we tell whether it is dark or light outside.[9] He might also have in mind that it is by sight that we perceive darkness and very bright objects, even though neither involves seeing colours. In *DA* II.10 422^{a}20–3 Aristotle writes: 'Sight is of both the visible and the invisible (for darkness is invisible, and sight discriminates this too), and further of that which is very bright (for this is invisible but in a different way from darkness).' Whichever way we interpret Aristotle's example, its point is clear: there is more to be perceived by sight than colours and coloured things. So while Plato may be correct to say that 'sight could certainly never *see* anything that has no colour', perceiving by sight is not restricted to seeing a colour or something coloured. Hence, it does not necessarily follow that the first-order seeing thing must be coloured in order to be perceived by sight.

The second solution consists in defusing the objection with Aristotle's theory of perception: the first-order seeing thing is, after all, coloured in a way. Each sense organ, Aristotle adds, receives perceptible form without matter. The evidence is that perceptions and representations are present in the sense organs even when the perceptibles themselves are gone. Insofar, then, as the eye receives a colour in an act of seeing, it can be said to be coloured. Thus the suggestion that the first-order seeing thing is coloured ceases to be problematic, and with it the idea that it is by sight that we perceive that we see. In fact, this seems to open the possibility that we *see* that we see.

To sum up what has been said so far about the *DA* III.2 passage: Aristotle offers three alternatives about how we perceive that we see.

[8] For a sound discussion of the sentence at ^{b}21–2, see Johansen (2006: 249–50).
[9] This interpretation of Aristotle's example was suggested to me by David Sedley.

We do so (i) by a sense other than sight; (ii) by sight, but not in a way that involves colour, that is, not by seeing; (iii) by sight, and in a way that does involve colour, that is, by seeing. We have seen that the first possibility is problematic on account of two unpalatable consequences: duplication of the senses perceiving the same special perceptible, and the infinite regress. Admittedly, neither of these two problems would arise if the common sense were a candidate for the 'other sense' by which we perceive that we see. Indeed, the whole passage would look very different had the common sense been on the table. As for the second and third possibilities, the passage does not seem to decide between them. If there is room left for the common sense in the passage, it will have to be found between the last two possibilities.

As we have seen in the previous chapter, *DSV* 2 explicitly says that it is not by sight that we see that we see, and that contradicts the third possibility in *DA* III.2. An elegant way to save Aristotle from contradiction is to accept Sedley's textual emendation at *DSV* 2 455^{a}17.[10] What the emended text of *DSV* 2 says is that it is not by sight that we see that we see *and hear*, so that there is no conflict between the two passages. If one hesitates to accept the emendation, however, one can resolve the contradiction along the line of interpretation spelled out in the previous chapter. That is, one can insist that in *DSV* 2 Aristotle does not deny that it is by sight that we perceive that we see, but only that we *see* that we see; in other words, what *DSV* 2 denies is that we perceive the activity of sight by virtue of its special function. Of course, this is only one step towards resolving the contradiction. What remains to be done is to interpret the third possibility in *DA* III.2 in such a way that there is no clash with the appropriately interpreted *DSV* 2 passage.

Johansen attempted to do just that in his paper from 2006. He argues that Aristotle's preferred view is indeed that we *see* that we see, yet that our second-order seeing is very different from our first-order seeing. Whereas our first-order seeing is a case of proper perception, since what is perceived is the special perceptible of sight, our second-order seeing is a case of accidental perception, according to Johansen, since 'it involves not just perceiving color but attributing this color to one's own sense of sight'.[11] Assuming that accidental perception is a common function of sight, Johansen can conclude that we indeed see that we see, although this second-order seeing, being a case of accidental perception, is due to sight's common function, and hence to the common sense. So in

[10] See Part III, Ch. 3, p. 166. [11] Johansen (2006: 260).

denying that it is by sight that we see that we see, in *DSV* 2 Aristotle denies only that it is by sight's special function that we perceive that we see, whereas by suggesting that it is by sight that we see that we see in *DA* III.2, Aristotle implies that it is by a common function of sight that we perceive that we see. Thus there is no contradiction between *DSV* 2 and *DA* III.2.

I am not comfortable with the idea that perceiving that we see is a form of accidental perception. My reservation does not come from the assumption that accidental perception is not really perception, or that it is perception but such that it necessarily involves concepts, as some commentators have held.[12] Rather, my reservation comes from the assumption that accidental perception is contingent in a way in which perception of seeing is not. I am unable to discuss accidental perception at any length here, but let it suffice to say two things. First, I take it that an animal needs to develop its ability to perceive accidentally, to acquire what it will subsequently associate with the special perceptibles in acts of accidental perception. How good an animal is at accidental perception thus depends on the range of special perceptibles it can perceive and on the range of things it can associate with the special perceptibles it perceives. If you have keen sight and good hearing, as well as extensive experience and a vast body of knowledge, you will perceive many more accidental perceptibles than I, and do so with fewer errors. The ability to perceive that we see, on the other hand, seems to come naturally and to require no development. It does not depend on the range of special perceptibles that one can perceive, and still less on the range of things one can associate with the special perceptibles. Consequently, there is little room for the possibility that, when actually engaged in seeing, one errs about perceiving that one sees. Second, accidental perception does not seem to be the sort of thing that follows upon each and every act of seeing or hearing. On the other hand, Aristotle thinks that every act of seeing or hearing is accompanied by second-order perception.[13] The claims I have just made about perceiving that one sees will be justified later.

[12] e.g. Beare (1906: 286), Hicks ((ed.)1907: 360–1), Block (1960: 94), Kahn (1966: 46, 64), Graeser (1978: 90).

[13] One could think of more specific objections to the claim that perceiving that we see is a form of accidental perception. Here is one. The colour seen can be associated with one's own sense of sight, but presumably also with another person's sense of sight, e.g. when we both look at the same object. Insofar as they are two acts of accidental perception, there is no difference between them; but surely my perceiving that I see is a very different sort of experience from my perceiving that the other person sees.

Johansen's interpretation of the third alternative in *DA* III.2, although ingenious, is based on tenuous grounds. In fact, I think it is extremely difficult to follow his strategy and try to provide a plausible interpretation of the third possibility in *DA* III.2 which would save it from contradicting the *DSV* 2 passage. A more promising strategy of aligning the two passages would be to argue that the third possibility in *DA* III.2 is not put forward as a serious option. There are at least two ways to argue that, and I find them both attractive independently of their role in resolving the contradiction between *DA* III.2 and *DSV* 2. First, one can exploit the dialectical dimension of the passage in *DA* III.2. Plato raised a difficulty which rests, among others, on the premiss that to perceive by sight is to see ('if to perceive by sight is to see . . .', ^{b}19). Aristotle's first reply ('to perceive by sight is not one thing', ^{b}20) is to contest that premiss. Aristotle's second reply ('the seeing thing is in a way coloured', ^{b}22) shows that the difficulty can be defused even if one accepts its premiss. Since Aristotle seems to accept the premiss only for the sake of argument, we should not think that his second reply carries any commitment.

Second, when Aristotle says that the organ of sight is coloured 'in a way' (ὡς κεχρωμάτισται), one can exploit the qualification and say that what is coloured 'in a way' can only be seen 'in a way'. Relying on the Aristotelian doctrine of reception of form without matter, one can maintain that seeing a coloured object out there is very different from seeing the in-a-way-coloured eye. The former involves reception of the object's perceptible form without matter, whilst the latter does not. Hence, the latter cannot be seeing in any strict sense.

Let us, then, proceed on the assumption that the third possibility in *DA* III.2 is not really an option. We are left with the second possibility, namely that we perceive that we see by sight, but not in a way that involves colour. The way in which we perceive colour is certainly due to the special function of sight, that is, we perceive colour by sight as an individual sense. What about the other way in which we perceive by sight, the way that does not involve colour? To what is that way of perceiving by sight due? There is no simple answer to this question, because perceiving by sight in that other way does not seem to be a simple thing, either. Although neither perceiving darkness nor perceiving very bright objects involves colour, these two perceptions seem to implicate sight in different ways. Sight is palpably affected by bright objects, so much so that excessively bright objects can destroy it.[14] Darkness, on the other hand, does not seem to affect sight at all. Leaving the case of very bright objects aside, I would like to argue that perceiving darkness is a common function of sight.

When we sit in a completely dark room with our eyes wide open, what do we see? We might be inclined to say that we see darkness, but strictly speaking we do not see anything. Our sight is not active because there is nothing that activates it, no perceptible form is received. But if our sight is not activated, how do we perceive darkness? One might be tempted to answer that perception of darkness amounts to the inactivity of sight, nothing more and nothing less. It takes little reflection to see that this answer cannot be right. Our sight is inactive also when we are asleep. Clearly we do not perceive darkness when we are in sleep, because then we are not aware of the state of our senses. So to perceive darkness we must be awake and aware of our sight's inactivity. This awareness of our sight's inactivity is the first, but not the only condition of perceiving darkness. Suppose someone suffered an injury whereby he lost his sense of sight. Lying awake in this traumatic state, surely he is aware of his sight's inactivity, but that does not amount to his perceiving darkness. A blind person is deprived of visual data because he has no sense of sight due to some malfunction in his sensory apparatus. A sighted person who perceives darkness, by contrast, is deprived of visual data because no such data are available due to external circumstances, notably the absence of light. What this situation shows is that perception of darkness requires the presence of sight. Although inactive at the moment, one's sense of sight must be 'on standby', as it were, fully functional, ready to become activated as soon as the external circumstances change and visual data become available again.

It is important to clarify these two conditions of perception of darkness. It might be suggested that perception of darkness requires awareness not only of sight's inactivity but also of sight's presence. In a way that is true, but one should not think that there is anything about our sight's inactivity itself that tells us whether our sight is inactive merely because no visual data are available or because it is incapacitated. To illustrate this, suppose that the unfortunate person from the previous passage had his optical nerve severed, without any other damage to his head. Suppose, furthermore, that he wakes up in a completely dark

[14] Cf. *DA* II.10 422^{a}20–31 and 12 424^{a}28–32. Some interpreters take Aristotle to make the same point in III.2 426^{a}30–^{b}7, but this is challenged by Barker (1981).

room and feels no pain or any other sensation that might indicate to him that he is blind. This person would be aware of his sight's inactivity, but could he tell whether he is blind or merely perceiving darkness? I do not think he could. He would not realize that he is blind until told so, or until he learns that such external circumstances obtain that he would see things had his sight been present.

Deprivation of sensory stimuli is not an alarming experience when we know that our senses are present. We have this knowledge usually because sensory deprivation ensues after stimulation, because it does not last long, and because we do not feel any pain or sensation that might suggest that something is wrong with us. However, when we do not know that our senses are in good shape, or if deprivation of sensory stimuli lasts for too long, it is likely to be a disturbing experience. So, in normal circumstances awareness of a sense's inactivity informs us about external circumstances such as darkness or silence; in abnormal circumstances it warns us that something might be wrong with our sense and the sensory apparatus.

Now this awareness of a sense's inactivity cannot be the work of the sense's special function, since this function is not exercised. It can only be the work of the sense's common function. So it seems that we perceive darkness by being aware of our sight's inactivity, we perceive silence by being aware of our hearing's inactivity, and so forth, and such awareness is supplied by the common sense.

This is exactly what we would expect. Since awareness of the activity of a sense is the work of the common sense, it is natural to suppose that awareness of the inactivity of that sense also is the work of the common sense. What I am suggesting, then, is that the common sense provides us with the awareness of both activity and inactivity of the senses. This view has long been attributed to Aristotle and to his successor Theophrastus. In the context of discussing how we perceive that we perceive, Priscian of Lydia writes that Theophrastus 'sets out his argument on the same lines as Aristotle, wanting the common sense to be that which has this extra awareness, since it perceives both the activity of each [sense] and its inactivity. For opposites are of the same [sense].'[15] Even before Priscian, some such view was advocated by Augustine: 'The sense of the eye does not see that it is seeing or not seeing, and hence it cannot judge what it lacks or what it enjoys; however, the inner sense warns the soul

[15] Translated by P. Huby in Priscian (1997: 31); the Greek text is Priscian (1886: 21.32–22.1) = FHSG 296.

of an animal to open the closed eye and provide what it perceives is missing.'[16]

We are now in a position to expand our minimalist assumption from the preceding chapter, namely that 'perceiving that we see and hear' amounts to the awareness of the activity of our senses. It involves not only perceiving that we see and hear (e.g. when we engage in a conversation), but also perceiving that we do *not* see and hear (e.g. when we find ourselves in a completely dark recording studio). So to perceive that we see and hear refers to the awareness we have of both the activity and inactivity of our senses. Indeed, when we are awake, we are aware not only of the activity of one, two, or any number of senses that happen to be actualized by their special perceptibles, but we are also aware of the inactivity of one, two, or any number of senses that happen not to be actualized by their special perceptibles. When we are asleep, by contrast, we are not aware of the inactivity of our senses. This is, I take it, what 'perceiving that we see and hear' really amounts to, both in *DSV* 2 and in *DA* III.2.

Let us try to accommodate this finding within Aristotle's theory. We have seen that Aristotle evokes the idea of reception of form without matter towards the end of our passage in *DA* III.2. The seeing thing is in a way coloured because the sense organ receives the perceptible form without matter. In an act of perception, then, the perceptible form of an external object is present in the sense organ too. Its presence in the sense organ explains why this form is available for perception even when the external object is gone. Johansen has argued that its presence in the sense organ explains also why it is the individual sense located in that sense organ that perceives its own acts of perception. When sight perceives itself seeing, Johansen maintains, it is perceiving the same perceptible form that it perceives in first-order vision, only now it is perceiving the sensible form as manifested in its own organ, the eye.[17]

However, we must keep in mind that Aristotle introduces the idea of reception of form without matter in the context of his reply to a difficulty the premisses of which he does not seem to share. Hence, we should pause before we follow Johansen and think that reception of form by the sense organ is the whole explanation of perceiving that we see. Recall Aristotle's observation from *DS* 2 (438^b12–16), that soldiers go blind when the channels behind their eyes are severed by a blow to

[16] Augustine, *De Libero Arbitrio* II.6.12 (Green) = *PL* XXXII.1247 (Migne).
[17] See Johansen (2006: 254).

the temple. As I have argued in Part I, Chapter 3, Aristotle's considered view is that no perception occurs unless a perceptual change arrives from a peripheral sense organ to the central sense organ—'the part receptive of all perceptibles' (*PA* II.1 647^{a}25–30). When a perceptual change arrives from the eyes, it produces a visual perception, when it arrives from the ears, it produces an auditory perception, and so forth.[18] Hence, a perceptible form has to be received by a peripheral sense organ and transduced to the central sense organ in order to be perceived. The central sense organ is thus crucially involved in every act of perception by an individual sense.

Now the central sense organ is also the seat of the common sense. We know that the common sense is necessarily up and running when we are awake, and I would like to suggest that its activity consists not only of unifying and differentiating perceptions from the individual senses, but more fundamentally of registering their presence or absence. When a perceptual change arrives to the central sense organ through a conduit which connects it with a particular peripheral sense organ, we have not only an act of first-order perception by the relevant individual sense, but also an act of second-order perception by the common sense. On the other hand, when no perceptual change arrives to the central sense organ through that conduit, we have no first-order perception by the relevant individual sense, yet we do have a second-order perception by the common sense—it is a perception of not having a first-order perception, which is precisely what makes one aware of the sense's inactivity.

What I am suggesting, then, is that the common sense is always active when we are awake, and a fundamental part of its activity consists of registering the activity or inactivity of the individual senses, that is, their 'monitoring'.[19] When the common sense shuts off in sleep, not only are

[18] See *DI* 3 461^{a}25–^{b}5 In this picture the origin of a perceptual change is of crucial importance, much like in contemporary neuroscience; cf. O'Shea (2005: 7): 'The brain interprets or decodes electrical signals according to their address and destination. We *see* an electrical signal coming from the eyes, *hear* electrical signals from the ears, and *feel* the electrical signals coming from touch sensitive cells in the skin.'

[19] One might object that my suggestion implies that the triple scheme of types of potentiality and actuality from *DA* II.5 is inapplicable to the common sense. What it implies, rather, is that the transition between first and second actuality of the common sense cannot be found in the waking state. That is to say, while the individual senses can go between first and second actuality in the waking state, the common sense cannot, because its transition between first and second actuality marks the shift between sleep (or other forms of temporary unconscious states) and waking.

all the individual senses shut off, but monitoring ceases and thus one becomes unaware of the inactivity of one's senses.

The account I have provided has several consequences worth bringing out. Since a necessary condition for an act of first-order perception seems to be a sufficient condition for an act of second-order perception—that is, the arrival of perceptual change at the central sense organ—it seems to follow that every first-order perception is accompanied by second-order perception. This is confirmed by more than one passage in Aristotle. In *DS* 2 437^{a}27–8 Aristotle says that 'it is not possible to be unaware of perceiving and seeing'.[20] There is a famous passage in *EN* IX.9 1170^{a}29–^{b}1: 'The one who sees perceives that he sees, the one who hears that he hears, one who walks that he walks, and similarly for all the other human activities there is something that perceives that we are active, so that we perceive that we perceive, and we think that we think, and [to perceive or think] that we are perceiving or thinking is [to perceive or think] that we exist.'[21] The way this passage reads suggests that every first-order cognitive act is accompanied by a second-order cognitive act of the corresponding type. In *Met.* XII.9 1074^{b}33–6 Aristotle says that 'knowledge, perception, opinion, and reasoning are always of something else, but of itself by the way'. This sentence can also be read as saying that, apart from its primary object, a cognitive capacity always has itself as a secondary object too.[22]

If it is true that every first-order perception is accompanied by second-order perception, then monitoring of the senses cannot be equated with Armstrong's reflex introspective consciousness, mentioned in the preceding chapter. Armstrong's example of the absent-minded truck-driver demonstrates that reflex introspective consciousness need not always accompany perceptual consciousness. More generally, all higher-order theories of consciousness assume that a first-order mental state *can* occur without a second-order mental state, since they are regarded as two different token mental states. This is precisely what

[20] Caston (2002: 757–8) finds a similar point in *Phy.* VII.2 244^{b}12–245^{a}2. Caston's interpretation of this passage is challenged, rightly in my view, by Johansen (2006: 264–5).

[21] Caston's (2002: 774–5) translation, slightly modified. I subscribe to Caston's view regarding Bywater's (1892: 64–5) famous emendation to the effect that we perceive not only that we perceive, but also that we think.

[22] So Caston (2002: 786). Johansen (2006: 265) objects that 'there is no need to read "always" across the contrast between primary and second function'.

enables such theories to 'distinguish awareness from mere psychology and conscious states/events from mere mentation'.[23]

In his important paper from 2002, Caston appreciates the advantages of higher-order perception theories of consciousness. The main advantage of such theories is that they take consciousness to be a case of intentionality, since second-order mental states are directed upon first-order mental states. However, such theories have some disadvantages, the main one being that they take consciousness to be a relational feature of mental states, whereas there is a strong intuition that it is an intrinsic feature of mental states. Caston argues that Aristotle has a notion of consciousness which preserves the advantages of higher-order perception theories while avoiding their disadvantages, a notion according to which each token mental state is directed both upon an object and upon itself. Because of its reflexive nature, every token mental state is higher-order while remaining intrinsic.[24]

So, according to Caston, 'Aristotle cannot accept an "inner sense" or internal scanner whose activities are distinct tokens from the activities they monitor', because reflexive awareness is intrinsic to the original perceptual activity.[25] However, Caston does not seem to ascribe reflexivity of the original perceptual activity to the individual sense: 'The perceptual system *sees* in virtue of its visual part. But it perceives that it sees in virtue of the nature of perception more generally.'[26] It follows that in a single token perceptual state, one type of content is achieved by the relevant individual sense, another by the common sense. This can be squared with our description of the perceptual capacity of the soul. We can say that each token perceptual state is achieved by the perceptual capacity of the soul as a whole, and that one aspect of that token (perception of an object) is achieved by one aspect of the perceptual capacity of the soul (individual sense), whereas the other aspect of that token (perception of perceiving) is achieved by the other aspect of the perceptual capacity of the soul (the common sense).

However, there is a catch in my account which undermines Caston's case. Even though first-order perceptions are always accompanied

23 Lycan (1997: 756).

24 Such a theory can be classified as a 'same-order perception theory of consciousness'; cf. Kriegel (2002; 2006) and Lurz (2003).

25 Caston (2002: 779). This is necessitated by Caston's interpretation of the infinite regress argument which relies on the activity reading of the whole passage; cf. nn. 4 and 7 above. I have offered a capacity reading which is at least as plausible as Caston's activity reading, and it includes a different interpretation of the regress argument.

26 Caston (2002: 779).

by second-order perceptions, second-order perceptions do not always accompany first-order perceptions. That is to say, there are second-order perceptions by the common sense that register the absence of first-order perceptions by the individual senses, which is how we perceive, for instance, darkness or silence. To many interpreters this would suggest quite strongly that first-order perception and second-order perception must be two distinct tokens. I doubt that Caston would be convinced, since he refuses to accept that mental states are individuated by their content.[27] However, if my account is correct, he would be compelled to admit that, while a token perceptual state cannot be exhausted by the content of first-order perception, it *can* be exhausted by the content of second-order perception. Caston finds it 'grossly counterintuitive to say that I am *aware* of a certain mental state, when no such state exists',[28] but I do not find it at all counterintuitive to say that I am aware of not being in a certain mental state. When I shut my eyes, I seem to be perfectly aware of not seeing anything.

The fact that second-order perception can occur without first-order perception has a number of repercussions for Caston's interpretation of Aristotle. For instance, the fact shows that reflexive consciousness, according to Aristotle, does not presuppose the existence of its objects, and this may open room for error. More importantly, the fact prompts us to acknowledge that monitoring has a certain degree of autonomy from the activity of the individual senses, and this seems to commit Aristotle to some sort of 'internal monitoring capacity', after all. I do not wish to say that this aligns Aristotle with the contemporary higher-order perception theorists of consciousness, since I agree with Caston's contention that every first-order perception is indeed accompanied by second-order perception. However, it does not make Aristotle a same-order perception theorist either, since there is no constitutive relation between first- and second-order perceptions such that the latter could not occur without the former.

Let us conclude with some general remarks on 'perceiving that we see and hear' as I have interpreted it. If my account of the Aristotelian explanation of monitoring of the senses is correct, it should follow that every animal is aware of the activity and inactivity of its senses, regardless of the number and sophistication of its senses, since every animal necessarily has a central sense organ and the common sense which controls the individual senses. Indeed, this is suggested by Aristotle's

[27] Caston (2002: 779). 781–2. [28] Ibid. 781.

perfectly general conclusion to his treatment of the perceptual capacity of the soul, following his discussion of perceiving that one perceives and perceptual discrimination in *DA* III.2. At 427ª14–16 he writes: 'Let this much be set forth, then, about the principle in virtue of which we say than an animal is capable of perceiving.' There is no suggestion here that the preceding discussion applies only to some animals.

Granted that all animals have the ability to monitor their senses, one may wonder what are the benefits from this ability. The benefit from being aware of the inactivity of one's senses is pretty obvious. In a number of situations animals find themselves deprived of sensory information due to some external or internal circumstance. The awareness of this deprivation prompts the animal to acquire information about its environment by other sense modalities, or to take measures leading to the reactivation of the senses. This enables the animal to cope with such situations and increase its chances of survival or recovery. The described benefit, however, is on a par with the benefit from first-order perceptions; the benefit of perceiving darkness, for instance, is of the same sort as the benefit of perceiving colour or coloured objects. However, are there any benefits from second-order perceptions insofar as they accompany first-order perceptions, that is, from being aware of the activity of one's senses?

One benefit from the awareness of the activity of the senses can be discerned if we consider the fact that animals frequently receive deficient sensory information, such as insufficiently clear, partial, or unexpected impressions. An animal needs to be aware that the activity of its sense is in some way deficient in order to make an attempt to acquire clearer or fuller sensory information. That animals are indeed aware of deficient activity of their senses is obvious from their behaviour. For example, people shade their eyes with their hands when observing objects against the glare of the sun, hounds cock their ears upon hearing a faint crack in the bushes, cats move closer to inspect novel objects by sight and smell. Such actions, I would argue, demonstrate the awareness of deficient activity of the senses, and the benefit of such awareness is that it allows an animal to take steps to acquire better sensory information and thus guide its behaviour more reliably.

Finally, I am inclined to think that the awareness even of the fully adequate activity of the senses has a far-reaching benefit. We must remember that we have not been talking about an animal's awareness of the activity of one of its senses in contrast with, or in isolation from, its awareness of the activity of another sense. Rather, we have been talking about an animal's unified awareness of the activity of any number of its senses that happen to be actualized. Without this unified awareness, activities and inactivities of the animal's senses would not be experienced as *its* activities and inactivities. And without experiencing them as its own, the link between perception, desire, and purposeful action would be severed. As Augustine writes, 'an animal would not move either to pursue or to avoid something unless it perceived that it is perceiving'.[29] John Sisko puts the same point differently: 'it is our reflexive higher-order awareness that links thought (and perception) to the self and, thus, links the self to the world.'[30] Although I am not entirely comfortable with the talk of 'self' in this context, it does seem to me that monitoring of the senses points at the notion of a subject of perceptual experience.[31] And it is this subject of perceptual experience that has desires and acts in accordance with them.

To conclude, in this chapter I have argued that Aristotle's formula, 'perceiving that we see and hear', should be understood as covering cases of perceiving that we see and hear clearly, cases of perceiving that we see and hear faintly, and also cases of perceiving that we do not see and hear at all. Assuming, moreover, that 'seeing and hearing' in the formula above are merely examples, I have advanced a general claim that Aristotle took animals to be aware of the activity of their senses, both when this activity is adequate and when it is inadequate, as well as of the inactivity of their senses, both when this inactivity is caused simply by the absence of sensory stimuli and when it is caused by an injury to the sensory apparatus. This awareness is what I have proposed to call 'monitoring of the senses', and I have argued that, in Aristotle's considered view, it is achieved by the common sense.

[29] Augustine, *De Libero Arbitrio* II.4.10 (Green) = *PL* XXXII.1246 (Migne).

[30] Sisko (2004: 520).

[31] So Wallace ((ed.)1882: pp. lxxx–lxxxii), Stewart (1892: II.391–2), Ross ((ed.) 1961: 35), Hamlyn ((ed.)1968: 122), Sisko (2004).

5

Other Roles of the Common Sense

In this chapter I would like to consider two perceptual operations which can be plausibly related to the common sense as I have defined it. These two perceptual operations are often regarded as functions of the common sense. In fact, one of them, perception of the common perceptibles, is usually regarded as the most salient function of the common sense. Here I explain why these two operations are not treated as functions of the common sense in this book, and what role, if any, the common sense plays in these operations.

5.1 PERCEPTION OF THE COMMON PERCEPTIBLES

One of the functions traditionally ascribed to the common sense is perception of the common perceptibles. This view is largely based on the reading of Aristotle's argument in *DA* III.1 425^{a}12–27, which has been analysed and criticized in Part II, Chapter 2. I have argued that the phrase *αἴσθησις κοινή* at 425^{a}27 refers to the sensitivity of the individual senses to the common perceptibles, not to some perceptual power by which the common perceptibles are perceived. That interpretation granted, one might still wonder whether that sensitivity shared by the individual senses is their common function, that is, something they owe to the common sense. My view is that they do not owe it to the common sense, at least not without qualification. To clarify and support that view, I should like to take a look at the closing passage of *DA* III.1.

At 425^{b}4 Aristotle raises the question of why we have more than one individual sense, and answers:

Is it in order that the perceptibles which accompany [the special perceptibles] and which are common—e.g. change, magnitude, and number—are less likely to escape our notice? For if sight were the only sense, and it was of white, they would be more likely to escape our notice and they all would seem to be the same because colour and magnitude always accompany each other. But as things are, since the common perceptibles are present also in another [kind of special] perceptible, this makes it clear that each of them is something different. (*DA* III.1 425^{b}5–11)

We have a plurality of the individual senses, Aristotle says, in order that the common perceptibles be 'less likely to escape our notice' (ὅπως ἧττον λανθάνῃ, ^{b}5). At first glance this reply is surprising, for two reasons. First, one would expect that we have a plurality of the individual senses primarily in order to perceive a greater variety of the *special* perceptibles.[1] While that is no doubt true, Aristotle's reply seems to be geared to the context of the second half of *DA* III.1. Having shown that there is no special sense for the common perceptibles, Aristotle now has to show that the five individual senses suffice for the perception of the common perceptibles. Second, among the five senses only touch and sight are sensitive to all common perceptibles.[2] Of the other three senses, hearing and smell do not seem to be sensitive to magnitude and shape. Besides, hearing, smell, and touch are quite poor at perceiving the common perceptibles. Sight, on the other hand, is said to be the sense 'through which we perceive the common perceptibles most of all' (*DS* 1 437^{a}8). Would it not be more appropriate, then, to say that we have sight in addition to touch, rather than a plurality of senses, in order that the common perceptibles are less likely to escape our notice? The answer to this worry might be that, according to Aristotle, sight presupposes all the other four senses, for there are animals with the other four senses, but no sense of sight.[3] To have the sense of sight in addition to touch, then, the animal must have the remaining three senses too. Thus it is not inappropriate to say that we have a plurality of individual senses in order that the common perceptibles are less likely to escape our notice.

Aristotle's reply to the initial question receives an explanation which is formulated as a counterfactual conditional: if we had only the sense

[1] Holding on to this expectation, Plutarch of Athens (*apud* Simplicius (1882: 186.27–31) and Philoponus (1897: 462.7–10)) argued that Aristotle does not raise the general question why we have a plurality of the senses, but the more specific question why we have a plurality of the senses by which we grasp the common perceptibles, rather than only one sense by which we do so.

[2] In *DA* II.6 418^{a}11 and 19 Aristotle says that the common perceptibles are common to *all* the senses (κοινὰ πάσαις), which seems to be an overstatement. I suppose that only change and rest, plurality and one are common to all the senses; cf. Brunschwig (1991: 459; 1996: 197–9).

[3] *DSV* 2 455^{a}7; *HA* IV.8 532^{b}32–533^{a}3.

of sight, the common perceptibles would be 'more likely to escape our notice' (ἐλάνθανεν ἂν μᾶλλον, b7). What this means, I take it, is that if we had only sight, we would be *less* sensitive to the common perceptibles, not that we would be *insensitive* to them.[4] To be less sensitive to the common perceptibles, moreover, is either to be sensitive to fewer types of common perceptible, or to be sensitive to fewer tokens of those types of common perceptible to which one is sensitive, or both. Now why does Aristotle think that if we had only sight we would be less sensitive to the common perceptibles? Aristotle's answer is that (i) 'they all would seem to be the same', which is in turn explained by saying (ii) that 'colour and magnitude always accompany each other'.

It is not very clear what (i) actually means, because it is uncertain what the scope of 'they all' (πάντα, b8) is, and what it means that they would 'seem to be the same' (ἐδόκει ταὐτὸν εἶναι). Given that the counterfactual posits sight as our only sense, and given that (ii) mentions colour and magnitude, I infer that 'they all' refers to all token colours and magnitudes. To say that they 'would seem to be the same', on the other hand, seems to mean that particular colours and particular magnitudes that accompany them would be conflated in perception. That is, magnitudes would not be differentiated from the colours that they accompany.

This is explained in (ii) by saying that colour and magnitude always accompany each other. Since you cannot see a colour without some magnitude or other, nor a magnitude without some colour or other, they would seem to be the same thing to you, and thus magnitudes would escape your notice. This sounds quite plausible. If sight were your only sense, you would not be sensitive to one type of common perceptible, namely magnitude, because you would have no means of differentiating tokens of magnitude from tokens of colour.

Aristotle's example of magnitude is not chosen arbitrarily. Apart from shape, magnitude is the only type of common perceptible a token of which accompanies every token of colour.[5] This is not the case with the other types of common perceptible. For example, it is not the case that

[4] I assume that there is no difference between saying that *we* would be less sensitive, and that our *sight* would be less sensitive to the common perceptibles. We are sensitive to the common perceptibles insofar as our sight and the other senses are sensitive to them.

[5] Cf. Plato, *Meno* 75b9–10: 'Let shape be for us that thing which, alone of the things that are, always accompanies colour' (trans. R. W. Sharples). Aristotle's choice of example may have been intended as a correction of Plato: magnitude is another thing that always accompanies colour.

you cannot see a colour without seeing some change or another, for you can, and often do, see a colour at rest. Indeed, you can see the same token of colour changing at one moment and resting at another. Since you can see colours with and without change, then, there is no reason to assume that colour and change would seem to be the same thing to you, and hence that change would escape your notice if sight were your only sense. Consequently, there is no reason to suppose that you would not be sensitive to change (and rest) as a type of common perceptible. The same, I suppose, applies to number and one.

What follows from this is that if we had only the sense of sight, we would be sensitive to fewer types of common perceptible; namely, we would not be sensitive to magnitude and shape. However, it seems that we would still be sensitive to change and rest, and to number and one. None of the latter four types of common perceptible is such that its tokens always accompany tokens of colour and vice versa,[6] and hence there is no reason to suppose that we would conflate them. Seeing some colours change and some rest, or even the same patch of white changing at one moment and resting at another moment, should make it perfectly clear that change (and rest) is something different from colour.

The last sentence in the quoted passage explains what makes us sensitive to magnitude and shape. 'As things are' (νῦν, ᵇ9) introduces the factual situation in which we have a plurality of individual senses, notably sight and touch. What makes it clear to us that magnitude, for instance, is something different from colour is that we observe magnitudes to accompany tangible qualities. By observing that the same feature, or the same type of feature, accompanies special perceptibles of different types, we learn that this feature, or this type of feature, is something different from each one of the special perceptibles.

Now to be able to observe that the same feature, or type of feature, accompanies colours and tangible qualities, my sight and touch cannot be isolated from one another. There must be some one thing which compares the reports of sight and touch and discerns what they have in common. In Plato's scheme this one thing is the soul which operates 'by itself', whereas in Aristotle's scheme it is the higher-order perceptual power which emerges from the unity of the perceptual capacity of the

[6] However, the latter four types of common perceptible come in two pairs, such that either one or the other member of each pair necessarily accompanies every token special perceptible. That is to say, every token special perceptible is either changing or resting, it is either a plurality or one.

soul. In other words, Aristotle's view is that the individual senses access their respective special perceptibles, whereas the common sense discerns their common accompaniments.

Many interpreters would approve of what I have just said. Indeed, many would claim that this is in fact how we perceive the common perceptibles.[7] But I disagree with that claim. What the common sense explains in this argument is *not* how we perceive the common perceptibles, but how we learn this the common perceptibles are something different from the special perceptibles they accompany. More precisely, it explains how we do that in the case of those common perceptibles which we would have no means of differentiating from colours if we had the sense of sight only. Since every colour we see is of some shape and magnitude or other, and every shape and magnitude we see is of some colour or other, the only way to differentiate shapes and magnitudes from colours is to draw on the sense of touch and observe that shapes and magnitudes accompany not only colours but also tangible qualities. This observation is afforded by the common sense which discerns common accompaniments of special perceptibles that belong to different senses. However, since the other types of common perceptible are *not* such that their tokens accompany every token of colour, as I have shown, we should have no difficulty differentiating them from colours, and hence no need to appeal to the common sense and its ability to discern common accompaniments of special perceptibles that belong to different types. What the common sense ultimately explains, then, is our sensitivity only to those types of common perceptible to which we would not be sensitive if we had only one individual sense.

Perhaps the common sense explains more than that. It might be suggested that comparing the reports of different senses concerning the common perceptibles gradually makes one sensitive to a greater number of tokens of various types of common perceptible. For instance, it might be argued that our senses of touch and sight are sensitive to a large variety of shapes due to frequent checking of tactile reports by visual reports and vice versa. If we accept this suggestion, and given that checking the reports of one individual sense by another individual sense relies on the common sense, it follows that the common sense enables us to be sensitive not only to a greater number of types of common perceptible, but also to a greater number of tokens of at least some types of common perceptible.

[7] Cf. Part II, Ch. 2, pp. 70–3.

Moreover, when we are not sure about the report of one sense concerning a token common perceptible, we normally check it by another sense, typically sight or touch. Aristotle describes such a case in *DI* 2 460^b20–2: 'By crossing of the fingers a single object appears as two, but even so we still deny that there are two things. For sight has more authority than touch. If touch stood alone, we would also judge the single object to be two.'[8] In this case a tactile report concerning the unity of the perceived object is checked and corrected by a visual report, which would not be possible without the common sense. It seems, therefore, that the common sense enables us to verify or correct reports of the individual senses concerning the common perceptibles, thereby increasing the accuracy of our perception of the common perceptibles.[9]

We can say, therefore, that the common sense enhances the sensitivity of the individual senses to the common perceptibles in various ways, but we have no grounds for saying that it is necessary for that sensitivity, let alone that it is what perceives the common perceptibles.

There is one passage which can be taken to oppose the stated relationship between the sensitivity to the common perceptibles and the common sense. We have seen that in *DSV* 2 455^a12–15 Aristotle says that the individual senses have special and common functions. He then introduces a 'common power accompanying all the individual senses'—that is, the common sense—as an explanation of the common functions of the individual senses. One could argue that the sensitivity to the common perceptibles is a common function of the individual senses, and consequently something to be explained by the common sense. If so, the relationship between the sensitivity to the common perceptibles and the common sense must be tighter than I have argued.

This inference is justified only if we assume that all common functions are equally related to the common sense, so that whatever is a common

[8] Translated by D. Gallop. Ross ((ed.)1961: 273) informs us that this is known in psychology as 'Aristotle's experiment'.

[9] This can be contrasted with Plato's view. In *Republic* X (602ce) Plato claims that our senses tend to be deceived by certain properties of things, most of which correspond to certain types of the Aristotelian common perceptibles, notably shape (602c10–11), magnitude, and number (602d8). We correct the reports of the senses concerning these properties, according to Plato, by measuring and counting, which are the work of the rational part of the soul. This seems to imply that non-rational animals cannot perceive the common perceptibles very accurately. With the notion of the common sense, which enables animals to correct the reports of one sense by another sense, Aristotle avoids this unpalatable implication. I thank Filip Grgić for drawing my attention to the passage from *Republic* X.

function, it is explained by the common sense. I do not think, however, that we have to make that assumption. True, there are some functions which are common to the individual senses owing to their being accompanied by the common sense, like perceiving that we see and hear, or discriminating heterogeneous special perceptibles. These are the only common functions explicitly mentioned in *DSV* 2, and they are indeed explained by the common sense. However, it is not necessary to assume that all common functions are like that. For instance, if the perception of the accidental perceptibles is also a common function (you can perceive the son of Diares by sight, hearing, and smell), and if the ability to perceive the accidental perceptibles relies on the sensory capacity of the soul which combines perception and imagination, as I have suggested, then this common function is not explained by the common sense. Similarly, if each individual sense has the resources to perceive at least some common perceptibles, as I have argued, then this common function is not explained by the common sense either. So I do not think that it is necessary to interpret the passage in *DSV* 2 in a way which is damaging to my case concerning the relationship between the sensitivity to the common perceptibles and the common sense.

5.2 ACCIDENTAL PERCEPTION

When we perceive something accidentally, our sense is not affected by that thing in virtue of being what it is, but in virtue of making an accidental unity with something that does affect the sense in itself. We can divide things that can be perceived accidentally into two large classes. First, there are things that cannot be perceived otherwise than by making an accidental unity with something that does affect the sense in itself. These are the accidental perceptibles, such as the son of Diares or his location. Second, there are things that can be perceived otherwise than by making an accidental unity with something that does affect the sense in itself. These are the special perceptibles, each token of which normally affects one sense in itself, but it can also, provided certain conditions, affect another sense by making an accidental unity with a special perceptible of that sense. For instance, bitter is properly perceived by taste, but it can also be accidentally perceived by sight.

Let me summarize what has been said earlier about the role of the common sense in perceiving each of the two classes of things that can be perceived accidentally. In Part III, Chapter 1 I have argued that in an act of simultaneous perception two heterogeneous perceptibles form an accidental unity. I have suggested that one easily gets from perceiving the accidental unity of two heterogeneous perceptibles to perceiving something in which both perceptibles coincide, that is, a physical object. It is plausible to think, I have argued, that the ability to perceive physical objects, which are accidental perceptibles of the fundamental sort, develops from simultaneous perception. Since simultaneous perception is due to the common sense, it follows that the role of the common sense is to supply the conditions for the development of an animal's ability to perceive the accidental perceptibles. Whether it plays any other role in the perception of the accidental perceptibles, I would hesitate to say. It does seem to me, though, that the unified sensory capacity of the soul, which combines the work of perception and imagination, plays a more prominent role in the development of the ability to perceive the accidental perceptibles.

As for accidental perception of a special perceptible of one sense by another sense—let us call this 'cross-modal perception' for brevity—it certainly presupposes simultaneous perception. 'The senses perceive each other's special perceptibles accidentally, not as such, but as one, when a perception occurs simultaneously in respect of the same thing, e.g. of bile that it is bitter and yellow, for it is not the task of a further [perception] to say that both are one' (*DA* III.1 $425^{a}30–^{b}3$). In an act of simultaneous perception of a drop of bile, for example, bitter and yellow form an accidental unity. Because they have once formed an accidental unity in an act of simultaneous perception, I take it, when we see yellow on a later occasion, we accidentally perceive bitter too.[10]

It is debatable just how complex cross-modal perception is, and on what cognitive resources it draws. For one, it seems to presuppose memory of some sort.[11] If the earlier act of simultaneous perception in which yellow and bitter formed an accidental unity left no trace in one's mind, there would be no basis for one's accidental perception of bitter upon seeing yellow. I am inclined to think, therefore, that the ability to perceive a special perceptible of one sense accidentally by another sense is also due to the unified sensory capacity of the soul which combines perception and imagination, rather than to the common sense. If so,

[10] I suppose that in order to accidentally perceive bitter by sight, the yellow must be sufficiently similar to the yellow of the previously perceived drop of bile.

[11] I add this qualification because cross-modal perception may not require memory as Aristotle understands it in the *DM*, i.e. as the ability to contemplate images as copies of things experienced in the past.

the role of the common sense in cross-modal perception is again only to supply the necessary conditions of cross-modal perception by way of simultaneous perception.

It may be objected to my claim that cross-modal perception is due to the unity of the sensory capacity of the soul, by pointing out that Aristotle explicitly says at 425^a30-1 that 'the senses perceive each other's special perceptibles accidentally, not as such, but as one'. This statement can be interpreted as saying that the perceptual capacity of the soul has to operate, not only as this or that individual sense, but also as a single thing, in order to accomplish cross-modal perception. This would effectively mean that cross-modal perception is accomplished by the common sense, that is, the higher-order perceptual power emerging from the unity of the perceptual capacity of the soul. No doubt this is a plausible interpretation of Aristotle's statement. However, it can also be interpreted as saying that cross-modal perception requires the individual senses to form some sort of unity, leaving it open whether this unity is achieved at the level of the perceptual capacity of the soul, or perhaps at the higher level of the sensory capacity of the soul, which comprises the perceptual and the imaginative capacities of the soul. It might be the case, of course, that Aristotle has failed to distinguish these two levels when he made the statement at 425^a30-1. That, however, should not stop us from making this distinction and applying it in the best interest of Aristotle's theory.

And even if we suppose, for the sake of argument, that cross-modal perception is performed by the common sense, I do not think that we should consider it a function of the common sense. Rather, it seems to be a coincidence of having a perceptual capacity of the soul which is a unity with some internal complexity. That is, if an animal has a soul with a perceptual capacity which is a unity conceptually divided into the individual senses, having once simultaneously perceived two heterogeneous perceptibles, the animal should be able to perceive the relevant special perceptible of one sense by another sense; but it does not seem to be the case that the animal has such a perceptual capacity of the soul in order to be able to perceive special perceptibles of one sense by another sense.

Conclusion

What, then, is the common sense, according to Aristotle? I hope that the central parts of this book have convinced the reader that an attempt to give a simple answer to this question is bound to be misleading. To get things right, we need to ask two different questions. First, what does Aristotle himself designate with the phrase 'common sense'? Second, what should *we* designate as the Aristotelian notion of the common sense?

(1) In reply to the first question, we would have to say that Aristotle designates three different things with the phrase 'common sense' (*κοινὴ αἴσθησις*) and its variants. (i) An individual sense, namely touch, is called a 'common sense' in *HA* I.3 489^{a}17. It is so called because it is shared by all animals, for the sense of touch is found in every individual animal of every species. Apart from the sense of taste, which is a modification of the sense of touch, the other three individual senses are not found in all species of animals. However, they are found in a number of different species, and hence they are shared by animals of these species. It follows that some individual senses, such as sight and hearing, are less common because they belong to fewer animals. The other individual senses are more common, because they belong to a greater number of animals. Indeed, touch is 'the most common sense', as *EN* III.10 1118^{b}1 puts it, because it is present in all animals without exception. At any rate, each and every individual sense, in this use of the phrase, can be designated as a 'common sense'. This inference is confirmed by *Met.* I.1 981^{b}14, where all the five individual senses are called the 'common senses'.

(ii) I have argued that Aristotle distinguishes aspects of the properly functioning individual senses according to types of features perceived. For instance, one aspect of the properly functioning sense of sight is its ability to perceive colours. This aspect is special to the sense of sight, since this ability is not found in any other sense. Another aspect of the properly functioning sense of sight is its ability to perceive the common perceptibles. Now this aspect is not proper to the sense of sight, since it is found in the other senses too, albeit perhaps in different degrees. That is to say, the sense of sight is able to perceive all types of common perceptible, and to do so better than any other sense. Apart from the sense of touch, which can also perceive all types of common perceptible, the other senses are able to perceive only some types. Nevertheless, since all individual senses have the ability to perceive at least some common perceptibles, this aspect of the properly functioning senses is common to all of them. I have shown that the phrase *αἴσθησις κοινή* is used once, in *DA* III.1 425^{a}27, precisely with reference to this shared ability of the individual senses to perceive the common perceptibles. Since this ability is only an aspect of the properly functioning senses, rather than a distinct sense on its own account, it would be misleading to translate the phrase in this particular use as 'common sense'. 'Common sensitivity' would be a more appropriate rendering.

I have insisted that there is nothing in this use of the phrase that restricts it to the ability of the individual senses to perceive the common perceptibles. Any ability shared by the individual senses could be, in principle at least, described as a 'common sensitivity'. For instance, if the ability to perceive the accidental perceptibles is shared by the individual senses, as I think it is, then this ability can also be described as a 'common sensitivity', for it is the senses' common sensitivity to features such as the son of Diares, his location, his action, and so on. This is easy to see once we understand that something is described as a 'common sensitivity' not because it is the sensitivity to the objects of perception that are called 'common', but rather because it is shared by several individual senses.

With this interpretation of the phrase *αἴσθησις κοινή* in *DA* III.1 425^{a}27, I challenge the standard interpretation according to which the phrase stands for a higher-order perceptual capacity which accompanies all the senses. Potentially even more controversial is my dissociation of the thing described in *DA* III.1 425^{a}27 as *αἴσθησις κοινή* from the higher-order perceptual capacity. I have argued in Part II, Chapter 2 and Part III, Chapter 5 that there is no need to suppose that the higher-order perceptual capacity accounts for the ability of the individual senses to perceive the common perceptibles. To be sure, the higher-order perceptual capacity enables the individual senses to perceive some common perceptibles that the senses would not be able to perceive were they not integrated in the perceptual capacity of the soul; perhaps the higher-order perceptual capacity enables the individual senses also to perceive a greater number of the common perceptibles, or to perceive them more accurately. However, Aristotle gives us no reason to think that an individual sense unaccompanied by the higher-order perceptual capacity would be entirely unable to perceive the common perceptibles.

(iii) I have discussed at some length three difficult passages in *PA* IV.10, *DM* 1, and *DA* III.7. These passages are difficult on philosophical grounds, and the latter two, especially the last, are difficult also on textual grounds. I have offered interpretations of these passages which make good sense of the texts in their received form, or at any rate as good sense as any other interpretation available. The upshot of my interpretations is that the phrase 'common sense' is used in *PA* IV.10 686^{a}31, *DM* 1 450^{a}10, and *DA* III.7 431^{b}5 consistently as a proper name for what I have called the 'sensory capacity of the soul'.

Recall that the sensory capacity of the soul, according to the framework set out in Part I, Chapter 4, is related to the perceptual capacity of the soul in the same way in which the latter is related to the individual senses. The individual senses are conceptually distinct parts or aspects of the perceptual capacity of the soul, and the perceptual capacity, along with the imaginative capacity, is a conceptually distinct part or aspect of the sensory capacity of the soul. Just as the perceptual capacity unifies the individual senses, so the sensory capacity unifies the perceptual and the imaginative capacity. Thus the sensory capacity of the soul is in fact the non-rational cognitive capacity of the soul, and in all three passages it is contrasted with its rational counterpart, the thinking capacity of the soul.

We can conclude, then, that Aristotle has three different uses of the phrase 'common sense', for he designates three quite different types of thing with that phrase. This is a conclusion whose importance for our subject can hardly be exaggerated. There are two implications of that conclusion which I wish to underscore, one minor and one major.

The minor implication is that such variation in use suggests that the phrase 'common sense' was not fixed as a technical term in Aristotle's mind. I hesitate to be more categorical about this implication, because in *PA* IV.10 686^{a}31, *DM* 1 450^{a}10, and *DA* III.7 431^{b}5, according to my interpretations of these occurrences, the phrase is used in a way which is characteristic of technical terminology, that is, consistently and as a proper name. The fact, however, that Aristotle's heirs, notably Theophrastus and Alexander of Aphrodisias, did *not* use the phrase 'common sense' with reference to the sensory capacity of the soul, reaffirms the minor implication.

The major implication of the aforementioned conclusion is that we should not suppose that the phrase 'common sense' always refers to the same thing, and hence we should not suppose that various functions which go beyond the individual senses taken separately are achieved all by the same thing. This should come as a great relief to interpreters of Aristotle's notion of the common sense, because the diversity of its functions has presented them with an acute problem. If the common sense is something that discharges perceptual functions as diverse as simultaneous perception and the perception of time—one having nothing to do with imagination, the latter crucially depending on it—then the notion of the common sense seems to be incoherent. As Deborah Modrak puts it: 'If there are no underlying similarities [viz. among its functions], then Aristotle's conception of the common sense seems ad hoc at best and arbitrary at worst.'[1] Indeed, the notion of the common sense as it is usually construed, with a motley set of functions attributed to it, seems very much arbitrary.

Fortunately, we do not need to saddle Aristotle with such a problematic notion of the common sense. I have argued that Aristotle's framework operates with a series of related but distinct notions to which diverse functions are attributed. What are these notions? First, we have the notion of the perceptual capacity of the soul. The perceptual capacity of the soul is a single thing only conceptually differentiated into the individual senses. Hence, it can operate as this or that individual sense, but it can also operate as a unity. When it operates as a unity, we can talk about a higher-order perceptual power which accompanies the individual senses. This higher-order perceptual power, then, is the second notion. The third notion is found one level up on the hierarchy of psychic capacities, and I have labelled it the 'sensory capacity of the soul'. The sensory capacity of the soul is a single thing only conceptually differentiated into the perceptual capacity of the soul and the imaginative capacity of the soul. Hence, it can do all the things that the perceptual capacity can do and all the things that the imaginative capacity can do, but it can also operate as a unity. When it operates as a unity, it can combine perception and imagination, and thus achieve feats of non-rational cognition manifest in some non-human animals. Here we can talk about a higher-order non-rational cognitive power, which is our fourth notion.

[1] Modrak (1987: 62).

Now functions that go beyond the individual senses taken separately can be divided into two kinds: perceptual ones narrowly speaking, in which imagination plays no part, and perceptual ones broadly speaking, in which the work of perception and imagination is combined. Obviously, functions of the former kind can be assigned to the first notion (the perceptual capacity of the soul), or more precisely to its conceptually distinct aspect captured by the second notion (the higher-order perceptual power which emerges from the unity of the perceptual capacity of the soul). Functions of the latter kind can be assigned to the third notion (the sensory capacity of the soul), or more exactly to its conceptually distinct aspect captured by the fourth notion (the higher-order non-rational power which emerges from the unity of the sensory capacity of the soul). Thus we do not assign both kinds of functions to a single thing, and in that way we save Aristotle from an incoherent notion of the common sense.

(2) Having distinguished those four notions, and having established that three times Aristotle refers to the third notion as the 'common sense', the answer to the second question seems obvious: we should designate the sensory capacity of the soul as the Aristotelian notion of the common sense. However, taking into account the historical development of the notion of the common sense, I think we should eschew the obvious answer and designate the second notion—the higher-order perceptual power emerging from the unity of the perceptual capacity of the soul—as the Aristotelian notion of the common sense. Aristotle's successors, as much as we can tell from the available evidence, confined the common sense to the perceptual capacity of the soul. Their notion was picked up and further developed by medieval philosophers and passed on to modern philosophers. The origin of what came to be known as *sensus communis* in psychological and physiological theories from the thirteenth until the eighteenth century should not be sought in the wider notion of the sensory capacity of the soul, but rather in the notion of the perceptual capacity of the soul, or most specifically in the notion of the higher-order perceptual power emerging from the unity of the perceptual capacity of the soul. This book was, therefore, devoted primarily to mapping that higher-order perceptual power and exploring its functions.

A systematic treatment of the sensory capacity of the soul would be a considerably more challenging but highly rewarding task. It would be more challenging because Aristotle's notion of imagination is notoriously problematic, and the functions discharged on account of the unity of the sensory capacity are bound to be more complex and wide-ranging; what Aristotle calls 'experience' (ἐμπειρία) is, I think, a good example of such a function. Nevertheless, this task would be rewarding because its successful execution would provide us with a complete account of non-rational cognition in Aristotle. I hope that this task will be undertaken in the future, and that the present book will contribute to the endeavour.

In the last Part of the book I have identified four distinct functions of the common sense: (1) simultaneous perception, (2) perceptual discrimination, (3) control of the senses, and (4) monitoring of the senses.

(1) Simultaneous perception is perception of two or more special perceptibles in a single act. This function is problematic for Aristotle because his theory of perception yields two restrictions: the objective restriction that only one special perceptible can produce a single act of perception, and the subjective restriction that whatever is grasped in a single act of perception is perceived as a single thing. Aristotle distinguishes two cases of simultaneous perception, that which involves heterogeneous perceptibles, such as white and sweet, and that which involves homogeneous perceptibles, such as white and black. His explanations of both cases must accommodate the stated restrictions.

I have argued that Aristotle's explanation of the former case is very reasonable. Two or more heterogeneous special perceptibles, each grasped by its corresponding individual sense, are perceived in a single act of the common sense. In that single act of the common sense they are perceived as forming a unity, which can be interpreted as Aristotle's reply to the problem of cross-modal binding. Simultaneous perception of heterogeneous perceptibles, I have suggested, is closely related to accidental perception: it is necessary for accidental perception of a special perceptible of one sense by another sense, and it is a likely origin of the ability to perceive the accidental perceptibles.

Contrary to some interpreters, I have maintained that Aristotle subscribes to the intuitive view that we *can* simultaneously perceive two or more homogeneous special perceptibles, and that we can do so without fusing the perceptibles into a mixture. However, his discussion hardly amounts to an explanation of this sort of simultaneous perception, and the explanation we can reconstruct from his discussion of perceptual discrimination is not satisfactory. First, his explanation is not satisfactory because he seems to believe that we simultaneously perceive two or more colours, for instance, not by the sense of sight, as one would naturally suppose, but by the common sense. He is forced to relegate simultaneous perception of homogeneous perceptibles to the common sense, I have maintained, because he is unwilling to meet the aforementioned restrictions by dividing an individual sense into different parts or aspects which grasp two or more homogeneous perceptibles. The trick that worked for heterogeneous perceptibles does not work for homogeneous perceptibles. Second, Aristotle's explanation is disappointing because he seems to think that we simultaneously perceive two or more colours, for example, only to the extent that we apprehend their common boundary. This does not seem to be a promising way of explaining how we bind colours—which often form elaborate patterns with multiple boundaries, or indeed without any clear boundaries—into coherent wholes.

(2) Perceptual discrimination refers to perceiving that two or more special perceptibles differ from one another. This function is problematic for similar reasons to the previous one. Aristotle assumes that special perceptibles can be perceptually differentiated only if they are present to the discriminating thing at the same time, that is, in a single act. This fundamental assumption of discrimination is problematic from our point of view, because quick succession of objects seems to be more conducive to their differentiation than their simultaneity. Nevertheless, Aristotle's explanation of perceptual discrimination of heterogeneous special perceptibles is tenable: two or more perceptibles, each apprehended by its corresponding individual sense, are differentiated from one another in a single act of the common sense.

It was clear to Aristotle, however, that this sort of explanation cannot work for perceptual discrimination of homogeneous special perceptibles, because two or more special perceptibles of the same kind cannot be present to the same individual sense at the same time. The analogy with a geometrical point was supposed to solve that problem. The upshot of that analogy, according to my interpretation, is that each individual sense apprehends only one special perceptible, yet the common sense uses the boundary of that special perceptible to differentiate it from the neighbouring special perceptible(s). This explanation is disappointing for the same reasons that make his explanation of simultaneous perception of homogeneous perceptibles disappointing.

It is clear that simultaneous perception and perceptual discrimination are two closely connected functions. The same conditions have to be satisfied in order to have these two functions discharged, so we can legitimately wonder whether one can ever occur without the other. Indeed, it seems that simultaneous perception of two special perceptibles, according to Aristotle, implies their differentiation from one another, for otherwise we would not have *two* special perceptibles that are perceived as forming a unity in a single act of the common sense. Similarly, perceptual discrimination of two or more special perceptibles implies that they form a unity of some sort, for otherwise they could not be accessed at the same time in order to be differentiated in a single act. Whether simultaneous perception and perceptual discrimination are two distinct acts of the common sense, or one act under two different descriptions, is an issue I do not wish to speculate on.

(3) In the state of waking, all the individual senses that a sentient being might possess are on, that is, they are either actualized by the corresponding objects or ready to become so actualized. In the state of sleep, by contrast, all the individual senses are off, that is, they are incapacitated, neither actualized nor ready to become actualized by the corresponding objects. Obviously, a mechanism of control is required for keeping the senses all on in the state of waking, and all off in the state of sleep. Aristotle finds the essential part of this mechanism in the common sense. The common sense is related to the individual senses in such a way that when it is on, all the individual senses are on, and when it is off, all the individual senses are off. So the common sense controls the individual senses because their status follows upon, or is dictated by, the status of the common sense.

It is important to add that this relationship between the common sense and the individual senses is asymmetrical, since it is not the case that when an individual sense is off, the common sense is off too. This is obvious from the fact that the loss of an individual sense does not knock one out. On the contrary, in typical circumstances one is fully aware of the loss of an individual sense, and one can only be aware of that because the common sense remains up and running. This brings us to the fourth function of the common sense.

(4) Our state of waking is characterized, according to Aristotle, by 'perceiving that we see and hear'. In my interpretation, 'to perceive that we see and hear' is to be aware of the activity of our senses of sight and hearing. Assuming that 'seeing' and 'hearing' are no more than examples, I have argued that 'to perceive that we see and hear' should be understood as the awareness of the activity of any number of our senses that happen to be actualized at a given moment. Assuming, moreover, that Aristotle was committed to the view that we are aware also of the

inactivity of our senses—whether because a sense is incapacitated or because it just happens not to be actualized at a given moment—I have maintained that the phrase 'perceiving that we see and hear' describes the awareness not only of the activity of the individual senses, but also of their inactivity. Indeed, when we are awake we are aware of the activity of those of our senses that happen to be active, and also of the inactivity of those of our senses that happen to be inactive. Similarly, when we are asleep we are unaware of the inactivity of our senses. Moreover, I have indicated that animals are aware not merely of activity or inactivity of their senses, but also of inadequate activity of their senses, and that this is also part of what Aristotle means by 'perceiving that we see and hear'. Thus I have maintained that 'perceiving that one sees and hears' is a distinct function which comprises the awareness of adequate activity of one's senses, of their inadequate activity, as well as of their inactivity, and I have called this function 'monitoring of the senses'.

There are two passages in which Aristotle discusses 'perceiving that we see and hear'. What he says in one passage (*DSV* 2) suggests that he assigns it to the common sense. What he says in the other passage (*DA* III.2), however, indicates that he assigns perceiving that we see to the sense of sight, and perceiving that we hear to the sense of hearing. I have argued, to put it shortly, that the latter passage is dialectical, and hence that we should not take it to express Aristotle's considered view on this matter. Aristotle's considered view is, rather, that the common sense enables us to perceive that we see and hear, that is, to be aware of the activity and inactivity of our senses.

I have tried to elaborate on this view and suggest how the common sense achieves this awareness. In short, the common sense is always active in the state of waking, and its activity consists of registering the activity and inactivity of the individual senses. This story can be supported by Aristotle's physiological theory. The common sense is located in the central sense organ, the heart or its analogue in bloodless animals, and it is connected with the connate media of the contact senses (the flesh and tongue) and with the peripheral organs of the distal senses through a network of channels. When the connate media or peripheral sense organs receive the form of an external object without matter, a change is set up and dispatched to the central sense organ. As the changes continually flow into the central sense organ from various regions of the body, the common sense registers their occurrence, and thus it affords the awareness of the activity of the senses. It registers their non-occurrence, on the other hand, as an interruption in the flow of perceptual changes from a particular region of the body, and thus it affords the awareness of the inactivity of the corresponding sense.

What follows from this picture is essentially that the common sense provides second-order perceptual awareness of first-order perception. This may tempt us to think that Aristotle, if I have interpreted him correctly, espouses a higher-order perception theory of consciousness like Armstrong's or Lycan's. There are at least two reasons why this temptation should be resisted. First, these higher-order perception theorists take consciousness to be second-order perception of all kinds of first-order mental state, whereas the common sense provides second-order perception of first-order *perceptual* states only. Hence, if we decide that the monitoring function of the common sense is a kind of consciousness, it is consciousness of perceptual states only. Second, those higher-order perception theorists take it that the relationship between second- and first-order states is contingent, in the sense that we can have a first-order mental state without a second-order perception directed at it. This allows them to account for unconscious or subconscious mental states, and to suggest that the difference between human and non-human consciousness is that mental states in humans are normally accompanied by second-order perceptions directed at them, whereas in other animals they are not. What follows from my interpretation, however, is that the relationship between second- and first-order states is not contingent in the sense that we can have first-order perceptions without second-order perceptions. Every first-order perception, according to my understanding of Aristotle, is accompanied by second-order perception. It follows that there are no unconscious or subconscious perceptions (at least not in the relevant sense), and that all animals, rational and non-rational alike, have their first-order perceptions accompanied by second-order perceptions. Indeed, the common sense is not something that distinguishes human from non-human souls, on any interpretation of Aristotle.

Now the fact that the relationship between first- and second-order perceptions is not contingent in the sense that we can have a first-order perception without a second-order perception, may tempt us to think that Aristotle subscribed to a form of the same-order theory of consciousness. What is distinctive of the same-order theories of consciousness is that they take the relationship between second- and first-order states to be non-contingent and in some way constitutive. However, we must resist this temptation too. We have seen that the common sense affords the awareness of the inactivity of the senses.

This clearly means that we can have second-order perceptions which do *not* accompany first-order perceptions. Hence, the relationship between first- and second-order perceptions is contingent, after all. It is not contingent in the sense that we can have a first-order perception without a second-order perception, as the contemporary higher-order perception theorists of consciousness maintain, but it *is* contingent in the sense that we can have a second-order perception without a first-order perception.

If we were pressed to align Aristotle's theory with higher-order or same-order theories of consciousness, I think we should align it with the former. These theories maintain a clear distinction between mental states of the two different orders and assign them to different faculties. In fact, Aristotle's theory seems to be an ancestor of the modern higher-order perception theories of consciousness, from Locke and Kant to Armstrong and Lycan. However, we must keep in mind that Aristotle's theory is importantly different from all modern theories of consciousness in that it is restricted to the awareness of perceptual states only. The fact that it does not allow for first-order perceptions without second-order perceptions may not distinguish it from the early modern theories,[2] but it certainly does distinguish it from the contemporary theories which are committed to the view that mental states can be unconscious. The fact, on the other hand, that Aristotle's theory allows for second-order perceptions without first-order perceptions seems to make it *sui generis*. I am inclined to think that this feature of Aristotle's theory carries an important yet unduly neglected insight, namely that consciousness is awareness of mental states but also of their lapses.

I have argued that the common sense's function of monitoring the senses can be related only to the contemporary notion of introspective consciousness as the awareness of current mental states, in particular the unreflective, spontaneous, and diffuse sort of awareness of current mental states.[3] This contemporary notion comprises the awareness of

[2] Descartes and Locke routinely speak of our being conscious of all our mental states. For example, Descartes writes in *Fourth Replies* (*Oeuvres de Descartes*, VII.246) that 'no thought can exist in us of which we are not conscious at the very moment it exists in us'; see also ibid. III.273, VII.107, 160, 232. Locke writes in his *Essay Concerning Human Understanding* (II.27.9) that it is 'impossible for any one to perceive, without perceiving, that he does perceive. When we see, hear, smell, taste, feel, meditate, or will any thing, we know that we do so'; see also ibid. II.1.10 and 19.

[3] Recall that Armstrong distinguishes 'reflex introspection' from 'introspection proper'. We have no reason to doubt that some non-human animals can achieve the former, whereas reflective, deliberate, and focused awareness of our mental states seems to be a human achievement. The same distinction has been underscored by Rosenthal, only he

mental states as diverse as perceptions, images, memories, thoughts, and emotions. The common sense's function of monitoring captures the segment of the awareness solely of perceptual states. I wish to conclude this book with two observations in this connection.

First, the view that the common sense provides the awareness only of perceptual states should be considered in opposition to Plato's view that the rational soul provides the awareness of all mental states. This opposition is motivated by Aristotle's wider project in which he seeks to explain complex behaviour of some animals without attributing rational capacities to them. I have suggested, if only cursorily, that the awareness solely of perceptual states allows an entity to experience reports of the senses as *its own*, and thus to view the world from a special, egocentric perspective which seems to be necessary for purposeful behaviour.

Second, the fact that the common sense's function of monitoring captures only a segment of the contemporary notion of introspective consciousness does not mean that this notion cannot be accommodated within Aristotle's psychology. Recall that Aristotle considers each individual soul to be a unity which is only conceptually divisible. There are two advantages of conceptual division of the soul. The first advantage is that, once the main parts or aspects of the soul are demarcated, each one of them can be regarded as a unified whole which is itself conceptually divided into parts or aspects at a lower level. Thus the perceptual capacity of the soul is found to be a unified whole conceptually divided into the individual senses. The unity of the perceptual capacity of the soul, we have seen, gives rise to the common sense which integrates and monitors the individual senses. The second advantage of conceptual division of the soul is that each main part or aspect of the soul can be treated as a conceptually distinct part or aspect of a unified whole at a higher level. The perceptual capacity of the soul can thus be regarded as a conceptual part or aspect of the sensory capacity of the soul. The sensory capacity of the soul, which is essentially the non-rational cognitive capacity of the soul, can in turn be treated as a conceptual part or aspect of the cognitive capacity of the soul. So the cognitive capacity of the soul is a unified whole conceptually divided into the sensory and the thinking capacity of the soul. The unity of the cognitive

confines the word 'introspection' to the latter form of being conscious of our mental states; cf. Rosenthal (1986; 2001).

capacity of the soul could, I suppose, provide for some sort of monitoring of all cognitive states. As for emotive states, Aristotle speaks of the desiderative capacity of the soul (τὸ ὀρεκτικόν), which can be treated as a conceptually distinct part or aspect of the sensory capacity, or perhaps, in the case of rational beings, of the cognitive capacity of the soul. Of course, all of this would require more argument, but it indicates that Aristotle's psychology could in principle accommodate the contemporary notion of introspective consciousness.

Appendix
Greek Texts

(a) *De Anima* III.1 425[a]14–29

ἀλλὰ μὴν οὐδὲ τῶν κοινῶν οἷόν τ' εἶναι αἰσθητήριόν τι ἴδιον, ὧν ἑκάστῃ αἰσθήσει αἰσθανόμεθα κατὰ συμβεβηκός, οἷον κινήσεως, στάσεως, σχήματος, μεγέθους, ἀριθμοῦ, ἑνός· ταῦτα γὰρ πάντα κινήσει αἰσθανόμεθα (οἷον μέγεθος κινήσει, ὥστε καὶ σχῆμα, μέγεθος γάρ τι τὸ σχῆμα, τὸ δ' ἠρεμοῦν τῷ μὴ κινεῖσθαι, ὁ δ' ἀριθμὸς τῇ ἀποφάσει τοῦ συνεχοῦς) καὶ τοῖς ἰδίοις· ἑκάστη γὰρ ἓν αἰσθάνεται αἴσθησις. ὥστε δῆλον ὅτι ἀδύνατον ὁτουοῦν ἰδίαν αἴσθησιν εἶναι τούτων, οἷον κινήσεως· οὕτω γὰρ ἔσται ὥσπερ νῦν τῇ ὄψει τὸ γλυκὺ αἰσθανόμεθα· τοῦτο δ' ὅτι ἀμφοῖν ἔχοντες τυγχάνομεν αἴσθησιν, ᾗ ὅταν συμπέσωσιν ἅμα γνωρίζομεν. εἰ δὲ μή, οὐδαμῶς ἂν ἀλλ' ἢ κατὰ συμβεβηκὸς ᾐσθανόμεθα, οἷον τὸν Κλέωνος υἱὸν οὐχ ὅτι Κλέωνος υἱός, ἀλλ' ὅτι λευκός, τούτῳ δὲ συμβέβηκεν υἱῷ Κλέωνος εἶναι· τῶν δὲ κοινῶν ἤδη ἔχομεν αἴσθησιν κοινήν, οὐ κατὰ συμβεβηκός· οὐκ ἄρ' ἐστὶν ἰδία· οὐδαμῶς γὰρ ἂν ᾐσθανόμεθα ἀλλ' ἢ οὕτως ὥσπερ εἴρηται.

15 *ὧν καὶ E* Torstrik *αἰσθανοιμεθ' ἂν* coni. Theiler *κατὰ* codd. Them. Simp.[lcp] Phil.[lc] edd.: *οὐ κατὰ* VetL Torstrik Biehl *οἷον . . .* 19 *συνεχοῦς* in parenthesi ponenda et ante *καὶ τοῖς ἰδίοις* lacunam esse censet Susemihl 16 *ἑνός* codd. Phil.[c] Ross[a] edd.: om. *V*[2] Them. Phil.[l] Soph. Ross[b] 17 *κινήσει*[1] codd. Simp.[c] Phil.[lp] Prisc. Soph. Ross[a] edd.: secl. Ross[b]: *κοινῇ* Torstrik *οἷον . . .* 19 *συνεχοῦς* in parenthesi ponit Gregoric cf. Simp.[p] 184.5–9 *ὥστε . . .* 18 *σχῆμα* in parenthesi ponit Ross[ab] 18 *μεγέθους* coni. Torstrik *τι ELSUVX* Phil.[c] Soph. edd.: *τι καὶ CWTy* Simp.[l] Sylburg Jannone *μὴ* om. *M* 23 *ᾗ* codd. Simp. [l] Phil.[l] Ross[ab] Jannone: *ᾗ καὶ E* edd. 24 *ἅμα γνωρίζομεν E* edd.: *ἀναγνωρίζομεν L* Bekker Trendelenburg Jannone: *γνωρίζομεν CWySUVX* Phil.[l] Simp.[p] Aldus Sylburg *εἰ δὲ μὴ . . .* 27 *εἶναι* in parenthesi ponit Förster Ross[a]: secl. Susemihl 25 *ᾐσθανόμεθα*: *SUVX* Simp.[l] edd.: *αἰσθανοίμεθα L* Jannone: *αἰσθανόμεθα ETUVWy* Phil.[c] Biehl Apelt *οἷον . . .* 27 *εἶναι* in parenthesi ponit Ross[b] 26 *λευκός CWyEL* Them. Phil.[p]: *λευκόν SUX*[1] *τούτῳ* codd. edd.: *τοῦτο ELVX* Phil.[p] 27 *ἤδη ἔχομεν αἴσθησιν Ey* Simp.[l] edd.: *ἔχομεν ἤδη αἴσθησιν LTUW* Phil.[l] Jannone: *ἔχομεν αἴσθησιν ἤδη SVX* Aldus Sylburg

Sigla codicorum manuscriptorum in Ross[b]
VetL = Translatio vetus latina
Prisc. = Priscian (1886: 21.16–20)
Susemihl = Susemihl (1884: 42)
Ross[a] = Ross ((ed.)1956)
Ross[b] = Ross ((ed.)1961)

(b) *De Memoria et Reminiscentia* 1 450^{a}9–14

s 450^{a} 9 μέγεθος δ' ἀναγκαῖον γνωρί-
10 ζειν καὶ κίνησιν ᾧ καὶ χρόνον, καὶ τὸ φάντασμα τῆς κοι-
νῆς αἰσθήσεως πάθος ἐστίν· ὥστε φανερὸν ὅτι τῷ πρώτῳ
αἰσθητικῷ τούτων ἡ γνῶσίς ἐστιν· ἡ δὲ μνήμη, καὶ ἡ τῶν νοη-
13 τῶν, οὐκ ἄνευ φαντάσματός ἐστιν, <καὶ τὸ φάντασμα τῆς
13a κοινῆς αἰσθήσεως πάθος ἐστίν>· ὥστε τοῦ νοητικοῦ κατὰ
συμβεβηκὸς ἂν εἴη, καθ' αὑτὸ δὲ τοῦ πρώτου αἰσθητικοῦ.

9 δ' om. *E* 10 καὶ^{2} om. *Y* καὶ τὸ . . . 11 πάθος ἐστίν codd. edd.: post 13 ἐστιν transp. Freudenthal Ross Laurenti: fort. secl. Kahn: καὶ τὰ φαντάσματα . . . 11 πάθος ἐστίν Mich.^{c} χρόνον codd. Mich.^{p} edd.: χρόνος E^{1} 11 ὥστε codd. edd.: ὥστε τοῦτο *a* Biehl GRTRoss: ὥστε τούτῳ *m* 12 τούτων codd. edd.: τούτου censet Freudenthal ἡ^{3} om. Mich.^{c} 13 φαντάσματος *bMP* Mich.^{c}: τῆς φαντασίας *EY* 13–13a καὶ τὸ . . . πάθος ἐστίν ex 10 transp. Freudenthal Ross Laurenti 13a τοῦ νοητικοῦ *P* VetL Biehl GRTRoss Mugnier: τοῦ νοουμένου codd. Mich.^{c} Soph. Siwek: τοῦ διανοουμένου Bywater Beare Hett: τοῦτο νόομεν *E*: τοῦ νοῦ μὲν F^{e} S^{d} *l* Förster Ross: νοοῦντος vel νοῦ coni. Zeller

Sigla codicorum manuscriptorum in Ross ((ed.)1955)
m (Bekkeri) = cod. Paris. 1921, saec. xiv
F^{e} (Siweki) = cod. Laur. Cast. 'Acquisti' 67, saec. xv
S^{d} (Siweki) = cod. Vindobon. Philos. 75, saec. xv
VetL = Translatio vetus latina
Bywater = Bywater (1901: 243)
Freudenthal = J. Freudenthal (1869: 368, 400)
Beare = Beare ((ed.)1908: ad 450^{a}13, n. 8)
Kahn = Kahn (1966: 60 n. 36)
Zeller = Zeller (1921: 548 n. 2)

(c) *De Anima* III.7 431b2–10

431b 2 τὰ μὲν οὖν εἴδη τὸ νοητικὸν ἐν τοῖς φαντάσμασι νοεῖ, καὶ ὡς ἐν ἐκείνοις ὥρισται αὐτῷ τὸ διωκτὸν καὶ φευκτόν, καὶ ἐκτὸς τῆς αἰσθήσεως, ὅταν ἐπὶ τῶν φαντασμάτων ᾖ, κινεῖται· οἷον αἰσθανόμενος τὸν φρυκτὸν ὅτι πῦρ, τῇ κοινῇ γνωρίζει, ὁρῶν κινούμενον, ὅτι πολέμιος· ὁτὲ δὲ τοῖς ἐν τῇ ψυχῇ φαντάσμασιν ἢ νοήμασιν, ὥσπερ ὁρῶν, λογίζεται καὶ βουλεύεται τὰ μέλλοντα πρὸς τὰ παρόντα· καὶ ὅταν εἴπῃ, ὡς ἐκεῖ τὸ ἡδὺ ἢ λυπηρόν, καὶ ἐνταῦθα φεύγει ἢ διώκει, καὶ ὅλως ἐν πράξει.

3 ἐν om. *y*   4 ἐκτὸς codd. Simp.[lp] edd.: ἔντος Aldus Camotius   αἰσθήσεως *LS* Simp.[l] Phil.[p] edd.: αἰσθήσεως ὄν *SUVXC* Jannone: αἰσθήσεως ὢν *Wy*   5 φρυκτὸν codd. Simp.[lcp] Phil.[c] edd.: φευκτὸν *TUVWX* Them. Sylburg: φυκτόν Camotius   ὅτι πῦρ unc. incl. Torstrik   τῇ κοινῇ *CWyLSUV* Simp.[l] Phil.[cp] Ross[a] edd.: τῇ κινήσει *Basil.* Torstrik: secl. Bywater Susemihl Hicks Hamlyn   γνωρίζει ὁρῶν κινούμενον codd. Simp.[l] Phil.[c] Ross[a] edd.: ὁρῶν κινούμενον γνωρίζει Simp.[p] Ross[b]   9 ἡδὺ ἢ λυπηρὸν codd. Simp.[l] Phil.[p] edd.: ἡδὺ ἢ τὸ λυπηρὸν *L*: λυπηρὸν ἢ ἡδὺ *W*   καὶ ἐνταῦθα *y*: ἐνταῦθα codd. Simp.[lc] edd.: ἐνταῦθα τὸ ἀγαθὸν ἢ κακόν coni. Torstrik   10 οὕτως coni. Trendelenburg   ἐν codd. Simp.[lc] edd.: ἓν Ross[ab] Jannone Lawson-Tancred

Sigla codicorum manuscriptorum in Ross[b]
Basil. = Editio basileensis tertia
Bywater = Bywater (1888: 61–2)
Susemihl = (1892: 110)
Ross[a] = Ross ((ed.)1956)
Ross[b] = Ross ((ed.)1961)

(d) *De Sensu et Sensibilibus* 7 449^{a}5–20

εἰ δὲ δὴ ἄλλῳ μὲν γλυκέος ἄλλῳ δὲ λευκοῦ αἰσθάνεται ἡ ψυχὴ μέρει, ἤτοι τὸ ἐκ τούτων ἕν τί ἐστιν ἢ οὐχ ἕν. ἀλλ' ἀνάγκη ἕν· ἓν γάρ τι τὸ αἰσθητικόν ἐστι μέρος. (τίνος οὖν ἐκεῖνο ἑνός; οὐδὲν γὰρ ἐκ τούτων ἕν.) ἀνάγκη ἄρα ἕν τι εἶναι τῆς ψυχῆς ᾧ ἅπαντα αἰσθάνεται, καθάπερ εἴρηται πρότερον, ἄλλο δὲ γένος δι' ἄλλου. ἆρ' οὖν ᾗ μὲν ἀδιαίρετόν ἐστι κατ' ἐνέργειαν, ἕν τί ἐστι τὸ αἰσθητικὸν γλυκέος καὶ λευκοῦ, ὅταν δὲ διαιρετὸν γένηται κατ' ἐνέργειαν, ἕτερον; ἢ ὥσπερ ἐπὶ τῶν πραγμάτων αὐτῶν ἐνδέχεται, οὕτως καὶ ἐπὶ τῆς ψυχῆς; τὸ γὰρ αὐτὸ καὶ ἓν ἀριθμῷ λευκὸν καὶ γλυκύ ἐστι, καὶ ἄλλα πολλά· εἰ γὰρ μὴ χωριστὰ τὰ πάθη ἀλλήλων, ἀλλὰ τὸ εἶναι ἕτερον ἑκάστῳ. ὁμοίως τοίνυν θετέον καὶ ἐπὶ τῆς ψυχῆς τὸ αὐτὸ καὶ ἓν εἶναι ἀριθμῷ τὸ αἰσθητικὸν πάντων, τὸ μέντοι εἶναι ἕτερον καὶ ἕτερον τῶν μὲν γένει τῶν δὲ εἴδει. ὥστε καὶ αἰσθάνοιτ' ἂν ἅμα τῷ αὐτῷ καὶ ἑνί, λόγῳ δ' οὐ τῷ αὐτῷ.

6 τὸ om. Alex.^{lc} ἐκ om. Biehl Mugnier τί *aPSUW* Alex.^{lc}: om. *LX* οὐχ ἕν *LMUWX* Alex.^{lc}: οὐθέν *SP*: οὔθ' ἕν *E* 7 ἕν^{2} om. *bP* Alex.^{c} 8 τινὸς . . . ἕν in parenthesi ponit Gregoric ἐκεῖνο *LMPSUX* Alex.^{c}: ἐκεῖνος *E* VLat: ἐκεῖ *W* ἕν^{1} *LP* Alex.^{c}: om. *aSUWX* ἄρα codd. Alex.^{c} edd.: δὲ coni. Biehl 9 ψυχῆς ᾧ Ross Beare: ψυχῆς, ᾧ Biehl GRTRoss Förster Hett Mugnier Siwek ἅπαντα codd. edd.: πάντα *P* Alex.^{c} 11 τί *bP* Alex.^{p}: om. Alex.^{c} VLat 13 ὥσπερ ἐπὶ codd. edd.: ὥσπερ *M*: ὡς περὶ Alex.^{c} 14 ψυχῆς; Ross Siwek: ψυχῆς. Biehl GRTRoss Hett Mugnier καὶ^{2} *bP* Alex.^{c}: om. *a* ἀριθμῷ . . . 17 ἓν om. *X* 15 πολλά· εἰ Ross Siwek: πολλά, εἰ Biehl GRTRoss Smith Förster Hett Mugnier γὰρ *LPSUW* Alex.^{c} edd.: om. *a* Biehl GRTRoss Hett Mugnier 16 τὸ codd. Alex.^{cp} edd.: τῷ *W* 18 τὸ codd. Ross Siwek: τῷ *LX* Biehl GRTRoss Förster Hett Mugnier καὶ ἕτερον codd. edd.: καὶ ἑτέρων coni. Beare 19 καὶ^{1} om. *W* τῷ αὐτῷ καὶ ἑνί codd. edd.: τὸ αὐτὸ καὶ ἕν *EMC^{c}* 20 τῷ αὐτῷ codd. edd.: τὸ αὐτό *MC^{c}m*

Sigla in Ross ((ed.)1955)
C^{c} (Siweki) = cod. Paris. 'Suppl. Grec. 332'
m (Bekkeri) = cod. Paris. 1921
VLat = Translatio vetus latina
Beare = Beare ((ed.)1908)

(e) *De Anima* III.2 427a9–14

ἀλλ’ ὥσπερ ἣν καλοῦσί τινες στιγμήν, ᾗ μία ἢ δύο, ταύτῃ καὶ διαιρετή. ᾗ μὲν οὖν ἀδιαίρετον, ἓν τὸ κρῖνόν ἐστι καὶ ἅμα, ᾗ δὲ διαιρετὸν ὑπάρχει, δὶς γὰρ τῷ αὐτῷ χρῆται σημείῳ ἅμα. ᾗ μὲν οὖν δυσὶ χρῆται τῷ πέρατι, δύο κρίνει καὶ κεχωρισμένα, ἔστιν ὡς κεχωρισμένῳ· ᾗ δὲ ἑνί, ἓν καὶ ἅμα.

10 *ὥσπερ ἓν* coni. Trendelenburg *ᾗ μία* edd.: *ἢ μίαν* Alex.[l]: *ἡ μία* Alex.[c] *ἢ CW* Alex.[l] VetL Biehl Rodier Hicks Förster Siwek Jannone: *καὶ L* Phil.[lp] Smith Ross[ab]: *καὶ ᾗ* Simp.[l] Bekker Trendelenburg Torstrik Hett: *ἡ μία, ᾗ δύο* coni. Rodier 11 *καὶ*[1] om. *L* *διαιρετή* codd. Alex.[l] Simp.[l] Phil.[l] edd.: *καὶ ἀδιαίρετος καὶ διαιρετή* Them. Torstrik Ross[ab] *ἀδιαίρετον EUWX* Soph. edd.: *ἀδιαίρετος CSUV* Alex.[l] Them: *ἀδιαίρετα y*[1] *καὶ ἅμα* om. *y* 12 *ὑπάρχει ELSUVXW* Alex.[l] Simp.[c] Bekker Trendelenburg Smith Hett Ross[ab]: *οὐχ ἓν ὑπάρχει Cy* Soph. VetL Rodier Hicks Apelt Siwek Jannone: *ὑπάρχει, οὐχ ἕν E* Aldus Sylburg *Basil.* Torstrik Biehl *δὶς γὰρ CW* Simp.[c] VetL Aldus Sylburg *Basil.* Torstrik Biehl Rodier Hicks Apelt Siwek Jannone: *δὶς ELSUVX* Alex.[l] Soph. Bekker Trendelenburg Förster Smith Hett Ross[ab]: *διὸ γὰρ y* 13 *δυσὶ* codd. Alex.[l] Simp.[lp] Soph. edd.: *ὡς δυσὶ* coni. Trendelenburg: *δὶς* Torstrik Förster Ross[ab] *κεχωρισμένα* codd. Alex.[l] Them. Simp.[l] Soph. edd.: *τὰ κεχωρισμένα C*: secl. Ross[a] 14 *κεχωρισμένῳ CL* edd.: *τῷ κεχωρισμένῳ* Alex.[l]: *κεχωρισμένως Uy* Simp.[lc](Laur. 85) Comotius Ross[ab]: *καιχωρισμένω E*: *κεχωρισμένων S* Bekker Simp.[lc](Ald.): *καὶ κεχωρισμένων X*: *τε καὶ κεχωρισμένα W*: *κεχωρισμένα* vel *κεχωρισμένως V*: *κεχωρισμένοις* Simp.[lc](corr. Hayduck): *κεχωρισμένον* Soph. coni. Trendelenburg *ἑνί, ἓν* coni. Christ Ross[ab] Hicks Hamlyn: *ἑνί, ἑνὶ* Smith: *ἕν, ἑνὶ CWy* Alex.[l] Simp.[lp] VetL Bekker Trendenlenburg Torstrik Förster Hett: *ἑνί* om. *U*: *ἓν* om. *ELSVX* Soph. Biehl Rodier Apelt Siwek Jannone *καὶ* om. Soph. Phil.[p]

Sigla codicorum manuscriptorum in Ross[b]
VetL = Translatio vetus latina
Basil. = Editio basileensis tertia
Alex. = Alexander (1897: 94.10–98.16)
Ross[a] = Ross ((ed.)1956)
Ross[b] = Ross ((ed.)1961)

(f) *De Anima* III.7 431^{a}20–^{b}1

τίνι δ' ἐπικρίνει τί διαφέρει γλυκὺ καὶ θερμόν, εἴρηται μὲν καὶ πρότερον, λεκτέον δὲ καὶ ὧδε. ἔστι γὰρ ἕν τι, οὕτω δὲ καὶ ὡς ὁ ὅρος. καὶ ταῦτα, ἓν τῷ ἀνάλογον καὶ τῷ ἀριθμῷ ὂν ἔχει πρὸς ἑκάτερον ὡς ἐκεῖνα πρὸς ἄλληλα. τί γὰρ διαφέρει τὸ ἀπορεῖν πῶς τὰ μὴ ὁμογενῆ κρίνει ἢ τὰ ἐναντία. οἷον λευκὸν καὶ μέλαν; ἔστω δὴ ὡς τὸ Α τὸ λευκὸν πρὸς τὸ Β τὸ μέλαν, τὸ Γ πρὸς τὸ Δ [ὡς ἐκεῖνα πρὸς ἄλληλα]· ὥστε καὶ ἐναλλάξ. εἰ δὴ τὰ ΓΔ ἑνὶ εἴη ὑπάρχοντα, οὕτως ἕξει ὥσπερ καὶ τὰ ΑΒ, τὸ αὐτὸ μὲν καὶ ἕν, τὸ δ' εἶναι οὐ τὸ αὐτό, κἀκεῖνα ὁμοίως. ὁ δ' αὐτὸς λόγος καὶ εἰ τὸ μὲν Α τὸ γλυκὺ εἴη, τὸ δὲ Β τὸ λευκόν.

22 *καὶ ὡς ὁ* codd. edd.: *καὶ ὁ* *C*^{1}*Xy* Jannone: *ἡ στιγμὴ καὶ ὁ* *W*: *καὶ* *L*: *ὥσπερ ὁ* Phil.^{p}: *ὥσπερ καὶ ὁ* Simp.^{p}: *ὡς ὁ* Ross^{ab}: *καὶ ἡ στιγμὴ καὶ ὅλως ὁ ὅρος* coni. Torstrik *ὅρος. καὶ* Bekker Biehl Apelt Rodier Hicks Siwek Hett Jannone: *ὅρος, καὶ* Trendelenburg Wallace Ross^{ab} *ἓν* codd. Simp.^{lc} Phil.^{l} edd.: *ἐν* *LSVX* Aldus Trendelenburg *καὶ τῷ* codd. Simp.^{l}(Ald.) Phil.^{lp} edd.: *ἢ τῷ* *Ly*: *ἢ* *UVWX* Simp.^{lc}: om. *S* 23 *ὂν* Simp.^{lc} VetL Freudenthal Neuhaeuser Biehl Apelt Rodier Hicks Siwek Hett Jannone: *ὃν* codd. Simp.^{l}(Ald.) Bekker Torstrik Trendelenburg Wallace Förster: *ὄντα* Ross^{ab} *ἔχει πρὸς ἑκάτερον* codd. Simp.^{l}(Ald.) Phil.^{l} edd.: *ἔχει πρὸς ἑκάτερα* *X* Simp.^{lc}: *ἔχει ἑκάτερον πρὸς ἑκάτερον* Madvig Ross^{ab} Smith: *ἔχει πρὸς ἑκάτερον ἐναντίον* coni. Freudenthal 24 *μὴ* *SUVXL* Simp.^{l}(Laur. 85) Phil.^{lp} Soph. VetL edd.: om. *CWy* Simp.^{l}(corr. Hayduck) Simp.^{p} Bekker Trendelenburg 25 *τὰ ἐναντία* codd. Simp.^{p} Phil.^{l} Soph. edd.: *τἀναντία* *SXWy* Simp.^{l} Bekker Trendelenburg *τὸ*^{1} codd. Simp.^{p} Phil.^{cp} edd.: *ἐν τῷ* *y* A, B, etc. codd. edd.: *πρῶτον, δεύτερον, κτλ.* Phil.^{c} 26 *ὡς* . . . 17 *ἄλληλα* codd. Phil.^{c} Bekker Trendelenburg: secl. Freudenthal Baeumker edd. 27 *ὥστε* codd. edd.: *οὕτως* *W*: *οὕτὰ* Simp.^{p} *τὰ* codd. Simp.^{p} edd.: om. *SUVX* ΓΔ codd. Simp.^{p} edd.: ΓΑ Ross^{ab} *ἑνὶ* codd. edd.: *ἓν* *T*: *ἐν* *Cy* 28 *καὶ τὰ* codd. Simp.^{p} edd.: *καὶ τὸ* *STV*: *κἂν εἰ τὰ* coni. Torstrik AB codd. Simp.^{p} edd.: ΔΒ Ross^{ab} 29 *καὶ ἕν* *CWyL* Phil.^{c} edd.: *καὶ* *S*: om. *UVX* *δ'* *CWyLV* Phil.^{c} edd.: *εἶναι* *SU*: om. *X* *κἀκεῖνα* Simp.^{p} Pacius Torstrik Hett Ross^{ab}: *κἀκεῖνο* *SUVXLWy* Phil.^{c} edd.: *κἀκεῖνος* *C*^{1} *ὁ δ'* . . . 1^{b} *λευκόν* codd. Simp.^{cp} edd.: om. Phil.^{p} *καὶ εἰ* codd. edd.: *κἂν εἰ* *SUVX* Simp.^{c} *τὸ μὲν* codd. edd.: *μὲν τὸ* *SUVX*: *τὸ* Simp.^{c}: *τὸ*^{2} et *τὸ*^{4} om. *W*

Sigla codicum manuscriptorum in Ross^{b}
T(Bekkeri) = Vaticanus 256
VetL = Translatio vetus latina

Freudenthal = J. Freudenthal (1869: 397–9 n. 10)
Baeumker = Baeumker (1877: 74 n. 3)
Neuhaeuser = Neuhaeuser (1878: 58–9)
Ross[a] = Ross ((ed.)1956)
Ross[b] = Ross ((ed.)1961)

Bibliography

I. ARISTOTLE'S TEXTS: EDITIONS, TRANSLATIONS, AND COMMENTARIES

APELT, O. (ed.)(1911). *Aristotelis De Anima Libri III*. Leipzig.

APOSTLE, H. G. (ed.)(1966). *Aristotle's Metaphysics*. Bloomington and London.

BALME, D. M., and GOTTHELF, A. (eds.)(2002). *Aristotle: Historia Animalium*, vol. 1. Cambridge.

BARNES, J. (ed.)(1985). *The Complete Works of Aristotle*, 2 vols., Princeton.

BEARE, J. I. (ed.)(1908). *Aristotle: The Parva Naturalia (De Sensu et Sensibili, De Memoria et Reminiscentia, De Somno, De Somniis, De Divinatione per Somnum)*. Oxford.

BIEHL, W. (ed.)(1884). *Aristotelis De Anima Libri III*. Leipzig.

—— (ed.)(1898). *Aristotelis Parva Naturalia*. Leipzig.

BONITZ, H. (ed.)(1848). *Aristotelis Metaphysica*, 2 vols., Bonn.

BYWATER, I. (ed.)(1894). *Ethica Nicomachea*. Oxford.

DROSSAART LULOFS, H. J. (ed.)(1943). *Aristotelis De Somno et Vigilia*. Leiden.

—— (ed.)(1947). *Aristotelis De Insomniis et De Divinatione per Somnum*. Leiden.

—— (ed.)(1965). *Aristotelis De Generatione Animalium*. Oxford.

DÜRING, I. (ed.)(1961). *Protrepticus: An Attempt at Reconstruction*. Göteborg.

FOBES, F. H. (ed.)(1919). *Aristotelis Meteorologicorum Libri Quattuor*. Cambridge, Mass.

FÖRSTER, A. (ed.)(1912). *Aristotelis De Anima*. Budapest.

—— (ed.)(1942). *Aristotelis De Sensu et De Memoria Libri*. Budapest.

GALLOP, D. (ed.)(1990). *Aristotle on Sleep and Dreams*. Peterborough.

HAMLYN, D. W. (ed.)(1968). *Aristotle: De Anima Books II and III*. Oxford.

HAMMOND, W. A. (ed.)(1902). *Aristotle's Psychology*. London and New York.

HETT, W. S. (ed.)(1935). *Aristotle: On the Soul, Parva Naturalia, On Breath*. Cambridge, Mass.

—— (ed.)(1936). 'On Indivisible Lines', in *Aristotle: Minor Works*. Cambridge, Mass.

HICKS, R. D. (ed.)(1907). *Aristotle: De Anima*. Cambridge, Mass.

JAEGER, W. (ed.)(1957). *Aristotelis Metaphysica*. Oxford.

JANNONE, A. and BARBOTIN, E. (eds.)(1966). *Aristote: De l'âme*. Paris.

JOACHIM, H. H. (ed.)(1926). *Aristotle: On Coming-to-Be and Passing-Away*. Oxford.

KING, R. A. H. (ed.)(2004). *Aristoteles: De Memoria et Reminiscentia*. Berlin.

LANGKAVEL, B. (ed.)(1868). *Aristotelis De Partibus Animalium*. Leipzig.

LAURENTI, R. (ed.)(1971). *Aristotele: I piccoli trattati naturali*. Bari.

LAWSON-TANCRED, H. C. (ed.)(1986). *Aristotle: De Anima (On the Soul)*. London.
LE BLOND, J.-M. (ed.)(1945). *Aristote, philosophe de la vie. Le livre premier du Traité sur les Parties des Animaux*. Paris.
LENNOX, J. G. (ed.)(2001). *Aristotle: On the Parts of Animals I–IV*. Oxford.
LOUIS, P. (ed.)(1956). *Aristote: Les parties des animaux*. Paris.
MINIO-PALUELLO, L. (ed.)(1949). *Aristotelis Categoriae*. Oxford.
MORAUX, P. (ed.)(1965). *Aristote: Du ciel*. Paris.
MUGNIER, R. (ed.)(1953). *Aristote: Petits traités d'histoire naturelle*. Paris.
NUSSBAUM, M. C. (ed.)(1978). *Aristotle's De Motu Animalium*. Princeton.
OGLE, W. (ed.)(1882). *Aristotle On the Parts of Animals*. London.
____ (ed.)(1911). *Aristotle: De Partibus Animalium*. Oxford.
PECK, A. L. (ed.)(1937). *Aristotle: Parts of Animals, Movement of Animals, Progression of Animals*. Cambridge, Mass.
____ (ed.)(1942). *Aristotle: Generation of Animals*. Cambridge, Mass.
____ and BALME, D. M. (eds.)(1965). *Aristotle: Historia Animalium*, 3 vols., Cambridge, Mass.
RODIER, G. (ed.)(1900). *Aristote: Traité de l'âme*, 2 vols., Paris.
ROSS, G. R. T. (ed.)(1906). *Aristotle: De Sensu and De Memoria*. Cambridge.
ROSS, W. D. (ed.)(1924). *Aristotle's Metaphysics*, 2 vols., Oxford.
____ (ed.)(1928). *The Works of Aristotle translated into English*. Vol. VIII: *Metaphysics*, 2nd edn., Oxford.
____ (ed.)(1949). *Aristotle's Prior and Posterior Analytics*. Oxford.
____ (ed.)(1955). *Aristotle: Parva Naturalia*. Oxford.
____ (ed.)(1956). *Aristotelis De Anima*, editio minor. Oxford.
____ (ed.)(1957). *Aristotelis Politica*. Oxford.
____ (ed.)(1958). *Aristotelis Topica et Sophistici Elenchi*. Oxford.
____ (ed.)(1959). *Aristotelis Ars Rhetorica*. Oxford.
____ (ed.)(1961). *Aristotle: De Anima*, editio maior. Oxford.
SEIDL, H. (ed.)(1995). *Aristoteles: Über die Seele*. Hamburg.
SMITH, J. A. (ed.)(1918). *Aristotle: On the Soul*. Oxford; repr. in Barnes (ed.)(1985).
SIWEK, P. (ed.)(1933). *Aristotelis De Anima Graece et Latine*. Rome.
____ (ed.)(1963). *Aristotelis Parva Naturalia Graece et Latine*. Rome.
SORABJI, R. (ed.)(1972). *Aristotle on Memory*. London; 2nd edn., London 2004.
STEWART, J. A. (1892). *Notes on the* Nicomachean Ethics *of Aristotle*, 2 vols., Oxford.
TAYLOR, A. E. (ed.)(1949). *Aristotle on His Predecessors, Being the First Book of His Metaphysics*. La Salle, Ill.
THEILER, W. (ed.)(1959). *Aristoteles: Über die Seele*. Berlin.
THILLET, P. (ed.)(2005). *Aristote: De l'âme*. Paris.
TORRACCA, L. (ed.)(1961). *Aristotele: Le parti degli animali*. Padua.
TORSTRIK, A. (ed.)(1862). *Aristotelis De Anima*. Berlin.

TREDENNICK, H. (ed.)(1933). *Aristotle: The Metaphysics*, vol. 1. Cambridge, Mass.

TRENDELENBURG, F. A. (ed.)(1877). *Aristoteles: De Anima*, 2nd edn., Berlin.

VAN DER EIJK, P. J. (ed.)(1994). *Aristoteles: De Insomniis, De Divinatione per Somnum*. Berlin.

WALLACE, E. (ed.)(1882). *Aristotle's Psychology*. Cambridge.

WALZER, R. R. and MINGAY, J. M. (eds.)(1991). *Aristotelis Ethica Eudemia*. Oxford.

II. ANCIENT AND MEDIEVAL COMMENTARIES ON ARISTOTLE: EDITIONS AND TRANSLATIONS

ALEXANDER OF APHRODISIAS (1887*a*). *De Anima*, ed. I. Bruns. Berlin.

—— (1887*b*). *De Anima Liber Mantissa*, ed. I. Bruns. Berlin.

—— (1897). *Quaestiones*, ed. I Bruns. Berlin.

—— (1901). *In Aristotelis De Sensu Commentarium*, ed. P. Wendland. Berlin.

—— (1994). *Quaestiones 2.16–3.15*, trans. R. W. Sharples. London.

—— (1996). *L'Anima*, trans. P. Accattino and P. Donini. Bari.

—— (2000). *On Aristotle on Sense Perception*, trans. A. Towey. London.

DAMASCIUS (1977). *The Commentary on Plato's* Phaedo, ed. L. G. Westerink, in *The Greek Commentaries on Plato's* Phaedo, vol. 2. Amsterdam.

MICHAEL OF EPHESUS (1903). *In Parva Naturalia Commentaria*, ed. P. Wendland. Berlin.

—— (1904). *In Libros De Partibus Animalium, De Animalium Motione, De Animalium Incessu Commentaria*, ed. M. Hayduck. Berlin.

PHILOPONUS (1897). *In Aristotelis De Anima Libros Commentaria*, ed. M. Hayduck. Berlin.

PRISCIAN OF LYDIA (1886). *Metaphrasis in Theophrastum*, ed. I. Bywater. Berlin.

—— (1997). *On Theophrastus on Sense-Perception*, trans. P. Huby; with Simplicius, *On Aristotle's On the Soul 2.5–12*, trans. C. Steel. London.

SIMPLICIUS (1882). *In Libros Aristotelis De Anima Commentaria*, ed. M. Hayduck. Berlin.

SOPHONIAS (1883). *In Libros Aristotelis De Anima Paraphrasis*, ed. M. Hayduck. Berlin.

—— (vulgo Themistius)(1903). *In Parva Naturalia Commentaria*, ed. P. Wendland. Berlin.

THEMISTIUS (1899). *In Libros Aristotelis De Anima Paraphrasis*, ed. R. Heinze. Berlin.

THOMAS AQUINAS (1948). *In Aristotelis De Anima Commentarium*, ed. M. Pirotta. Rome.

—— (1951). *Aristotle's De Anima in the Version of William of Moerbeke and the Commentary of St. Thomas Aquinas*, trans. K. Foster and S. Humphries. London.

III. SECONDARY LITERATURE

ACKRILL, J. L. (1972/3). 'Aristotle's Definitions of *psuchê*'. *Proceedings of the Aristotelian Society*, 73: 119–33; repr. in Barnes, Schofield, and Sorabji (eds.)(1979): 65–75; and in J. L. Ackrill, *Essays on Plato and Aristotle*. Oxford 1997: 163–78.

ANNAS, J. (1986). 'Aristotle on Memory and the Self'. *Oxford Studies in Ancient Philosophy*, 4: 99–118; repr. in Nussbaum and Rorty (eds.)(1992): 297–311.

—— (1992). *Hellenistic Philosophy of Mind*. Berkeley, Los Angeles, and Oxford.

ANTON, J. P. and KUSTAS, G. L. (eds.)(1971). *Essays in Ancient Greek Philosophy*. New York.

ARMSTRONG, D. M. (1968). *A Materialist Theory of the Mind*. London.

—— (1997). 'What is Consciousness?', in Block, Flanagan, and Güzeldere (eds.)(1997): 721–8.

AUGUSTINUS, A. (1956). *De Libero Arbitrio*, ed. W. M. Green. Vienna.

—— (1993). *On the Free Choice of the Will*, trans. T. Williams. Indianapolis and Cambridge.

BAEUMKER, C. (1877). *Des Aristoteles Lehre von dem äusseren und inneren Sinnesvermögen*. Leipzig.

BALME, D. (1987*a*). 'The Place of Biology in Aristotle's Philosophy', in Gotthelf and Lennox (eds.)(1987): 9–20.

—— (1987*b*). 'Teleology and Necessity', in Gotthelf and Lennox (eds.)(1987): 275–85.

BARKER, A. (1981). 'Aristotle on Perception and Ratios'. *Phronesis*, 26: 248–66.

BARNES, J. (1972). 'Aristotle's Concept of Mind'. *Proceedings of the Aristotelian Society*, 72: 101–14; repr. in Barnes, Schofield, and Sorabji (eds.)(1979): 32–41.

—— (ed.)(1995). *The Cambridge Companion to Aristotle*. Cambridge.

—— SCHOFIELD, M., and SORABJI, R. (eds.)(1979). *Articles on Aristotle. Volume 4: Psychology and Aesthetics*. London.

BAYNE, T. and CHALMERS, D. (2003). 'What Is the Unity of Consciousness?', in A. Cleeremans (ed.), *The Unity of Consciousness: Binding, Integration, and Dissociation*. Oxford: 23–58.

BEARE, J. I. (1897–8). 'Notes on Aristotle's *Parva Naturalia*'. *Hermathena*, 10: 455–73.

—— (1906). *Greek Theories of Elementary Cognition from Alcmaeon to Aristotle*. Oxford.

BENARDETE, S. (1975). 'Aristotle *De Anima* III.3–5'. *Review of Metaphysics*, 28: 611–22.

BENNETT, M. R. and HACKER, P. M. S. (2003). *Philosophical Foundations of Neuroscience*. Oxford.

BERNARD, W. (1987). 'Philoponus on Self-Awareness', in R. Sorabji (ed.), *Philoponus and the Rejection of Aristotelian Science*. London: 154–63.

Block, I. (1960). 'Aristotle and the Physical Object'. *Philosophy and Phenomenological Research*, 21: 93–101.

____(1961*a*). 'Truth and Error in Aristotle's Theory of Sense-Perception'. *Philosophical Quarterly*, 11: 1–9.

____(1961*b*). 'The Order of Aristotle's Psychological Writings'. *American Journal of Philology*, 82: 50–77.

____(1964). 'Three German Commentators on the Individual Senses and the Common Sense in Aristotle'. *Phronesis*, 9: 58–63.

____(1965). 'On the Commonness of the Common Sensibles', *Australasian Journal of Philosophy*, 43: 189–95.

____(1988). 'Aristotle on the Common Sense: A Reply to Kahn and Others'. *Ancient Philosophy*, 8: 235–49.

Block, N. (1995). 'On a Confusion about a Function of Consciousness'. *Behavioural and Brain Sciences*, 18: 227–87.

____Flanagan, O., and Güzeldere, G. (eds.)(1997). *The Nature of Consciousness: Philosophical Debates*. Cambridge, Mass.

Bolton, R. (1978). 'Aristotle's Definitions of the Soul: *De Anima* II 1–3'. *Phronesis*, 23: 258–78.

____(2005). 'Perception Naturalized in Aristotle's *De Anima*', in Salles (ed.)(2005): 209–44.

Bonitz, H. (1870). *Index Aristotelicus*. Berlin.

Bos, A. P. (2003). *The Soul and Its Instrumental Body: A Reinterpretation of Aristotle's Philosophy of Living Nature*. Leiden.

Bostock, D. (1988). *Plato's Theaetetus*. Oxford.

Bradshow, D. (1997). 'Aristotle on Perception: The Dual-Logos Theory'. *Apeiron*, 30: 143–61.

Brentano, F. (1867). *Die Psychologie des Aristoteles*, Mainz; English edn., *The Psychology of Aristotle*, trans. R. George. Berkeley, 1977.

Brittain, C. (2002). 'Non-Rational Perception in the Stoics and Augustine'. *Oxford Studies in Ancient Philosophy*, 22: 253–308.

____(2005). 'Common Sense: Concepts, Definition and Meaning In and Out of the Stoa', in D. Frede and B. Inwood (eds.)(2005), *Language and Learning: Philosophy of Language in the Hellenistic Age*. Cambridge: 164–209.

Broackes, J. (1999). 'Aristotle, Objectivity, and Perception'. *Oxford Studies in Ancient Philosophy*, 17: 57–113.

Broadie, S. (1993). 'Aristotle's Perceptual Realism', in Ellis (ed.)(1993): 137–60.

Brunschwig, J. (1991). 'Les Multiples Chemins aristotéliciens de la sensation commune'. *Revue de Métaphysique et de Morale*, 96: 455–74.

____(1996). 'En quel sens le sens commun est-il commun?', in Viano (ed.)(1996): 189–218.

____(2000). '*Metaphysics* Λ 9: A Short-Lived Thought-Experiment?', in D. Charles and M. Frede (eds.), *Aristotle: Metaphysics Lambda*. Oxford: 275–306.

Burnyeat, M. F. (1976). 'Plato on the Grammar of Perceiving'. *Classical Quarterly*, 26: 29–51.

—— (1990). *The Theaetetus of Plato*. Indianapolis and Cambridge.

—— (1992). 'Is an Aristotelian Philosophy of Mind Still Credible? (A Draft)', in Nussbaum and Rorty (eds.)(1992): 15–26.

—— (1995). 'How Much Happens When Aristotle Sees Red and Hears Middle C? Remarks on *De Anima* II.7–8', in M. C. Nussbaum and A. O. Rorty (eds.), *Essays on Aristotle's De Anima*, expanded paperback edn. Oxford: 421–34.

—— (2001). 'Aquinas on "Spiritual Change" in Perception', in Perler (ed.)(2001): 129–53.

—— (2002). '*De Anima* II, 5'. *Phronesis*, 47: 28–90.

Bynum, T. W. (1987). 'A New Look at Aristotle's Theory of Perception'. *History of Philosophy Quarterly*, 4: 163–78.

Bywater, I. (1885). 'Aristotelia'. *Journal of Philology*, 14: 40–52.

—— (1888). 'Aristotelia III'. *Journal of Philology*, 17: 53–74.

—— (1892). *Contributions to the Textual Criticism of Aristotle's Nicomachean Ethics*. Oxford.

—— (1901). 'Aristotelia IV'. *Journal of Philology*, 28: 242–4.

Cashdollar, S. (1973). 'Aristotle's Account of Incidental Perception'. *Phronesis*, 18: 156–75.

Caston, V. (1996). 'Why Does Aristotle Need Imagination?'. *Phronesis*, 41: 20–55.

—— (1997). 'Epiphenomenalisms, Ancient and Modern'. *Philosophical Review*, 106: 309–63.

—— (1998). 'Aristotle and the Problem of Intentionality'. *Philosophy and Phenomenological Research*, 58: 249–98.

—— (1999). 'Aristotle's Two Intellects: A Modest Proposal'. *Phronesis*, 44: 199–227.

—— (2001). 'Aristotle's Argument For Why the Understanding Is Not Compounded with the Body'. *Proceedings of the Boston Area Colloquium in Ancient Philosophy*, 16: 135–75.

—— (2002). 'Aristotle on Consciousness'. *Mind*, 111: 751–815.

—— (2004). 'More on Aristotle on Consciousness: Reply to Sisko'. *Mind*, 114: 523–33.

—— (2005). 'The Spirit and The Letter: Aristotle on Perception', in Salles (ed.)(2005): 245–320.

—— (2006). 'Aristotle's Psychology', in M. L. Gill and P. Pellegrin (eds.)(2006), *A Companion to Ancient Philosophy*. Oxford: 316–46.

Charles, D. (1988). 'Aristotle on Hypothetical Necessity and Irreducibility'. *Pacific Philosophical Quarterly*, 69: 1–53.

—— (1991). 'Teleological Causation in the *Physics*', in L. Judson (ed.)(1991), *Aristotle's Physics: A Collection of Essays*. Oxford: 101–28.

Charles, D. (2000). *Aristotle on Meaning and Essence*. Oxford.
Charlton, W. (1980). 'Aristotle's Definition of Soul'. *Phronesis*, 25: 170–86.
____(1981). 'Telling the Difference Between Sweet and Pale'. *Apeiron*, 15: 103–14.
Cherniss, H. (1944). *Aristotle's Criticism of Plato and the Academy*, 2 vols., Baltimore.
Code, A. and Moravcsik, J. (1992). 'Explaining Various Forms of Living', in Nussbaum and Rorty (eds.)(1992): 128–45.
Cohen, S. M. (1992). 'Hylomorphism and Functionalism', in Nussbaum and Rorty (eds.)(1992): 57–74.
Coles, A. (1997). 'Animal and Childhood Cognition in Aristotle's Biology and the *Scala Naturae*', in Kullman and Föllinger (eds.)(1997): 287–324.
Coope, U. (2005). *Time for Aristotle: Physics IV.10–14*. Oxford.
Cooper, J. M. (1970). 'Plato on Sense-Perception and Knowledge: *Theaetetus* 184–6'. *Phronesis*, 15: 123–44.
____(1975). Review of R. Sorabji (ed.), *Aristotle On Memory*. *Archiv für Geschichte der Philosophie*, 57: 63–9.
____(1982) 'Aristotle's Natural Teleology', in M. Schofield and M. C. Nussbaum (eds.), *Language and Logos*. Cambridge: 197–222.
____(1985). 'Hypothetical Necessity', in Gotthelf (ed.)(1985): 151–67.
____(1987). 'Hypothetical Necessity and Natural Teleology', in Gotthelf and Lennox (eds.)(1987): 243–74.
Cornford, F. M. (1935). *Plato's Theory of Knowledge*. London.
____(1937). *Plato's Cosmology*. London.
Dasen, V. (1993). *Dwarfs in Ancient Egypt and Greece*. Oxford.
De Corte, M. (1932). 'Notes exégetiques sur la théorie aristotélicienne du *sensus communis*'. *New Scholasticism*, 6: 187–214.
De Haas, F. A. J. (2005). 'The Discriminating Capacity of the Soul in Aristotle's Theory of Learning', in Salles (ed.)(2005): 321–44.
Descartes, R. (1897–1913). *Oeuvres de Descartes*, ed. C. Adam and P. Tannery, 11 vols., Paris.
____(1998). *The World and Other Writings*, trans. S. Gaukroger. Cambridge.
Devereux, D. and Pellegrin, P. (eds.)(1990). *Biologie, logique et métaphysique chez Aristote*. Paris.
Düring, I. (1943). *Aristotle's De Partibus Animalium*. New York and London.
____(1961). 'Aristotle's Method in Biology: A Note on *De Part. An.* I 1, 639b30–640a2', in S. Mansion (ed.), *Aristote et les problèmes de méthode*. Louvain: 213–21.
Ebert, T. (1983). 'Aristotle on What is Done in Perceiving'. *Zeitschrift für Philosophische Forschung*, 37: 181–98.
Ellis, J. (ed.)(1993). *Ancient Minds, Southern Journal of Philosophy* Supplementary Vol. 31. Memphis, Tenn.
Engmann, J. (1976). 'Imagination and Truth in Aristotle'. *Journal of the History of Philosophy*, 14: 259–66.

ESFELD, M. (2000). 'Aristotle's Direct Realism in *De Anima*'. *Review of Metaphysics*, 54: 321–36.

EVERSON, S. (ed.)(1991). *Companions to Ancient Thought 2: Psychology*. Cambridge.

—— (1997). *Aristotle on Perception*. Oxford.

FORTENBAUGH, W. W. (1970). 'On the Antecedents of Aristotle's Bipartite Psychology'. *Greek, Roman, and Byzantine Studies*, 11: 233–50.

FRAMPTON, M. F. (1991). 'Aristotle's Cardiocentric Model of Animal Locomotion'. *Journal of the History of Biology*, 24: 291–330.

FREDE, D. (1992). 'The Cognitive Role of *Phantasia* in Aristotle', in Nussbaum and Rorty (eds.)(1992): 279–95.

FREDE, M. (1987). 'Observations on Perception in Plato's Later Dialogues', in id., *Essays in Ancient Philosophy*. Oxford: 3–8.

—— (1990). 'The Definition of Sensible Substances in *Metaphysics* Z', in Devereux and Pellegrin (eds.)(1990): 113–29.

—— (1992). 'On Aristotle's Conception of the Soul', in Nussbaum and Rorty (eds.)(1992): 93–107.

—— (1996*a*). 'Aristotle's Rationalism', in M. Frede and G. Striker (eds.), *Rationality in Greek Thought*. Oxford: 157–73.

—— (1996*b*). 'La Théorie aristotélicienne de l'intellect agent', in Viano (ed.)(1996): 377–90.

FREELAND, C. (1992). 'Aristotle on the Sense of Touch', in Nussbaum and Rorty (eds.)(1992): 227–48.

FREUDENTHAL, G. (1995). *Aristotle's Theory of Material Substance: Heat and Pneuma, Form and Soul*. Oxford.

FREUDENTHAL, J. (1863). *Über den Begriff des Wortes Phantasia bei Aristoteles*. Göttingen.

—— (1869). 'Zur Kritik und Exegese von Aristoteles'. *Rheinisches Museum*, 24: 81–93, 392–419.

FRIEDMAN, W. J. (1990). *About Time: Inventing the Fourth Dimension*. Cambridge, Mass.

—— (1993). 'Memory For the Time of Past Events'. *Psychological Bulletin*, 113: 44–66.

GAUKROGER, S. (1981). 'Aristotle on the Function of Sense Perception'. *Studies in History and Philosophy of Science*, 12: 75–89.

GERSON, L. P. (2004). 'The Unity of Intellect in Aristotle's *De Anima*'. *Phronesis*, 49: 348–73.

GOTTHELF, A. (ed.)(1985). *Aristotle on Nature and Living Things*. Pittsburgh.

—— and LENNOX, J. G. (eds.)(1987). *Philosophical Issues in Aristotle's Biology*. Cambridge.

—— (1987). 'First Principles in Aristotle's *Parts of Animals*', in Gotthelf and Lennox (eds.)(1987): 167–98.

Graeser, A. (1978). 'Aristotle's Framework of Sensibilia', in Lloyd and Owen (eds.)(1978): 69–97.

Granger, H. (1990). 'Aristotle and the Functionalist Debate'. *Apeiron*, 23: 27–49.

____(1993). 'Aristotle and Perceptual Realism', in Ellis (ed.)(1993): 161–71.

Gregoric, P. (2003). 'Aristotle on the Common Sense'. D.Phil. thesis. Oxford.

____(2005). 'Plato's and Aristotle's Explanation of Human Posture'. *Rhizai*, 2: 183–96.

____ and Grgic, F. (2006). 'Aristotle's Notion of Experience'. *Archiv für Geschichte der Philosophie*, 88: 1–30.

Gundert, B. (2000). 'Soma and Psyche in Hippocratic Medicine', in Wright and Potter (eds.)(2000): 13–35.

Guthrie, W. K. C. (1981). *Aristotle: An Encounter*. Cambridge.

Hamilton, W. (1852). 'Note A', in Reid (1852): 742–803.

Hamlyn, D. W. (1959). 'Aristotle's Account of Aesthesis in the *De Anima*'. *Classical Quarterly*, 9: 6–16.

____(1968). 'Koine Aisthesis'. *The Monist*, 52: 195–209.

Hardie, W. F. R. (1976). 'Concepts of Consciousness in Aristotle'. *Mind*, 85: 388–411.

Harris, C. R. S. (1973). *The Heart and the Vascular System in Ancient Greek Medicine from Alcmaeon to Galen*. Oxford.

Hartman, E. (1977). *Substance, Body and Soul*. Princeton.

Hasher, L. and Zacks, R. T. (1979). 'Automatic and Effortful Processes in Memory'. *Journal of Experimental Psychology: Human Learning and Memory*, 97: 220–9.

Henry, P. (1960). 'Une comparison chez Aristote, Alexandre et Plotin', in E. R. Dodds (ed.), *Les Sources de Plotin*. Geneva: 427–49.

Heath, T. (1921). *A History of Greek Mathematics*, 2 vols., Oxford.

Huby, P. M. (1999). *Theophrastus of Eresus, Commentary volume 4: Psychology*. Leiden, Boston, and Cologne.

Huxley, T. H. (1879). 'On Certain Errors Respecting the Structure of the Heart Attributed to Aristotle'. *Nature*, 21: 1–5.

James, W. (1983). *The Principles of Psychology*, paperback edn., with introduction by G. E. Miller. Cambridge, Mass.

Johansen, T. K. (1998). *Aristotle on the Sense-organs*. Cambridge.

____(2000). 'Body, Soul, and Tripartition in Plato's *Timaeus*'. *Oxford Studies in Ancient Philosophy*, 19: 87–111.

____(2004). *Plato's Natural Philosophy: A Study of the Timaeus–Critias*. Cambridge.

____(2006). 'In Defense of Inner Sense: Aristotle on Perceiving that One Sees'. *Proceedings of the Colloquium on Ancient Philosophy*, 21 (2005): 235–76.

KAHN, C. H. (1966). 'Sensation and Consciousness in Aristotle's Psychology'. *Archiv für Geschichte der Philosophie*, 48: 43–81; also in Barnes, Schofield, and Sorabji (eds.)(1979): 1–31.
____ (1992). 'Aristotle on Thinking', in Nussbaum and Rorty (eds.)(1992): 359–80.
____ (2005). 'Aristotle versus Descartes on the Concept of the Mental', in Salles (ed.)(2005): 193–208.
KAMPE, F. F. (1870). *Die Erkenntnisstheorie des Aristoteles*. Leipzig.
KANAYAMA, Y. (1987). 'Perceiving, Considering, and Attaining Being'. *Oxford Studies in Ancient Philosophy*, 5: 29–81.
KEMP, S. and FLETCHER, G. J. O. (1993). 'The Medieval Theory of the Inner Senses'. *American Journal of Psychology*, 106: 559–67.
KOSMAN, A. L. (1969). 'Aristotle's Definition of Motion'. *Phronesis*, 14: 40–62.
____ (1975). 'Perceiving That We Perceive: *On the Soul III.2*'. *Philosophical Review*, 84: 499–519.
____ (1987). 'Animals and Other Beings in Aristotle', in Gotthelf and Lennox (eds.)(1987): 360–91.
____ (1992). 'What Does the Maker Mind Make?', in Nussbaum and Rorty (eds.)(1992): 343–58.
KRIEGEL, U. (2002). 'Consciousness, Permanent Self-Awareness, and Higher-Order Monitoring'. *Dialogue*, 41: 517–40.
____ (2006). 'The Same-Order Monitoring Theory of Consciousness', in U. Kriegel and K. Williford (eds.), *Self-Representational Approaches to Consciousness*. Cambridge, Mass.: 143–70.
KULLMANN, W. and FÖLLINGER, S. (eds.)(1997). *Aristotelische Biologie. Intentionen, Methoden, Ergebnisse*. Stuttgart.
LABARRIÈRE, J.-L. (1984). 'Imagination humaine et imagination animale chez Aristote'. *Phronesis*, 29: 17–49.
____ (1990). 'De la *phronesis* animale', in Devereux and Pellegrin (eds.)(1990): 405–28.
____ (2000). 'Sentir le temps, regarder un tableau. Aristote et les images de la mémoire', in C. Darbo-Peschanski (ed.), *Constructions du temps dans le monde grec ancien*. Paris: 269–83.
LANG, H. S. (1980). 'On Memory: Aristotle's Corrections of Plato'. *Journal of the History of Philosophy*, 18: 379–93.
LAUTNER, P. (1992). 'Philoponus, *In De Anima* III: Quest for an Author'. *Classical Quarterly*, 42: 510–22.
____ (1994). 'Rival Theories of Self-awareness in Later Neoplatonism'. *Bulletin of the Institute of Classical Studies*, 39: 107–16.
____ (2000). 'Plutarch of Athens on κοινὴ αἴσθησις and *Phantasia*'. *Ancient Philosophy*, 20: 425–46.
____ (2002). 'Status and Method of Psychology According to the Late Neoplatonists and their Influence During the Sixteenth Century', in C. Leijenhorst,

C. Lüthy, and J. M. Thijssen (eds.), *The Dynamics of Aristotelian Natural Philosophy from Antiquity to the Seventeenth Century*. Leiden: 81–108.

—— (2004). 'The *koinē aisthēsis* in Proclus and Ps.-Simplicius', in P. Adamson, H. Baltussen, and M. W. F. Stone (eds.), *Philosophy, Science and Exegesis in Greek, Arabic and Latin Commentaries*, vol. 1. London: 163–74.

—— (2005). 'The *Timaeus* on Sounds and Hearing, With Some Implications for Plato's General Account of Sense-perception'. *Rhizai*, 2: 235–53.

Lear, J. (1988). *Aristotle: The Desire to Understand*. Cambridge.

Lennox, J. G. (2001). *Aristotle's Philosophy of Biology: Studies in the Origins of Life Science*. Cambridge.

Lloyd, G. E. R. (1975). 'Alcmaeon and the Early History of Dissection'. *Sudhoffs Archiv*, 59: 113–47; also in Lloyd (1991): 167–93.

—— (1978). 'The Empirical Basis of the Physiology of the *Parva Naturalia*', in Lloyd and Owen (eds.)(1978): 215–39.

—— (1991). *Methods and Problems in Greek Science*. Cambridge.

—— (1992). 'Aspects of the Relationship Between Aristotle's Psychology and his Zoology', in Nussbaum and Rorty (eds.)(1992): 147–67.

—— (1996). *Aristotelian Explorations*. Cambridge.

—— and Owen, G. E. L. (eds.)(1978), *Aristotle on Mind and the Senses: Proceedings of the Seventh Symposium Aristotelicum*. Cambridge.

Locke, J. (1975). *An Essay Concerning Human Understanding*, ed. P. H. Nidditch. Oxford.

Lories, D. (1991). 'Des sensibles communs dans le "De Anima" d'Aristote'. *Revue Philosophique de Louvain*, 89 (4th ser., no. 83): 401–20.

Lurz, R. W. (2003). 'Neither hot nor cold: An Alternative Account of Consciousness'. *Psyche*, 9: http://psyche.cs.monash.edu.au/v9/psyche-9-01-lurz.html.

Lycan, W. G. (1997). 'Consciousness as Internal Monitoring', in Block, Flanagan, and Güzeldere (eds.)(1997): 755–71.

Magee, J. M. (2000). 'Sense Organs and the Activity of Sensation in Aristotle'. *Phronesis*, 45: 306–30.

Maudlin, T. (1986). '*De Anima* III.1: Is Any Sense Missing?'. *Phronesis*, 31: 51–67.

Menn, S. (2002). 'Aristotle's Definition of Soul and the Programme of the *De anima*'. *Oxford Studies in Ancient Philosophy*, 22: 83–139.

Modrak, D. (1981*a*). 'An Aristotelian Theory of Consciousness?'. *Ancient Philosophy*, 1: 160–70.

—— (1981*b*). '*Koinē Aisthēsis* and the Discrimination of Sensible Difference in *De Anima* III.2'. *Canadian Journal of Philosophy*, 11: 404–23.

—— (1981*c*). 'Perception and Judgement in the *Theaetetus*'. *Phronesis*, 26: 35–54.

—— (1986). '*Phantasia* Reconsidered', *Archiv für Geschichte der Philosophie*, 68: 47–96.

Modrak, D. (1987). *Aristotle: The Power of Perception*. Chicago.
—— (1991). 'The *Nous*–Body Problem in Aristotle'. *Review of Metaphysics*, 44: 755–74.
Molnár, Z. (2004). 'Thomas Willis (1621–1675), the Founder of Clinical Neuroscience'. *Nature Reviews Neuroscience*, 5: 329–35.
Mueller, I. (1970). 'Aristotle on Geometrical Objects'. *Archiv für Geschichte der Philosophie*, 52: 156–71.
Murphy, D. (2005). 'Aristotle on Why Plants Cannot Perceive'. *Oxford Studies in Ancient Philosophy*, 29: 295–339.
Neuhaeuser, J. (1878). *Aristoteles' Lehre von dem sinnlichen Erkenntnissvermögen und seinen Organen*. Leipzig.
Nussbaum, M. C. and Rorty, A. O. (eds.)(1992). *Essays on Aristotle's De Anima*. Oxford.
O'Shea, M. (2005). *The Brain: A Very Short Introduction*. Oxford.
Osborne, C. (1983). 'Aristotle *De Anima* 3.2: How Do We Perceive That We Perceive?'. *Classical Quarterly*, 33: 401–11.
—— (1998). 'Perceiving White and Sweet (again): Aristotle: *De Anima* 3.7, 431a20–b1'. *Classical Quarterly*, 48: 433–46.
—— (2000). 'Aristotle on the Fantastic Abilities of Animals in *De Anima* 3.3'. *Oxford Studies in Ancient Philosophy*, 19: 253–85.
Oser-Grote, C. M. (2004). *Aristoteles und das Corpus Hippocraticum: Die Anatomie und Physiologie des Menschen*. Stuttgart.
Owen, G. E. L. (1976). 'Aristotle on Time', in P. Machamer and R. Turnbull (eds.), *Motion and Time, Space and Matter*. Columbus, Ohio: 3–27.
Owens, J. (1971*a*). 'Aristotle's Definition of the Soul', in R. B. Palmer and R. Hamerton-Kelly (eds.), *Philomathes*. The Hague: 125–45.
—— (1971*b*). 'The Universality of the Sensible in the Aristotelian Noetic', in Anton and Kustas (eds.)(1971): 462–77.
—— (1980). 'Form and Cognition in Aristotle'. *Ancient Philosophy*, 1: 17–28.
—— (1981). 'Aristotelian Soul as Cognitive of Sensibles, Intelligibles and Self', in J. R. Catan (ed.), *Aristotle: The Collected Papers of Joseph Owens*. New York: 81–98.
—— (1982). 'Aristotle on Common Sensibles and Incidental Perception'. *Phoenix*, 36: 215–36.
Peck, A. L. (1942). 'Appendix B: σύμφυτον πνεῦμα', in *Aristotle: Generation of Animals*, ed. A. L. Peck. Cambridge, Mass.: 576–93.
—— (1953). 'The Connate *Pneuma*: An Essential Factor in Aristotle's Solutions to the Problems of Reproduction and Sensation', in E. A. Underwood (ed.), *Science, Medicine, and History*, vol. 1. London: 111–21.
Perler, D. (ed.)(2001). *Ancient and Medieval Theories of Intentionality*. Leiden.
Philippe, M. D. (1971). '*Phantasia* in the Philosophy of Aristotle'. *Thomist*, 35: 1–42.

Platt, A. (1921). 'Aristotle on the Heart', in C. Singer (ed.), *Studies in the History and Method of Science*, vol. 2. Oxford: 521–32.

Preus, A. (1968). '*On Dreams* 2, 459b24–460a33, and Aristotle's *opsis*'. *Phronesis*, 13: 175–82.

Rees, D. A. (1971). 'Aristotle's Treatment of Φαντασία', in Anton and Kustas (eds.)(1971): 491–504.

Reid, T. (1852). *The Works of Thomas Reid*, ed. W. Hamilton. Edinburgh.

Rosenthal, D. M. (1986). 'Two Concepts of Consciousness'. *Philosophical Studies*, 49: 329–59; repr. with revisions in Rosenthal (2005): 21–45.

—— (2001). 'Introspection and Self-Interpretation'. *Philosophical Topics*, 28: 201–33; repr. in Rosenthal (2005): 103–31.

—— (2005). *Consciousness and Mind*. Oxford.

Ross, W. D. (1949). *Aristotle*, 5th edn., London.

Salles, R. (ed.)(2005). *Metaphysics, Soul, and Ethics in Ancient Thought: Themes from the Work of Richard Sorabji*. Oxford.

Scaltsas, T. (1996). 'Biological Matter and Perceptual Powers in Aristotle's *De Anima*'. *Topoi*, 15: 25–37.

Schiller, Jerome (1975). 'Aristotle and the Concept of Awareness in Sense-perception'. *Journal of the History of Philosophy*, 13: 283–96.

Schofield, M. (1978). 'Aristotle on Imagination', in Lloyd and Owen (eds.)(1978): 99–129; repr. in Barnes, Schofield, and Sorabji (eds.)(1979): 103–32, and in Nussbaum and Rorty (eds.)(1992): 249–77.

Schwyzer, E. (1950). *Griechische Grammatik: Syntax and syntaktische Stilistik*. Munich.

Shaw, J. R. (1972). 'Models for Cardiac Structure and Function in Aristotle'. *Journal of the History of Biology*, 5: 355–88.

Silverman, A. (1989). 'Color and Color-Perception in Aristotle's *De Anima*'. *Ancient Philosophy*, 9: 271–92.

—— (1990). 'Plato on Perception and "Commons"'. *Classical Quarterly*, 40: 148–75.

Sisko, J. E. (1996). 'Material Alteration and Cognitive Activity in Aristotle's *De Anima*'. *Phronesis*, 41: 138–57.

—— (1997). 'Space, Time, and Phantasms in Aristotle, *De Memoria* 2, 425b 7–25'. *Classical Quarterly*, 47: 167–75.

—— (1998). 'Alteration and Quasi-alteration'. *Oxford Studies in Ancient Philosophy*, 16: 331–52.

—— (1999). 'On Separating the Intellect from the Body: Aristotle's *De Anima* iii.4, 429a20–b5'. *Archiv für Geschichte der Philosophie*, 81: 249–67.

—— (2003). 'Taste, Touch, and Temperance in *Nicomachean Ethics* 3.10'. *Classical Quarterly*, 53: 135–40.

—— (2004). 'Reflexive Awareness *Does Belong* to the Main Function of Perception: Reply to Victor Caston'. *Mind*, 113: 513–21.

Slakey, T. J. (1961). 'Aristotle on Sense Perception'. *Philosophical Review*, 70: 470–84.

Solmsen, F. (1950). 'Tissues and Soul'. *Philosophical Review*, 59: 435–68.

—— (1955). 'Antecedents of Aristotle's Psychology and Scale of Beings'. *American Journal of Philology*, 76: 148–64.

—— (1957). 'The Vital Heat, the Inborn Pneuma, and the Aether'. *Journal of Hellenic Studies*, 57: 119–23.

—— (1961). 'Greek Philosophy and the Discovery of the Nerves'. *Museum Helveticum*, 18: 150–97.

Sorabji, R. R. (1971). 'Aristotle on Demarcating the Five Senses'. *Philosophical Review* 80: 55–79; repr. in Barnes, Schofield, and Sorabji (eds.)(1979): 76–92.

—— (1972). 'Aristotle, Mathematics, and Colour'. *Classical Quarterly*, 22: 293–308.

—— (1974). 'Body and Soul in Aristotle'. *Philosophy*, 49: 62–89.

—— (1980). *Necessity, Cause, and Blame*. London.

—— (1983). *Time, Creation and the Continuum*. London.

—— (1991). 'From Aristotle to Brentano: The Development of the Concept of Intentionality'. *Oxford Studies in Ancient Philosophy*, suppl. vol. 1991: 227–59.

—— (1992). 'Intentionality and Physiological Processes: Aristotle's Theory of Sense-Perception', in Nussbaum and Rorty (eds.)(1992): 195–226.

—— (1993). *Animal Minds and Human Morals: The Origins of the Western Debate*. London.

—— (2001). 'Aristotle on Sensory Process and Intentionality: A Reply to Myles Burnyeat', in Perler (ed.)(2001): 49–61.

—— (2004). 'Introduction to the Second Edition', in R. Sorabji (ed.), *Aristotle on Memory*, 2nd edn., London: pp. viii–xxvi.

—— (ed.)(1990). *Aristotle Transformed*. London.

Sprague, R. K. (1989). 'Aristotle and Divided Insects'. *Méthexis*, 2: 29–40.

Steel, C. (1997). 'The Author of the Commentary On the Soul', in *Priscian: On Theophrastus on Sense-Perception* with *'Simplicius': On Aristotle On the Soul 2.5–12*, trans. P. Huby and C. Steel. London: 105–40.

Stigen, A. (1961). 'On the Alleged Primacy of Sight in Aristotle'. *Symbolae Osloenses*, 37: 15–44.

Susemihl, F. (1884). 'Bericht über Aristoteles und die ältesten Akademiker und Peripatetiker für 1880–1882'. *Jahresbericht über die Fortschritte der classischen Alterthumswissenschaft*, 30: 1–98.

—— (1892). 'Bericht über Aristoteles und die ältesten Akademiker und Peripatetiker für 1880–1882'. *Jahresbericht über die Fortschritte der classischen Alterthumswissenschaft*, 67: 78–184.

Taormina, D. P. (2002). 'Perception du temps et mémoire chez Aristote (*De memoria et reminiscentia*, 1)'. *Philosophie Antique*, 2: 33–61.

Tarán, L. (1981). *Speusippus of Athens: A Critical Study with a Collection of the Related Texts and Commentary*. Leiden.

Taylor, A. E. (1928). *A Commentary on Plato's Timaeus*. Oxford.

Tracy, T. (1983). 'Heart and Soul in Aristotle', in J. P. Anton and A. Preus (eds.), *Essays in Ancient Greek Philosophy II*. Albany, NY: 321–39.

Turnbull, K. (1996). 'Aristotle on Imagination: *De Anima*, iii.3'. *Ancient Philosophy*, 14: 319–34.

Van der Eijk, P. J. (1995). 'Hart en hersenen, bloed en pneuma'. *Gewina*, 18: 214–29; Engl. trans. 'The Heart, the Brain, the Blood and the *Pneuma*: Hippocrates, Diocles and Aristotle on the Location of Cognitive Processes', in Van der Eijk (2005): 119–35.

—— (1997). 'The Matter of Mind: Aristotle on the Biology of "Psychic" Processes and the Bodily Aspects of Thinking', in Kullmann and Föllinger (eds.)(1997): 221–58; repr. in Van der Eijk (2005): 206–37.

—— (2000). 'Aristotle's Psycho-physiological Account of the Soul–Body Relationship', in Wright and Potter (eds.)(2000): 57–77.

—— (2005). *Medicine and Philosophy in Classical Antiquity: Doctors and Philosophers on Nature, Soul, Health and Disease*. Cambridge.

Vander Waerdt, P. A. (1985). 'The Peripatetic Interpretation of Plato's Tripartite Psychology'. *Greek, Roman, and Byzantine Studies*, 26: 283–302.

—— (1987). 'Aristotle's Criticism of Soul-Division'. *American Journal of Philology*, 108: 627–43.

Verbeke, G. (1978). 'Doctrine du pneuma et entéléchisme chez Aristote', in Lloyd and Owen (eds.)(1978): 191–214.

—— (1985). 'La Perception du temps chez Aristote', in *Aristotelica. Mélanges offerts à Marcel De Corte*. Brussels and Liege: 351–77.

Vernon, M. D. (1962). *The Psychology of Perception*. Harmondsworth.

Viano, C. (ed.), *Corps et âme. Sur le De Anima d'Aristote*. Paris.

Ward, J. K. (1988). 'Perception and *Logos* in *De Anima* II.12'. *Ancient Philosophy*, 8: 217–33.

—— (1996). 'Souls and Figures: Defining the Soul in *De anima* ii 3'. *Ancient Philosophy*, 16: 113–28.

Watson, G. (1982). 'Phantasia in Aristotle *De Anima* III.3'. *Classical Quarterly*, 32: 100–13.

Webb, P. (1982). 'Bodily Structure and Psychic Faculties in Aristotle's Theory of Perception'. *Hermes*, 110: 25–50.

Wedin, M. V. (1988). *Mind and Imagination in Aristotle*. New Haven and London.

Wee, C. (2002). 'Has Aristotle's Mind Been Changed?'. *Archiv für Geschichte der Philosophie*, 84: 212–22.

Whiting, J. E. (2002). 'Locomotive Soul: The Parts of Soul in Aristotle's Scientific Works'. *Oxford Studies in Ancient Philosophy*, 22: 141–200.

Wiesner, J. (1985). 'Gedächtnis und Denkobjekte—Beobachtungen zu Mem. 1, 449 b 30–450 a 14', in J. Wiesner (ed.), *Aristoteles Werk und Wirkung*, vol. 1. Berlin: 168–90.

Wolfson, H. A. (1935). 'The Internal Senses in Latin, Arabic and Hebrew Philosophic Texts'. *Harvard Theological Review*, 28: 69–133.

Woolf, R. (1999). 'The Coloration of Aristotelian Eye-Jelly: A Note on *On Dreams* 459b–460a'. *Journal of the History of Philosophy*, 37: 385–91.

Wright, J. P. and Potter, P. (eds.)(2000). *Psyche and Soma: Physicians and Metaphysicians on the Mind–Body Problem from Antiquity to Enlightenment*. Oxford.

Yntema, D. B. and Trask, F. P. (1963). 'Recall as a Search Process'. *Journal of Verbal Learning and Verbal Behavior*, 2: 65–74.

Zeller, E. (1921). *Die Philosophie der Griechen in ihrer geschichtlichen Entwicklung*; II.2. *Aristoteles und die alten Peripatetiker*, 4th edn., Leipzig; English edn., *Aristotle and the Earlier Peripatetics*, trans. B. F. C. Costelloe and J. H. Muirhead, 2 vols., London and New York 1897.

Index of Passages

(Page numbers in bold indicate a translation of the passage in question.)

General Index

(This index does not include, save exceptionally, authors mentioned only in references.)